mediterranean PALEO COOKING

First Published in 2014 by Victory Belt Publishing Inc.

Copyright © 2014 Caitlin Weeks, Nabil Boumrar, Diane Sanfilippo

ISBN 13: 978-1-628600-40-7

Food Photography & Cover Design by Diane Sanfilippo

Interior Design by Diane Sanfilippo, Boryana Yordanova, and Yordan Terziev

Inside Portraits: Michelle Lange

Printed in the U.S.A.

RRD 0114

mediterranean PALEO COOKING

OVER 150 FRESH COASTAL RECIPES
FOR A RELAXED, GLUTEN-FREE LIFESTYLE

CAITLIN WEEKS, NC, CHEF NABIL BOUMRAR
and DIANE SANFILIPPO,
NEW YORK TIMES BESTSELLING AUTHOR OF *PRACTICAL PALEO*

VB

VICTORY BELT PUBLISHING, INC.

LAS VEGAS

contents

dedication

Nabil

This book is dedicated to my mother, Omi, who is sweet and warm and worked so hard to stretch every dollar and feed me and my eight brothers and sisters nutritious food. She inspired my love of cooking with her instinctual cooking skills, which she combined with lots of love to take simple foods such as fresh vegetables and basic cuts of meat to new heights.

Caitlin

When I first met Nabil's mother, I knew we would get along because some of her favorite foods are liver and lamb ribs. During our visit she would often say "Mange, mange, mange!" Translation: "Eat, eat, eat!" It was so gracious of Nabil's mother and sisters to cater to our dietary requests during our visit, and I will never forget the wonderful weeks we spent together.

Nabil's mother, Omi.

acknowledgments

Caitlin

I want to thank my husband, Nabil Bourmar, who inspired me to undertake this project with his delectable and nutritious home-cooked dishes. I would like to thank my dad for being the rock in my life. Thank you to my stepmom for being a good example and for keeping me in line, and to my mom for broadening my horizons and teaching me to follow my heart. I also want to thank my sister, Ellen Weeks, for being my sidekick all these years, and my late Grandma Weeks, who made me feel so loved. Thanks also to my ninety-two-year-old grandma, Ava Taylor, for showing me the right way to do things.

Thank you to Diane Sanfilippo for always believing in me and pushing me to do more than I thought I could. I would also like to thank my blogger friends—especially Karen Sorenson, Vanessa Romero, Carol Lovett, and Hannah Healy—who helped me stay on track with their daily encouragement. Thanks also to my lifelong friend Megan Davis, for being a cornerstone of support in my life. Thank you to Sandrine Love for helping me organize the beginning steps towards my first e-book.

I want to thank my teachers at University School of Nashville for six great years of elementary education. I would like to thank my professors at University of Tennessee for showing me that a degree in speech communication really can be used in any field. I want to thank my teacher Frank Rolek, who guided me when I wanted to turn towards a health and fitness career, and my nutrition mentors, Diane Fischler and Jodi Friedlander at Bauman College, who

set the bar high. I want to thank my first nutritionist, Dixie Raile, for starting me on an ancestral diet. I want to thank my friend Brad Crooks for being supportive of my California dreams.

Finally, I want to thank all my readers and fans who have followed me from a newsletter to a website that's now a full-time job that I wake up excited to do every day.

Nabil

I want to thank my wife, Caitlin Weeks, who has helped me dream bigger and reach for the stars. You are the light of my life.

Thank you to my sisters, Nacera, Samia, Siva, and Nora, for being wonderful people to grow up with. Thank you to my oldest brother, Arezki, for showing me how to work hard and follow my dreams; to my little brother, Massimo, for being a good friend; and to my brother Rachid for pushing me to be a better person. Thank you to my brother Mourad for his help when I first came to San Francisco. Thank you to my late father for being consistent and strong; I think of you and miss you every day. I want to thank my mom for her overflowing love; I wish I could be at home with you every day.

I would like to thank all my knowledgeable teachers at San Francisco City College Culinary School and Earl Darny, my baking mentor, for teaching me skills I will have for life. I want to thank my coworkers in the kitchen at the Omni Hotel for their hard work and for pushing me to learn all I can. And to all my San Francisco friends, who have become like family, many thanks.

introduction

nabil's story

I grew up in Algiers, Algeria, a city of 3.5 million people on the Mediterranean Sea. I am a middle child in a family of eleven; we liked to joke that we had enough family members for an entire soccer team. My mother and sisters did most of the cooking while I was growing up, but I always watched them prepare dishes with an interested eye, and I went to the farmers market with my mother to buy fresh local fish, grass-fed meats, pastured eggs, and seasonal organic produce. My parents and grandparents grew up in rural agricultural communities in the mountains, where they raised goats and sheep and lived off the land—they even made their own olive oil from their own olive groves—and at a young age I was exposed to many foods that aren't part of the typical American diet, such as sardines, liver, raw milk, and grass-fed butter. Between watching my mother and sisters cook, visiting the market with my mother, and learning about food from my parents and grandparents, I discovered early on the importance of wholesome, fresh, local food.

My first job, at age sixteen, was making pizza in a restaurant, and from then on I knew I wanted to work with food. I came to the US in 2004 to visit my older brothers in San Francisco, and after a few weeks I decided I liked the Bay Area and made arrangements to stay a while. One of my brothers helped me get a job as a cook at an Italian restaurant, where I learned to prepare foods such as omelets, paninis, soups, and pasta.

I went on to attend the well-known culinary school at San Francisco City College and graduated in 2010. Several doors opened for me upon graduation, and I'm happy to have worked with some world-class mentors. Currently I am a chef at a large hotel in downtown San Francisco, and I love learning and growing each day with the talented team I am a part of.

caitlin's story

I grew up in Nashville, Tennessee, where I was raised by my dad and stepmom after my parents divorced when I was three years old. The divorce was rough for me, and I began to gravitate towards food for comfort. While my dad instilled in me a desire to be adventurous and open to new cuisine—a good foundation for a future foodie—I spent a lot of time with my beloved paternal grandmother, who indulged me in everything from Pringles to biscuits and gravy. Those are some of my best memories, but there's no denying that I was already becoming pudgy by age six.

I started dieting in high school, attempting to survive all day on diet soda and low-cal frozen meals. I did lose weight, but I was always cranky and had difficulty concentrating. In college I took a break from dieting, and by the time I graduated I was up to 240 pounds, which was a lot to carry on my five-foot-eight frame. I remember standing on stage during the graduation ceremony and feeling so proud of my accomplishment and yet so ashamed of my weight.

After college I felt like it was finally time to focus on getting my weight back down. I went to Weight Watchers and was able to lose about eighty pounds over twelve months on the program. I learned some valuable things there about planning ahead and avoiding sugar, but I also ate a lot of processed food during that time, which most likely impacted my long-term health.

Meanwhile, I was working a few sales jobs in Nashville, feeling restless and longing for adventure. Friends who lived in San Francisco mentioned that they needed a roommate, so I took a leap, packed up, and moved out west. I was excited to find that people in the Bay Area were more active and interested in their health, and I decided that I wanted to help other people lose weight and feel better. I became a certified personal trainer and was very happy and fulfilled in my work for seven years.

Although I loved being a personal trainer, over time I began to notice that food was incredibly influential in the results my clients saw, and I became passionate about helping people eat better. I enrolled in a rigorous two-year program at Bauman

College in Berkeley to become a nutrition consultant and graduated in 2010.

Around the same time that I started the program, I became really involved in running, completing two half-marathons, and started eating a pescetarian diet—vegetarian but with the addition of fish. I thought I was being really healthy, but I discovered much later that my diet contained large amounts of soy and was often short on the important nutrients found in animal protein and healthy fats.

I started to feel incredibly fatigued and needed a whole pot of coffee to get going in the morning. I sought advice from several doctors and was diagnosed with Hashimoto's thyroiditis, an autoimmune condition in which the immune system mistakenly attacks the thyroid. I saw a naturopathic doctor who prescribed a protocol of supplements and a natural thyroid hormone replacement, which made a huge difference in my energy levels in just two weeks.

The illness motivated me to seek out a nutritionist, who urged me to try a healing, whole-foods diet to restore my stamina and balance my blood sugar. When I learned that the diet included grass-fed meat and coconut oil, I didn't need much convincing! In fact, I was excited to try something new that would keep me from feeling hungry and tired all the time. Later I learned that this way of eating had a name: "the Paleolithic diet." Also at the suggestion of my nutritionist, I reduced my stress and spent more time meditating and connecting with nature. I also changed my exercise routine to include more weight training and shorter bursts of activity in place of long-distance running. After following this new eating and exercise regimen for a while, I finally started to feel like myself again. My cravings for grains and sugar fell off, and

my low energy and other autoimmune symptoms were on the mend. I also saw improvements in my thyroid lab markers. Staying healthy and in shape was, and is, a bit more challenging with hypothyroidism, but focusing on healing from the inside out helps a lot.

In retrospect, I believe that my excessive running and nutrient-poor diet exacerbated my thyroid problems. This realization made me want to spread the word and help others who might not know that what they think of as a healthy diet and lifestyle could actually be hurting their health. I started my popular blog, *Grass Fed Girl*, in the fall of 2010 to offer an alternative to mainstream nutritional information.

better together

We met in a café in San Francisco in 2006. I (Caitlin) was drawn to Nabil's big green eyes and deep, masculine voice, and Nabil later told me that his knees buckled when he first met me. Nabil's English was not very clear yet, but we figured it out with a lot of hand signals and body language. After a romantic first date at a restaurant on the Hyde Street cable car line, where hundreds of Hollywood movies have been filmed, we were inseparable, and we were married later that year.

Cooking is one of our shared passions, and Nabil has taught me how to make many of his favorite dishes. I love to try to re-create his mother's cooking to make him feel at home, even though he is thousands of miles away from his family. We're also both very active—Nabil has always been an athlete and loves being outdoors, and because of my weight and health issues, exercise and staying fit are very important to me.

In 2011 Nabil became concerned about his health because of his family history and some moderate weight gain, and I convinced him to try a thirty-day Paleo challenge. He dropped fifteen pounds in that first month! He also had more energy and was better able to focus at work, and his weight stayed stable even when he was too busy to exercise. He was a convert.

In the fall of 2012, Juliet Starrett from San Francisco CrossFit asked us to teach a cooking class together. It turned out to be an amazing experience that brought us together on a whole new level. Nabil's experience as a chef and my experience as a nutritionist led to a natural combination of Mediterranean cooking and Paleo principles. The result? Food that was healthy, fun, and tasty, and a class that was lively and exciting. One attendee commented that our familiar husband-and-wife banter reminded them of Ricky and Lucy Ricardo from *I Love Lucy.*

After the wonderful experience of teaching together, it seemed only natural to write a cookbook that combined Nabil's family cuisine with the health principles that I teach my clients and blog readers. The idea for *Mediterranean Paleo Cooking* was born.

Creating a Cookbook

Nabil and I decided to create an e-cookbook of Paleo-friendly Mediterranean recipes. We spent hours in coffee shops writing down recipes, and Nabil cooked all the food in our tiny apartment kitchen, with his mom on the phone making sure we were on the right track. I tackled the photography, despite my limited skills, and bought lots of colorful plates and linens at thrift stores to serve as backdrops. We hired a designer to help us put it all together into a pretty package, I put the e-book on my website, and it sold hundreds of copies.

We always loved the idea of seeing our book in print, though. Enter Diane Sanfilippo.

Collaborating with Diane

Diane and I met in 2010. We went to the same nutrition school, though we were in different classes, and I often saw her business cards in the personal training studio where I worked. They led me to her website, where she'd posted interesting thoughts about health and nutrition, and I emailed her and asked if she wanted to grab a tea. It turned out that she lived around the corner from me and we had many of the same interests, and we quickly became friends. Diane encouraged me to start *Grass Fed Girl* to get the word out about ancestral nutrition and efficient exercise, and even after she moved back to New Jersey, we stayed close.

When Nabil and I finished the e-book of recipes, we sent a copy to Diane. She was so impressed with the work we had done that she sent it to her publisher, who was interested in helping us turn it into a printed book but agreed with Diane that the presentation could use an upgrade.

Diane has an eye for design and is a fantastic self-taught photographer, and she invited us to her house in New Jersey for a reshoot of all the photos. We were cooking and Diane was setting up and taking photographs for nearly a month, but we had an amazing time. We knew from the beginning that Diane would elevate the project with her many talents, and we were absolutely right.

The book you now hold in your hands is the result of a ton of hard work and a lot of love. We hope that both the work and the love shine through, and that these recipes bring you both the fresh, bright flavors of the Mediterranean and the good health that comes from Paleo dining.

mediterranean cuisine

The flavors of the Mediterranean are very diverse and, due to the expansive geographical area that the region covers, are influenced by many different cultures.

But there are some standard features of Mediterranean cuisine. It generally relies heavily on local and seasonal ingredients, from produce and herbs to grazing animals and wild seafood. Warm spices such as cumin, cinnamon, coriander, paprika, turmeric, and saffron are lit up by the bright flavors of fresh herbs like cilantro, parsley, and mint. Olives and olive oil are plentiful and used throughout the Mediterranean for tajines, salads, soups, and dips. Salty anchovies, sardines, and other fatty fish show up in the cuisine of many seaside towns and villages because they are affordable and add a unique depth of flavor to almost any dish.

regional flavor variations

In North Africa, food is often flavored with bright, fragrant herbs and warm spices, but it is not usually spicy. There is an emphasis on combining sweet flavors such as cinnamon with the earthy flavors of cumin and coriander. Saffron is commonly used in North Africa and Spain, which gives dishes a beautiful orange color and deep, full-bodied flavor. Dishes are often finished with a generous sprinkling of fresh herbs like cilantro or parsley to brighten up the flavors. This can be especially helpful on slow-cooked meats or soups, where the freshness of the herbs adds a special pop to the deep flavors.

In the Middle Eastern countries that line the Mediterranean Sea, there is ample use of garlic and sesame seeds. One of the foundational ingredients in Middle Eastern dishes is tahini, which has a unique tangy flavor and silky texture—much like a nut butter—and adds richness and body to recipes.

In Italy many dishes are tomato-based, and oregano, olive oil, parsley, basil, and thyme are prominent flavors. Asian influences can be seen in **Moroccan** food with the use of turmeric and ginger. **The Balkans** are known for their use of paprika and capers. **Provence,** a coastal region of France, is well known for its contributions to Mediterranean flavors, such as pungent sage and rosemary as well as licorice-flavored fennel.

Each dish's country of origin affects its flavors, and it's common to find nuanced differences among similar recipes across the entire region, with slight variations in the ingredients and even slightly varied names for the same basic dish. Chakchouka (also spelled *shakshouka* and sometimes dubbed "Eggs in Purgatory"), for example, is a dish widely known throughout the Mediterranean that consists of eggs poached in a cumin-spiced sauce of tomatoes, onion, and peppers. The dish is a staple in many coastal areas, and locals vary the basic recipe by using different types of peppers, adding potatoes or artichoke hearts, substituting other spices, or topping it with cheese. (In the recipe on page 76, Nabil added meatballs to make it a more filling and complete meal.)

the origins of our recipes

The recipes in this book are based on the food Nabil grew up with in his home country of Algeria in North Africa. Nabil was raised on the coast of the Mediterranean Sea, and the food of this region is heavily influenced by flavors from southern Europe and the Middle East. Throughout history, North Africa has been invaded and occupied many times by many distinct cultures, from Spain to Arabia to, most recently, France, which colonized Algeria from 1830 to 1962, and they all left their mark on the cuisine. The food of the Maghreb (the northwest region of Africa) is full of distinct flavors such as saffron, ginger, and, most importantly, cinnamon. This region is also known for its great nutritional treasures, such as fresh seafood, especially sardines and shellfish, olive oil, and almonds.

Nabil's family is Berber, a tribal people who today mostly live in the rugged mountains of Algeria and Morocco. Some claim that Berbers are descendants of Viking sailors who came to North Africa a thousand years ago. Many of the traditional Berber recipes

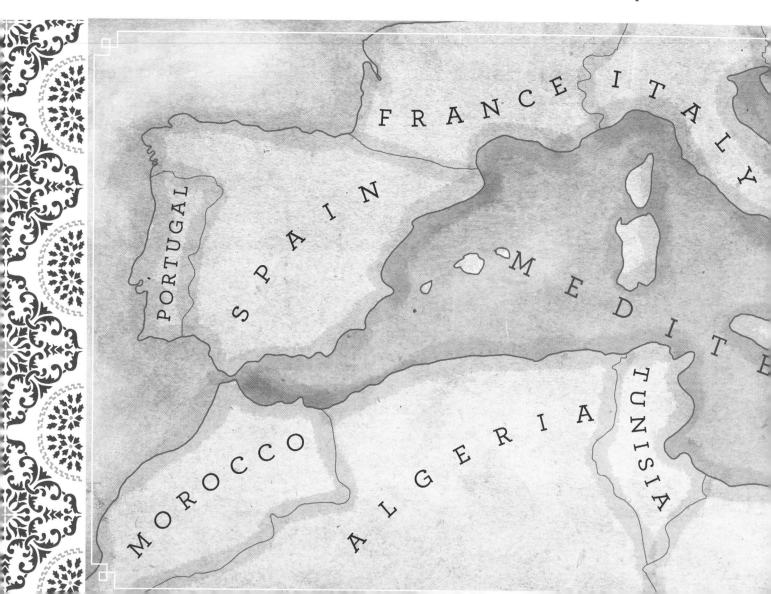

that Nabil learned from his mother and grandmother were passed down from generation to generation but were never written down—until now. We're excited to share some of our favorites with you in the recipes section!

In April 2013, Nabil and I had a once-in-a-lifetime opportunity to travel to North Africa together to visit his family in Algeria. We had been married for seven years at that point, but I hadn't met most of his family and I'd never been to that part of the world. Far from the dry and dusty North Africa of my imagination, Algeria is filled with green fields and beautiful parks, with animals grazing on the side of the road. Nabil's mother and sisters treated me like a queen and cooked all the grain-free dishes they could come up with. (By the end of the

trip, the family was very accustomed to hearing me say "No khobz"—"No bread"!)

And the food there is some of the best that I have ever eaten. While we in the States are slowly learning to seek out locally grown food, people in Algeria are already there, because buying food from local farms is cheaper than bringing it in from far away. Every day fresh meat and vegetables are brought to the markets from surrounding farms, and seafood is sold the same day it is caught. I tasted mouthwatering dishes like grilled sardines straight from the sea, grass-fed lamb ribs, and seasonal vegetables, many of which I'd never seen before. People in Algeria still hold on to their traditional methods of cooking and traditional, nutrient-dense foods, and

together they make for some of the most amazing dishes I've ever had.

North Africa is particularly known for flavorful, slow-cooked meat and vegetable dishes made in a clay pot called a *tajine*. It consists of a large cone-shaped cover on top of a flat base, and the lid circulates the heat back into the food as it cooks. The dishes traditionally made in a tajine are also called *tajines*, but they can be cooked in any type of stockpot or Dutch oven, too. Making your first tajine can be intimidating, but it's really a fairly simple method: meat (usually on the bone) is seared with onions in some fat, then broth is added

to the pot and heated to a slow simmer. Finally, vegetables are added to the broth when the meat is tender, allowing the flavors to meld together beautifully.

In this book, you'll find flavor combinations that are most representative of those Nabil grew up eating. It's our aim to showcase the unique tastes of his country's cuisine while presenting you with recipes that are accessible and exciting, and hopefully they'll even teach you entirely new uses for all of the amazing spices you have in your pantry.

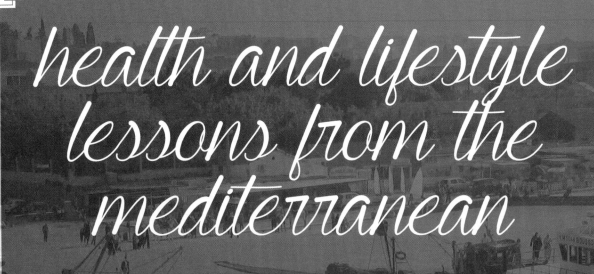

health and lifestyle lessons from the mediterranean

Researchers have known for a long time that people in Mediterranean countries such as Crete, Sardinia, Greece, Morocco, and southern Italy live longer and healthier lives than those in other Western countries. Studies conducted in the 1950s, '60s, and '70s attribute that to what nutritionists call "the Mediterranean diet." That's a huge factor, but I think the lifestyle I observed in Nabil's bustling, friendly neighborhood in Algiers also plays a big role. As we in the US have abandoned timeless methods of healthy food preparation and adopted a lifestyle—too often centered around sitting in a cube under fluorescent lights, chained to digital screens—that is not compatible with our physiology, rates of illnesses such as heart disease and cancer have risen dramatically. We can learn a lot from the way people in Mediterranean countries traditionally live, eat, work, and play.

8 keys to health

Slower Pace

During my two weeks in North Africa, I noticed that there was a lot less hustle and bustle. People seemed to have hours to stand around talking, and it was common to have neighbors over for tea and a long chitchat for no particular reason. There was much less running all over town between meetings and activities. Value was placed on just *being*, not always *doing*.

It took me a week or so to adjust to the slowed-down lifestyle, but when I did, I never wanted to come back. I loved spending hours walking around, browsing the street markets, and sitting in the park. The relaxed pace seemed to help keep everyone from getting stressed out, and I often think that Americans could benefit a great deal from taking a break from our usual fast-forward lifestyle.

Slowing down isn't just relaxing, it's also good for us. Chronic stress can affect the brain, making us more aggressive and angry. Overproduction of stress hormones can contribute to higher blood pressure and dangerous abdominal belly fat. Ever wonder why you tend to get sick just when you're at your busiest? It's because stress can depress the immune system, making us more prone to illness. There is also a great deal of current research that links stress with digestive problems, and many people suffer from insomnia when under chronic stress. Maybe we should follow the lead of people in the Mediterranean and slow down, taking more time to enjoy each other and our lives.

Strong Family Connections

As soon as I got off the plane in Algeria, I was struck by the strength of Nabil's family's connections and bonds. His family is very large, boisterous, and gregarious. They are very close and help each other out with child care, cooking, and cleaning. Nabil's unmarried siblings live at home with their mother, and the married children live close by. All day long at his mother's house there were group meals and children everywhere underfoot. The sense of connection within the family was very touching, and most families in America don't have that kind of day-to-day family experience. Missing that connection could easily contribute to the feelings of isolation and depression that are so common in our society. In fact, many studies have shown that social connection is one of the largest contributors to good health—it's more critical than anything we can ingest.

Seasonal Eating

Near Nabil's childhood home is a farmers market full of seasonal fruits and vegetables. His family shops at these stalls every day and brings home bags of fresh produce to cook. There's no need to wonder if something is in season—if it's not in season, it just isn't there. And even outside the farmers market, many people sell fresh produce right from their overflowing pickup trucks. I was amazed at the abundance and variety of produce that was grown locally, right near the city.

Active Lifestyles

Here in the US, most of us have a lifestyle that goes something like this: get out of bed, get in the car, go to work, sit all day at our desks, go home, pig out on the couch while watching the latest episode of *Dancing with the Stars*, go to bed, and repeat. In comparison, while we were visiting Nabil's family, we walked an average of four or five miles a day. We walked to get food, to go to the post office, and to visit friends. We also had to walk up three flights of stairs to get to his family's flat. Every day involved much more activity than a normal day even in my walking-friendly neighborhood in the Bay Area. With that level of activity incorporated into daily life, staying fit and healthy is much easier.

Less Reliance on Technology

Although there is plenty of technology in North Africa, it's less pervasive than in the States—it doesn't seem to have everyone under its spell the way it does here. (During my visit to Algiers, I seemed to be the only person in the house using wi-fi!) People are more present and in touch with what's happening around them, not what's happening on the screens of their smartphones. They're more excited about talking to family and experiencing nondigital life.

Cooking at Home

Eating outside of the home is not as common in North Africa as it is in the States; it tends to be expensive, and there aren't many options. There is also a higher value placed on family dinners and generational togetherness. Eating at home not only helps strengthen the family bond, it keeps us healthier and more nourished. Plus, cooking skills and family recipes are passed on from generation to generation.

Healthy Fats

Researcher Ancel Keys launched the American fear of fat in the 1950s when he hypothesized that low rates of heart disease in Mediterranean countries stemmed from a lower consumption of animal fats. But countries in this region—including Italy, Greece, Morocco, Spain, and France—have always prized animal fats. Butter, duck fat, and beef tallow all have been traditionally used for cooking in these diverse culinary cultures, and a traditional Mediterranean diet would never have called for people to skim their milk, throw out their egg yolks, or eat skinless chicken breasts to avoid saturated fat, especially in times of food scarcity.

The real lesson to take away from Keys' Mediterranean diet studies is that the subjects ate no processed foods, such as vegetable oils, or refined sugar, like high fructose corn syrup. They ate natural foods that were in season and purchased from local farmers, not the genetically modified foodlike products that we have today. People living in the countries touching the Mediterranean Sea were not historically fat-phobic and didn't count every calorie; they just ate wholesome foods without synthetic manipulation.

Nose-to-Tail Eating

In Algeria, there is a respect for animals and an understanding that they should be utilized to the fullest. It was commonplace for Nabil's family to gather in the kitchen to butcher a lamb after it had been slaughtered on the back porch. They would use all the organs to make slow-cooked tajines. Americans often see this as disgusting or backward, but there is a great deal of

nutritional wisdom in using the bones, organs, and even blood of an animal.

Vitamin and mineral deficiencies are at the root of many health problems. Thyroid problems, for instance, are due in part to zinc and selenium deficiency. Vitamin D deficiency can lead to cancer and immune dysregulation, while osteoporosis is thought to be caused by a lowered intake and absorption of calcium, magnesium, and vitamin D. The list goes on and on, so it is a good idea to increase the nutrient density of your diet with the richest food sources available—animals.

Bones contain minerals, vitamins, and gelatin that are not available from other foods, and organs, especially liver, are chock full of nutrients. Liver has almost twice the daily recommended amount of folate, and yet it's often seen as a throwaway food in the US. In North Africa, on the other hand, grilled liver is a popular street food. Grilling liver neutralizes the flavor that some people find off-putting, making it tasty and easy to eat. It was so refreshing to see that younger generations are still enjoying liver in North Africa, even though it's a hard sell back in the States.

The essential practices of the Mediterranean diet and lifestyle, such as preparing food from scratch, preparing and eating meals in big groups, consuming in-season produce, and staying active every day, are all essential for long-term health. They're also, no coincidence, fundamental to the way people lived in ancient times. Our Paleo ancestors didn't sit around browsing Facebook all day, and they moved a lot more and sat down much less. If we borrow these ideas and practices from Mediterranean cultures, we will all be better off and live longer, healthier lives.

the paleo diet

The Paleo diet is based on the idea that humans evolved on a diet of wild or grass-fed animals, fowl, eggs, fish, shellfish, vegetables, fruit, nuts, and seeds. Our bodies are designed to thrive on these Paleolithic foods, and they give us a proper balance of vitamins, minerals, phytochemicals, and antioxidants. Once grains and legumes became a major part of the human diet with the introduction of agriculture about 10,000 years ago, human health began to steadily decline.

health benefits of eating paleo

The Paleo diet can have a hugely beneficial effect on health. Here are a few of the reasons why.

No Grains and Legumes

Even though today we often think of whole grains and legumes as healthy foods, they actually create digestive dysfunction. They're full of lectins, phytates, and gluten, which cause intestinal inflammation that can block the absorption of other vitamins and minerals. Even worse, in what's known as *leaky gut syndrome*, they can cause holes to form in the intestinal lining, allowing undigested food and toxins into the bloodstream and prompting an immune response that can lead to a whole host of chronic diseases. Many people who suffer from gas, bloating, diarrhea, and constipation notice that these symptoms improve after a few weeks on the Paleo diet.

If you're wondering how you will get enough fiber without consuming corn, wheat, or oats, don't worry—fruits and vegetables contain eight times the fiber in whole grains. Fiber is plentiful on a balanced Paleo diet full of vegetables and seasonal fruits.

Unrefined Carbohydrates

While carbohydrates are not unhealthy in and of themselves—many ancient cultures thrived while getting a high percentage of their calories from carbohydrates—the problem comes when we replace nutrient-dense foods with processed and refined carbohydrates, which over time can cause insulin resistance and metabolic syndrome. Many people find that decreasing their intake of carbohydrates, increasing their intake of fat and protein, and eating higher-quality foods are instrumental in helping them regain their health or lose weight. The Paleo diet is naturally lower in carbohydrates than the Standard American Diet because it is free of processed foods such as corn syrup and wheat flour.

Everyone is different, though, and it's important to figure out the amount of carbohydrates that's right for your activity level and to maintain normal blood sugar. Even more important is to make sure you're getting your carbohydrates from vegetables and fruit, not from grains or processed food.

Healthy Ratio of Omega-6 to Omega-3

Many people worry that dietary fat causes heart disease, but studies have shown that inflammation is more closely associated with cardiovascular issues than are saturated fat and cholesterol. The ratio of omega-6 fatty acids (found in vegetable oils) to omega-3 (found in fish and eggs) can be a major factor—too much omega-6 relative to omega-3 can lead to a number of inflammation-related diseases, including cardiovascular disease. A Paleo diet that is full of grass-fed meat and wild fish will naturally balance the ratio of omega-6 to omega-3, while consuming vegetable oils (including corn, canola, and soybean oils, which are frequently found in salad dressings and processed foods) can tip the scale too far toward omega-6.

Nose-to-Tail Eating

Our ancient ancestors wasted no part of the animal, which meant they ate the parts we tend to avoid today: the organs. As it happens, these are the most nutrient-dense parts of the animal. The liver, for instance, is full of calcium, vitamin A, vitamin D, folic acid, and vitamin B12. A well-formulated Paleo diet incorporates these nutrient-rich foods.

Optional but Healthy Dairy

When it comes to Paleo, dairy is a gray area. Some experts think we evolved the enzymes to break it down effectively over the past 50,000 years, but there's no denying that many people today are lactose-intolerant, and even more are sensitive to dairy. To make sure you can tolerate dairy well, it's a good idea to remove it from your diet entirely for thirty days and add it back in slowly, watching for reactions such as upset stomach, breakouts and rashes, and headaches.

If you can tolerate dairy, the Paleo way is to consume raw, grass-fed, organic dairy—not dairy from conventional feedlot confinement operations, where cows are overcrowded and pumped full of hormones and antibiotics. (There's more on the benefits of dairy on page 44.)

learning from dr. weston a. price

For evidence of how an ancestral diet affects health, we can look to the findings of Weston A. Price, a dentist from Cleveland, Ohio, who traveled the world in the 1920s and '30s looking for the cause of the rampant tooth decay and dental abnormalities he saw in his practice.

Price studied remote tribes to find out why they were free of modern disease and dental cavities. He found that people who had little access to Western foods were the healthiest, with strong, straight teeth and almost no modern illnesses such as cancer, diabetes, and heart disease. Every tribe Price observed prized animal foods such as butter, raw milk, organ meats, seafood, and even insects. (Interestingly, he never found an isolated people that existed on plant foods alone.) Of course the diets he observed varied depending on the region, but what was absent from the diets was the same everywhere: the processed foods, vegetable oils, and refined sugar that are staples of the modern Western diet.

Price found that these tribes' traditional diets provided at least four times the amount of calcium and other important minerals, such as magnesium and potassium, as the Western diet, and at least ten times the amount of fat-soluble vitamins (found in foods such as butter, fish, eggs, shellfish, and organ meats). Fat-soluble vitamins are crucial for a strong immune system, precise eyesight, healthy fertility, good digestion, supple skin, and strong bones.

Some remote cultures did eat grains and beans, but far less than we eat on the modern Western diet, and they first put them through a meticulous sprouting and soaking process to reduce the levels of antinutrients, which can cause inflammation in the gut lining and prevent the absorption of crucial minerals and vitamins, causing health problems such as goiters and osteoporosis. Many cultures also soaked and sprouted nuts and seeds, which is a good idea if they are eaten often or as a main part of the diet.

Price recorded numerous accounts of tribes who were very fertile, resistant to chronic disease, very fit, and had perfect teeth—when they were following their traditional diets. But after the introduction of Western food, these tribes experienced a major decline in health in less than one generation.

mediterranean and paleo fusion

This cookbook combines the principles of the Paleo diet and regional Mediterranean cuisine. Together they emphasize a nourishing, whole-foods lifestyle and create a powerhouse nutritional program—not to mention delicious, flavorful foods.

Nabil's family went out of their way to make sure I could stick to my Paleo diet during our visit to Algeria, but I don't think it was very difficult because so much of their diet already consisted of real food. The traditional Mediterranean diet is rich in whole foods, such as fresh vegetables, seasonal fruits, wild fish, and dairy. It also stresses foods that are high in good fats, such as olive oil and nuts, and doesn't shun red meat and saturated fat. In fact, a traditional Mediterranean diet includes grass-fed meats such as goat and lamb, eaten nose to tail; animal fats such as butter and duck fat; and raw dairy with the cream on top. There is still a focus on traditional foods and healthy fats in southern Europe, North Africa, and the Middle East, and these regions reject the fat phobia that has permeated American culture.

All these features of the Mediterranean diet are also features of the Paleo diet (with the possible exception of dairy, which is a gray area in Paleo—though as we'll discuss on page 44, raw dairy is becoming more popular). You'll find that the recipes in this book heavily emphasize the following foods, both for their taste and nutritional content.

a winning combination

Meat, Poultry, and Eggs

Red meat began to be vilified in America in the 1950s, when researchers blamed its saturated fat and cholesterol for causing heart disease. As it turns out, though, these aren't the true roots of heart disease—inflammation, caused by numerous factors but especially vegetable oils, is a much larger factor. A Mediterranean Paleo diet features meat from healthy, grass-fed animals, which is full of essential nutrients that are hard to get from any other source.

Poultry, too, has its place in both Paleo and Mediterranean cooking as a great source of protein and a delicious and versatile meat. And all the fantastic nutrients in eggs come from the yolks, so use the whole egg, not just the whites!

A note on pork: Nabil doesn't eat pork for religious reasons, and it's generally not consumed in his home country of Algeria, or in North Africa in general—so none of the recipes in this book include pork. However, you're welcome to adapt them to use pork if you like. Ground pork can be substituted for any ground meat, and pork bacon can easily be substituted for the lamb bacon we used.

Offal

Traditional cultures prized organ meats because they knew they were the richest sources of important minerals and vitamins. In North Africa, grilled or slow-cooked liver is served everywhere—during my travels I was offered liver at almost every meal. Organ meats are high in zinc and selenium, which are important for thyroid health, and vitamins A and D, which support a healthy immune system. They are also a good source of omega-3 fatty acids.

Offal has fallen out of favor in the current low-fat paradigm, which demonizes animal foods and saturated fat. It's no coincidence that as we've abandoned nose-to-tail eating, rates of diabetes, obesity, and autoimmune diseases have skyrocketed. For optimal health it is very important to embrace offal, which are the most nutrient-dense foods on earth. If you've been turned off by offal in the past, don't worry; this book includes many recipes that will make you change your mind.

Seafood

Mediterranean cuisine features a ton of seafood, which can be an incredibly nutritious (and delicious) part of a Paleo diet. Wild fish and shellfish are full of healthy fats and fat-soluble vitamins that support the immune system, and most shellfish are rich in iodine and zinc, which are great for fertility and help protect against cancer. Seafood is also one of the few food sources of vitamin D, and just one serving of small fish, such as sardines or anchovies, contains the recommended daily amount of calcium. It's a good idea to eat twelve to sixteen ounces of wild seafood each week.

Seasonal Fruits and Vegetables

It almost goes without saying that fruits and vegetables are incredibly nutrient-dense, but they're also delicious, especially when eaten in season. Tomatoes, kale, beets, spinach, zucchini, and many, many more are all common in Mediterranean dishes and are great sources of vitamins and minerals.

Nuts and Seeds

Nuts can be a great snack and a good part of the Paleo diet, but be careful not to overuse them—don't fall into the trap of eating a few handfuls of nuts instead of cooking a nutritious meal. They also contain hard-to-digest antinutrients, which can cause problems for many people. Soaking them in water overnight can help to reduce antinutrients that cause inflammation, making them easier to digest. Almonds, pine nuts, pistachios, and others are part of a traditional Mediterranean diet, and when eaten in moderation, they can be a tasty part of your Paleo diet, too.

Bone Broth

Bone broth is an essential part of a healing, traditional diet, and when it's homemade, it adds layers of flavor to food. Bones are a great source of minerals that help stave off many diseases, and bone broth helps to heal the digestive tract and provides collagen for glowing, youthful skin. Plus, the natural flavor can't be matched. You will find several versions of bone broth in this book, including beef, chicken, and fish broth, all of which can be either used as a base for a dish or consumed alone.

Fermented Foods

In North Africa, it is common to preserve an abundance of summer vegetables through old-fashioned methods such as fermentation, which has the added benefit of producing beneficial probiotic bacteria. These bacteria enhance the digestibility of the preserved vegetables and increase their vitamin levels.

They also are beneficial for the digestive system. The overuse of antibiotics kills the helpful bacteria in the gut, and combined with processed food and too much stress, that can set the stage for poor gut function. In fact, having too little beneficial bacteria in the large intestine can contribute to malabsorption of nutrients and irritable bowel syndrome. Some experts also believe that our overly hygienic lifestyle has decreased the diversity of bacteria in our guts, which means that our immune systems aren't primed to recognize harmful bacteria, making us more susceptible to pathogens and viruses. Fermented foods help with all that by seeding the gut with helpful bacteria.

Fermented foods such as raw sauerkraut have become more popular recently and can be found in stores, but store-bought versions are much more expensive, and because traditional preparation methods can have unpredictable results, food manufacturers now use vinegar as a base and/or pasteurize the vegetables to preserve them. These modern methods do not produce the beneficial bacteria that are very much needed for balanced health.

When purchasing sauerkraut from the store, be sure it is raw and unpasteurized. Bubbies is a brand that is widely available in the refrigerated section of the supermarket.

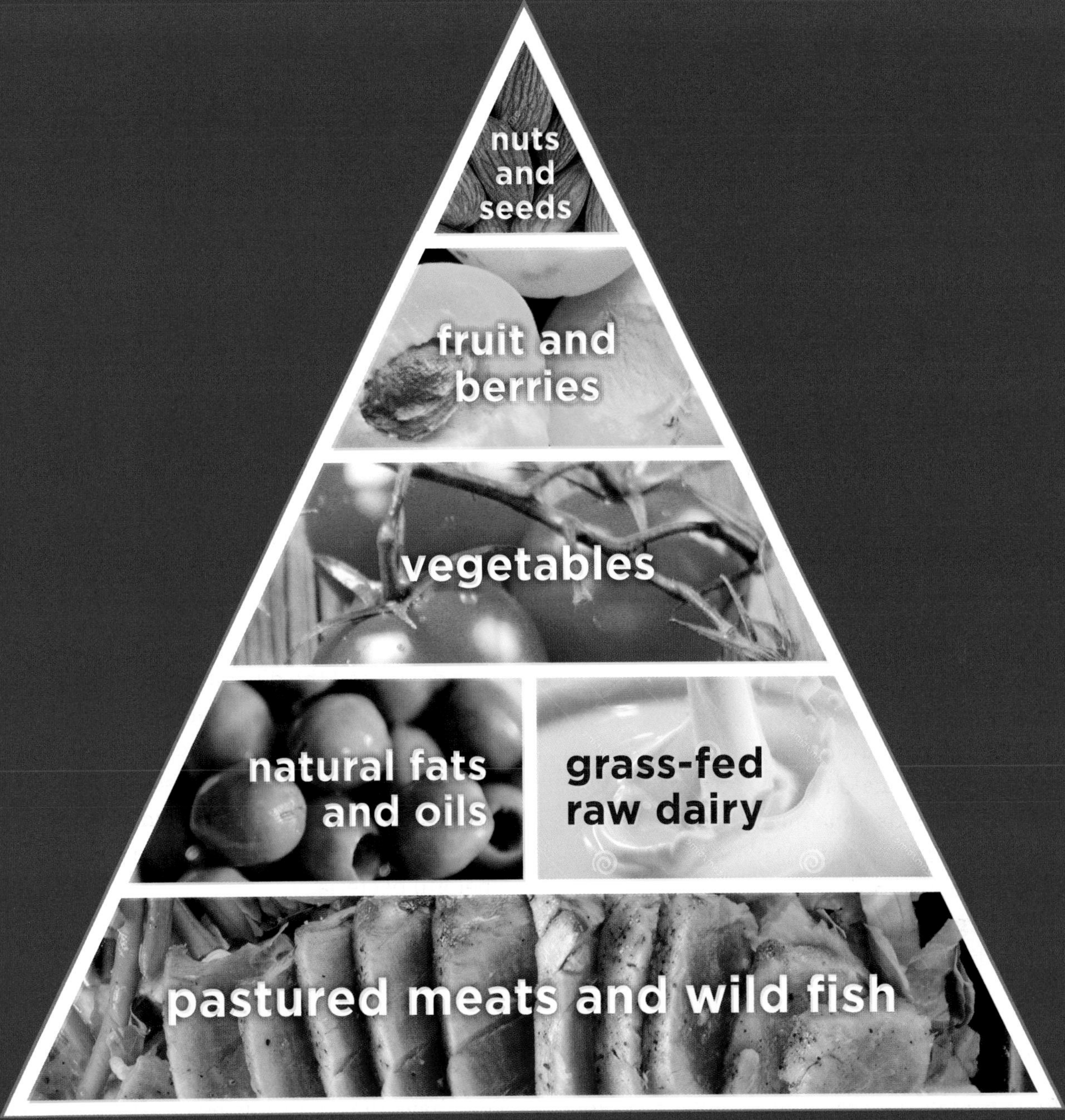

nuts
and
seeds

fruit and
berries

vegetables

natural fats
and oils

grass-fed
raw dairy

pastured meats and wild fish

mediterranean
PALEO PYRAMID

It is important to listen to your intuition and come up with a nutritional plan that's right for you. Experiment with different foods and ratios of protein, carbohydrates, and fat. The goal of this book is to help you have vibrant health while making the journey as palate-pleasing as possible.

stocking a mediterranean paleo kitchen

Finding quality foods can be a challenge, and it's often something that we have to perfect over time. If you're just starting to eat real, unprocessed food, follow the guidelines we offer in the following pages, and give yourself time to adjust and figure out how to work within your budget. Don't stress if your food is not 100 percent organic or grass-fed right away; just try to incorporate more and more well-sourced food over time. It can also be helpful to tap into your local Weston A. Price community to find resources for local, sustainably grown food. Visit the Weston A. Price Foundation website to find a nearby chapter of the foundation: www.westonaprice.org/get-involved/find-local-chapter/.

shopping for quality foods

Red Meat

Meat from concentrated animal feeding operations (CAFOs) is less beneficial than meat from animals eating their natural diet of grass or foraging for food in nature. For starters, when cows are fed corn even for just a few weeks, which is common at a feedlot, the fatty acid composition of their meat changes from a near-perfect one-to-one ratio of omega-6 fatty acids to omega-3s to a twenty-to-one ratio. As we talked about earlier, foods that are so heavily tipped towards omega-6 create rampant inflammation in people, and that's been found to be a major contributor to heart disease, diabetes, cancer, and more. Organic, pastured, and 100 percent grass-fed animals have a much more balanced ratio of omega-6 to omega-3.

What's more, anabolic hormones such as testosterone and estradiol, as well as synthetic combinations, are given to conventionally raised cattle to make them grow faster. Those hormones are transferred to us when we eat the meat, and they are powerful endocrine disrupters that can affect fetal and early childhood development. Growth hormones for cattle have been banned in the European Union but have not been adequately studied in the US and are still used here.

Antibiotics are also given to conventionally raised cattle, to combat the infections that are rampant in the unnatural and overcrowded conditions of feedlots, where cattle often stand in their own waste. Grain-fed animals also have a higher incidence of bacterial contamination because they're not eating their natural diet of grass, and that causes problematic changes in their digestive systems—so they need more antibiotics to stay healthy. It is also well known that antibiotics make livestock gain weight faster, so like hormones, they're used to increase a cow's sale value.

Grass-fed animals are not only healthier and happier than grain-fed ones, their meat is also much better for us. It contains a powerful antioxidant called *conjugated linoleic acid* (CLA), which is helpful for burning fat and has been studied for its cancer-fighting properties. Many people take CLA as a supplement, but it is best to get it from whole foods, such as grass-fed beef and raw milk, to benefit from nutritional cofactors such as vitamins A, D, E, and K, zinc, and selenium.

If you do buy nonorganic grain-fed beef on a regular basis, look for the leaner cuts to avoid some of the toxins that are stored in the fat, and supplement meals with healthy fats by cooking it in grass-fed butter or coconut oil.

Red Meat Quality Options

Best: 100 percent grass-fed and organic, or animals that are able to forage for their natural diet

Good: Organic (raised on organically grown feed and non-GMO corn and soy, without the use of hormones or antibiotics)

Baseline: No hormones or antibiotics (may still be fed GMO corn and soy and may not have an ideal fatty acid composition)

Worst: Conventionally raised, grain-fed animals whose feed could include GMO corn, soy, sugar, and Neotame (similar to aspartame) and who are given antibiotics and hormones to make them gain weight faster

a word about GMOs

Genetically modified foods were introduced by big agricultural companies in the mid-1990s and have never been proven to be safe for human consumption. Genetically modified organisms are created by merging the DNA of different species of plants or animals with bacteria and virus genes, which creates combinations that do not occur in nature. Many people report health improvements after eliminating genetically modified foods from their diets. Genetic modifications are most commonly found in crops such as corn, soy, sugar beets, cotton (and therefore cottonseed oil), and rapeseed (the source of canola oil), and these are prevalent in processed foods and animal feed. The best form of protection from GMOs is to buy organic. Genetically modified foods are banned in many countries around the world, and hopefully as awareness grows they will be outlawed in North America as well.

Poultry

Rotisserie chicken is one of Nabil's favorite foods—he grew up eating it from roadside stands in his home country—but I am always concerned about the quality of chicken in the US. Chicken and turkey have an undeserved health halo left over from the low-fat craze of the 1990s. Most poultry are raised in appalling, overcrowded conditions where they must be fed antibiotics to keep from getting sick. Overuse of antibiotics can cause rapid weight gain in the birds, sometimes leaving them unable to walk. (Fortunately, US law prohibits giving poultry hormones.)

Chickens are not vegetarians by nature, and they should get much of their nutrition from bugs and worms. In a commercial chicken factory, though, they have no access to grass to hunt for bugs, and their feed consists of corn and soy at best and animal by-products such as ground-up bones, animal parts, and even poop (yes, poop) at worst. Some experts think that the isoflavones in soy feed are passed on to people when we eat poultry, negatively affecting estrogen levels. Corn and soy are also the most commonly genetically modified crops, which have never been proven safe for consumers.

Commercial factories also deplete the amount of vitamins A and D that can otherwise be found in chicken and turkey, because the birds are not exposed to sunlight and are unable to receive nutrition from insects. Although "cage-free" and "free-range" chickens may have some outdoor access, these labels are voluntary and not regulated, so it's difficult to know just how "free-range" these birds really are and therefore how much sunlight, grubs, and insects they get.

For the best, healthiest poultry, look for ones that have been raised in pasture, where they get plenty of sunlight and tasty bugs and worms. Also be sure to get air-chilled chicken, which is rapidly cooled in a refrigerator. Conventional chicken, in contrast, is cooled in cold chlorinated baths, and because all the birds are thrown in the same water, there's a higher risk of bacterial contamination. Proponents of air-chilling also believe that it makes for crispier skin and a better-tasting bird.

Think about expanding your poultry beyond chicken and turkey, too. Ducks and geese can be great additions to a Paleo diet if they are pastured and given organic feed.

Poultry Quality Options

Best: Pastured on grass with soy-free, organic feed, and air-chilled

Good: Organic and free-range

Baseline: Free-range (birds have some access to outside but may still receive GMO feed), no antibiotics or hormones

Worst: Conventionally raised (no access to sunshine and bugs and fed GMOs and antibiotics)

Eggs

The best and most nutritious eggs come from poultry that's pastured, with plenty of access to sunshine, bugs, and worms. These eggs are higher in omega-3 fatty acids, vitamin D, and antioxidants such as lutein and vitamin E than those from chickens that are raised indoors. Not to mention, many people find they taste better!

Sometimes eggs are marketed as "omega-3-enriched," which means that the hens were fed flax, but this omega-3 is unlikely to be absorbed by humans, so there's no need to pay more for this feature.

There is some evidence that the isoflavones in soy poultry feed can be transferred to the meat and eggs, which can affect estrogen levels and cause problems for many people. The best way to avoid this is to seek out eggs from pastured, soy-free hens.

Eggs Quality Options

Best: Organic, pastured, soy-free

Good: Pastured, non-organic

Baseline: Organic, cage-free

Worst: Store-bought conventional

Seafood

To reduce your exposure to mercury, choose wild fish that are lower on the food chain. The selenium in fish does provide some protection from mercury, but for the most part try to avoid larger species such as swordfish, ahi tuna, shark, and tilefish.

Farmed fish are fed an unnatural diet of corn and soy, which dramatically diminishes their omega-3 content. They're also often raised in overcrowded pens that damage the environment and concentrate contaminates from the feed in their fat stores. At the same time, many of the world's oceans are overfished, so it's important to choose not just wild fish but sustainably caught wild fish. A great resource is an app from the Monterey Bay Aquarium called Seafood Watch, which recommends certain kinds of fish based on a set of criteria designed to help keep oceans healthy. The recommendations are updated every six months, so check back every so often to make sure you have the most recent information.

"Wild-caught" fish are raised in captivity and then released; they're better than farmed fish, but not as a good as wild.

Seafood Quality Options

Best: Wild fish from the US and Canada, wild shrimp from Oregon or Washington, farmed mussels and oysters

Good: Wild fish from other countries, wild-caught fish, wild shrimp, farmed shellfish from the US and Canada, certain sustainably farmed fish

Worst: Farmed fish and farmed shellfish from other countries; research each source to evaluate the quality of the fish

Fruits and Vegetables

The best way to find quality produce (and save money at the same time) is to go directly to the source: local farms or farmers markets. Seasonal, local produce is best for our health because the longer food is shipped or stored, the more nutrients it loses. Seek out organic produce, too—avoiding pesticides is best for both us and the planet, and organic farms do not fertilize their crops with sewage sludge, which is definitely not something I want coming in contact with my food.

Irradiation is often used on nonorganic produce to kill pathogens, but it reduces nutrients and damages natural enzymes, which makes fruits and veggies hard to digest. Irradiation can also produce free radicals that interact with pesticides on the food to create new compounds called *unique radiolytic products* (URPs), which could have detrimental effects on health. Currently, all irradiated food must be labeled as such, but changes to that rule may be in the works at the FDA, and the best way to avoid irradiated food is to buy organic.

If you can't find organic produce in your area or your budget does not allow for it, refer to the Dirty Dozen and Clean 15 lists provided by the Environmental Working Group (ewg.org). These lists tell you which fruits and vegetables carry the most and least amounts of pesticides, so you can make the best choices.

Fruits and Vegetables Quality Options

Best: Organic and in season, from a local farm or farmers market

Good: Organic from the grocery store

Baseline: Local, nonorganic, pesticide-free

Worst: Conventionally grown

Nuts and Seeds

Buy soaked nuts and seeds if you can find them. Soaking helps reduce lectins and phytates, compounds that can cause inflammation and prevent the absorption of nutrients. If you can't find nuts and seeds that have already been soaked, you can soak them yourself in water for twelve to twenty-four hours.

Choose raw nuts in their most unprocessed forms to avoid additives and processed, chemical-laden coatings. Roasted nuts are often cooked in vegetable oils, which are associated with inflammation and several chronic diseases—but even if they don't include additional oils, the oils in the nuts themselves can oxidize at high heat, so it's better to consume roasted nuts in moderation.

When choosing which nuts to buy, consider their ratios of omega-6 to omega-3 fats; as we've discussed, a ratio that's too far tilted toward omega-6 can drive inflammation in the body. Macadamia nuts have one of lowest omega-6 to omega-3 ratios, while almonds and walnuts are on the higher end of the spectrum.

Nuts and Seeds Quality Options

Best: Raw, organic, and soaked

Good: Raw, conventionally grown

Baseline: Conventionally grown, roasted

Worst: Store-bought, covered in processed oils or sugar

Dairy

Dairy hasn't always been popular in the Paleo community because humans didn't start consuming it until the domestication of animals during the Neolithic era, after our bodies had already evolved on a hunter-gatherer diet. But that is slowly changing as the health benefits of certain types of dairy come to light. Full-fat milk is a good source of vitamin K2, which has benefits for heart health, and of vitamins A and D, which support the immune system.

It's important to keep in mind that I'm specifically referring to full-fat milk here. Low-fat and fat-free milk have to go through more processing to remove the fat, which degrades the milk and reduces its vitamin content. Plus, vitamins A and D need fat to be properly absorbed, and the fat in milk helps prevent a blood sugar spike that could otherwise be caused by lactose, the sugar found in milk. And if that's not enough to convince you to stick to full-fat milk, keep this in mind: a quarter of the fat in milk is monounsaturated fat, the same healthy kind that is in olive oil, and the rest contains CLA, which is beneficial for the heart, helps prevent diabetes and cancer, and has been studied extensively as a weight loss aid.

Raw dairy is even better. Raw, grass-fed milk provides beneficial bacteria for the digestive tract, and it has a beneficial ratio of omega-3 to omega-6. Pasteurization originally came into fashion because so many dairies had unsanitary conditions that caused contamination of the milk, but raw milk today is very safe and closely regulated, and many people who are sensitive to conventional milk products can consume raw, grass-fed dairy without any problems.

But to make sure you can tolerate any dairy, raw or conventional, try removing it from your diet entirely for thirty to sixty days, to give your body a chance to heal from any problems it may have caused. Then add it back in slowly, monitoring your reactions.

Dairy Quality Options

Best: Full-fat raw milk from grass-fed cows, raw cheese, raw homemade yogurt and kefir

Good: Pasteurized full-fat grass-fed milk, grass-fed cheese, grass-fed yogurt and kefir

Baseline: Organic milk, organic cheese, organic yogurt and kefir

Worst: Conventional milk, low-fat milk, skim milk, milk with GMO growth factors such as rBST, conventional cheese and yogurt

Mediterranean Spices, Herbs, and Flavorings

Sometimes all it takes is sea salt and pepper to make everyday ingredients seem new again, and with a variety of fresh spices and herbs, you can make endless combinations of palate-pleasing dishes. Try to use them quickly and replace them often for the best flavor, and keep them in a cool, dry place. Avoid prepackaged spice blends or rubs; they may contain hidden ingredients such as MSG, corn, soy, and wheat.

A list of the most important spices and herbs to keep on hand and their health benefits is below.

Mediterranean Spices, Herbs, and Flavorings Quality Options

Best: Organic fresh herbs and organic dry spices

Good: Organic dried herbs

Baseline: Conventional dried herbs without other ingredients

Worst: Prepackaged spice rubs

Cilantro is full of minerals, folate, vitamin C, and the antioxidant quercetin. Its aromatics work well with other spices, giving dishes a fresh taste.

Cinnamon has been shown to have several health benefits: it helps stabilize blood sugar, reduces sugar cravings, fights candida in the body, and kills bacteria that can contaminate food. It is a sweet spice that comes from the bark of the cinnamon tree, and we often use it to flavor meats, soups, tajines, and sweets. Chefs prefer ceylon cinnamon because it is sweeter and usually fresher.

Cumin promotes the production of digestive enzymes and is helpful for clearing impurities through the liver. It is a spice from the parsley family that has a bitter taste and is often used in Mediterranean cooking; it's great with ground beef and stews.

Ginger is known to help nausea, heartburn, and indigestion. It is used in our book as a spicy addition to soups and stews.

Mint helps soothe the symptoms of irritable bowel syndrome and can be beneficial in controlling asthma. Mint tea is commonly served in the Middle East and North Africa after dinner. Mint gives savory dishes a refreshing and unique taste.

Orange blossom water is created when fresh bitter-orange blossoms are distilled for their essential oil. It has several uses in the Middle East—to mask the high mineral content of the water there, as a freshener for hygienic purposes, to soothe stomach upset in babies—but in cooking, its most important use is in wedding cookies, where its use is partially symbolic because orange blossoms are bridal bouquet flowers.

Paprika helps increase iron absorption from foods. Originally from Turkey, it's made from dried red pepper and gives savory dishes a hint of color and spice. Try to buy organic, sun-dried paprika, which is higher in vitamin C.

Ras el hanout is a mix of spices commonly used in North Africa, including cardamom, clove, cinnamon, chili powder, coriander, cumin, pepper, paprika, fenugreek, and turmeric. There's no exact definition of which spices are in ras el hanout; it is up to each cook to assemble it according to their preference. Versions of this spice combo can be bought at Middle Eastern groceries, however, and it is great on meat and fish.

Rose water was first made by medieval chemists in Persia by steam-distilling rose petals for drinking and perfume; rose water was a by-product. It is used to create a greater depth of flavor in cookies and sweets.

Saffron contains carotenoids, which are helpful in preventing aging and reducing oxidative stress in the body. Saffron is very popular in the Mediterranean region because it is an abundant native plant, and it gives a distinct flavor and color to dishes. It is more expensive outside the Mediterranean, but only a pinch is needed to give savory dishes an amazing taste.

Sea salt contains important minerals such as calcium and magnesium, which are essential for strong bones and a healthy heart. It's also rich in trace minerals such as selenium and zinc, which support a healthy thyroid and metabolism. Iodized salt, however, is heavily refined and devoid of these minerals, and it often contains anticaking agents. In the Standard American Diet, most salt intake comes from processed foods, but since a Paleo diet eliminates those sources, there's plenty of room for salting food to taste with a high-quality Celtic, Himalayan, or unprocessed sea salt. Salt was prized by ancient Mediterranean cultures, and it is important to salt your food for health and for the best flavor.

Turmeric has been shown to be as effective as some anti-inflammatory drugs, without their dangerous side effects. It can be used as a cheaper alternative to saffron, and it gives a great color to savory dishes. This spice is best absorbed when eaten with black pepper.

freezer friendly

Batch cooking and freezing is a great time-saving option for Paleo families who are busy during the workweek. The slow-cooked dishes and soups in our book are very good when frozen and reheated. Many dishes can be frozen in plastic bags or glass containers, then reheated on the stovetop or in a toaster oven.

how to choose healthy fats

Unprocessed fats are essential for steady energy, well-regulated hormones, optimal brain function, and responsive nerves. In contrast, though, processed fats—especially vegetable and crop oils, such as corn, canola, soybean, and cottonseed oils—not only lack these benefits, they're actually bad for you.

Processed oils are made in factories with high heat, which creates free radicals and trans fats. Free radicals damage cells and trans fats are associated with a ton of health problems, from obesity to cancer to heart disease and more—it's no coincidence that there's been a steady increase in heart disease since processed oils were introduced in the early 1900s. What's more, the chemicals used to refine processed oils can pollute the finished product.

It is best to rely on natural, unprocessed fats that have been safely consumed for thousands of years, such as coconut oil, grass-fed butter, and fat from pastured animals.

When choosing a fat, ask yourself the following questions:

- **Is it minimally processed?**
- **Did my great-great-grandparents eat it?**
- **Does it taste really good?**

The answer to all three questions should be "yes"!

Oils to Use for Cooking

Coconut oil

Palm oil

Butter/ghee

Unprocessed lard

Tallow (beef/lamb fat)

Poultry fat

Oils to Use Cold

Olive oil (or low heat only)

Sesame oil

Avocados, avocado oil

Nut-based oils

Seed-based oils

Nut and seed butters

Oils to Avoid

Hydrogenated oils (e.g., Crisco)

Margarine

Diet butters

Buttery spreads

Spray butter substitutes

Canola oil

Corn oil

Vegetable oil

Soybean oil

Grapeseed oil

Sunflower oil

Safflower oil

Rice bran oil

Peanut oil

Mediterranean Paleo Shopping List

Meats

Beef, organic, grass-fed

Bison or buffalo, grass-finished

Cold cuts, organic, gluten-free

Eggs, pastured, organic, soy-free

Goat, grass-fed

Lamb, grass-fed

Organ meats, pastured

Poultry, pastured, organic

Shellfish

Wild fish

Wild game (all kinds)

Nuts, Seeds, and Nut/Seed Butters

Almond butter

Almonds

Brazil nuts

Cashews

Chestnuts

Chia seeds

Golden flax seeds

Macadamia nuts

Pecans

Pine nuts

Pistachios

Pumpkin seeds

Sesame seeds

Sesame paste (tahini)

Sunflower seed butter

Sunflower seeds

Walnuts

A printer-friendly version of this list, along with shopping lists for the meal plans (64–71), can be found at MediterraneanPaleoCooking.com.

Fats and Oils

Beef tallow, grass-fed

Butter, grass-fed, organic

Chicken fat

Coconut butter

Coconut oil

Duck fat

Ghee

Lard

Palm oil

Palm shortening

Eat but don't heat

Avocado oil

Flax oil

Macadamia nut oil

Olive oil, cold-pressed

Sesame oil, cold-pressed

Walnut oil, cold-pressed

Nonstarchy Vegetables

Arugula

Artichokes

Asparagus

Bell peppers

Broccoli

Brussels sprouts

Cauliflower

Chard

Chiles

Chives

Celery

Cucumbers

Eggplants

Garlic

Green beans

Kale

Lettuce

Leeks

Mushrooms

Okra

Olives

Onions

Peas, fresh

Pumpkin

Radishes

Rutabaga

Seaweed

Shallots

Spaghetti squash

Spinach

Snow peas

Tomatoes

Turnips

Turnip greens

Watercress

Yellow squash

Zucchini

Starchy Vegetables

Acorn squash

Beets

Butternut squash

Carrots

Cassava (yuca)

Delicata squash

Parsnips

Plantains

Sweet potatoes

Tapioca

Yams

Fruits

Apples
Apricots
Avocados
Berries
Cherries
Cranberries
Dried fruit, unsweetened
Figs
Grapes
Grapefruit
Lemons
Limes
Melons
Nectarines
Oranges
Peaches
Pears
Persimmons
Plums
Pomegranates

Beverages

Almond milk, homemade
Bone broth, homemade
Coconut milk, full-fat
canned or homemade
Coconut water
Coffee (water-processed if
decaf)
Herbal and green tea
Kombucha (fermented tea)
Water, filtered, mineral
Water kefir

Fresh Herbs

Basil
Cilantro
Mint
Oregano
Parsley
Rosemary
Tarragon
Thyme

Spices

Black pepper
Chili powder
Cinnamon
Cloves
Cumin
Ginger
Marjoram
Nutmeg
Paprika
Saffron
Turmeric
Vanilla beans
Vanilla extract, gluten-free

Fermented Foods

Coconut yogurt
Kvass
Pickles
Sauerkraut, raw

Condiments and Sauces

Mustard, gluten- and MSG-
free
Coconut aminos
Vinegars (apple cider, red
wine, balsamic), gluten-free

Dairy

Butter, grass-fed, organic,
cultured
Cheese, raw, grass-fed,
organic
Kefir, grass-fed, organic
Milk, raw, grass-fed, organic
Sour cream, grass-fed,
organic
Whipping cream, raw,
organic, no carrageenan
Yogurt, grass-fed, organic

Sweeteners

Coconut palm sugar
Honey, raw
Maple syrup, grade B
Molasses
Stevia, organic, green leaf or
powder, without additives

Flours

Coconut flour
Blanched almond flour,
almond meal
Tapioca flour
Arrowroot flour
Cashew meal

recommended cooking equipment

When you commit to a Paleo lifestyle, you may find that it's helpful to have certain tools in your kitchen. While they aren't all necessary, these are the tools we recommend you have on hand to make your life in the kitchen easier.

Baking sheet	High-speed blender	Salad spinner
Cast-iron skillet	Immersion blender	Slow cooker
Cheesecloth	Microplane grater	Stainless-steel sauté pan
Cooking string	Parchment paper	Steamer pot
Food processor	Pasta machine	Stockpot
High-quality knife	Pizza stone	Tajine or Dutch oven

Commonly Used Ingredient Swaps

Beans → Green beans, green peas

Burger buns → Lettuce wraps, Mini Pitas (page 142)

Butter → Grass-fed butter, ghee, coconut oil, olive oil

Canola oil, soybean oil, corn oil → Avocado oil, olive oil, sesame oil

Couscous, rice → Cauliflower Couscous (page 332), cauliflower rice

Flour → For baking: blanched coconut flour, blanched almond flour; for thickening: tapioca flour or arrowroot flour

Hummus → Roasted Garlic Cauliflower Hummus (page 118), pumpkin, carrots, or parsnips

Milk, cream → Almond milk, coconut milk, cashew milk

Pasta → Zucchini Noodles (page 178), spaghetti squash noodles (see page 192), Paleo Pasta (page 172)

Pizza → Mediterranean Paleo Pizza (page 166)

Pita → Mini Pitas (page 142)

Potato chips → Kale chips, endive, sliced jicama, plantain chips

Store-bought mayo → Aioli (page 384), Easy Homemade Olive Oil Mayo (page 385)

Wine → Apple cider vinegar, lemon juice

Soy sauce → Coconut aminos, fish sauce

Sugar → Maple syrup, honey, coconut sugar, stevia extract powder

Tomato sauce, tomato paste → Basic Tomato Sauce (page 182), Autoimmune-Friendly No-Mato Sauce (page 187), cooked or canned pumpkin

how to use the recipes in this book

recipe elements

1 The color-coded margin indicates the type of dish.

2 Recipe name, preparation and cooking times, servings (yield where applicable), and a short description of the recipe from Caitlin and/or Nabil.

3 Ingredients list. Refer to the special diets key if you have dietary restrictions.

4 Preparation instructions.

5 Special notes regarding the health benefits of some ingredients, where to find ingredients, preparation techniques, and other important information.

6 Allergen/dietary restriction swaps for ingredients. You may also choose to omit ingredients on your own if you know you cannot eat them, but they may change the essence of the dish greatly. Significant omissions or replacements that should be made for your needs will be noted in the chart. Here is a breakdown of the chart:

Nut-free: The recipe has no nuts.

Egg-free: The recipe has no eggs.

Low FODMAP: This modification is low in "fermentable oligosaccharides, disaccharides, monosaccharides, and polyols," which are short-chain carbohydrates in certain foods that can exacerbate digestive issues. Please refer to pages 54 to 56 for more detailed information.

AIP-friendly: The recipe conforms to the autoimmune Paleo protocol, which is free of nuts, seeds and seed-based spices, nightshades, and eggs. See page 58 for more information.

SCD/GAPS: This recipe is suitable for the Specific Carbohydrate Diet and Gut and Psychology Syndrome diet, gut-healing programs that exclude carbohydrate foods with disaccharides or polysaccharides that can contribute to poor digestion. See page 57 for more information.

Lower carb: This recipe is suitable for people who are following a lower carbohydrate lifestyle and may want to avoid starchy vegetables, high-glycemic fruits, and sweeteners. See page 60 for more information.

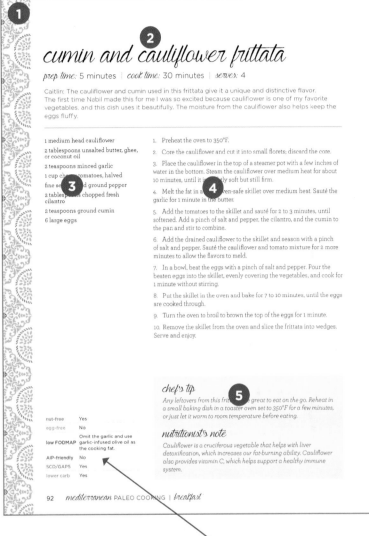

2

cumin and cauliflower frittata

prep time: 5 minutes | *cook time:* 30 minutes | *serves:* 4

Caitlin: The cauliflower and cumin used in this frittata give it a unique and distinctive flavor. The first time Nabil made this for me I was so excited because cauliflower is one of my favorite vegetables, and this dish uses it beautifully. The moisture from the cauliflower also helps keep the eggs fluffy.

1 medium head cauliflower
2 tablespoons unsalted butter, ghee, or coconut oil
2 teaspoons minced garlic
1 cup cherry tomatoes, halved
fine sea salt and ground pepper
2 tablespoons chopped fresh cilantro
2 teaspoons ground cumin
6 large eggs

1. Preheat the oven to 350°F.

2. Core the cauliflower and cut it into small florets; discard the core.

3. Place the cauliflower in the top of a steamer pot with a few inches of water in the bottom. Steam the cauliflower over medium heat for about 10 minutes, until it is mostly soft but still firm.

4. Melt the fat in an oven-safe skillet over medium heat. Sauté the garlic for 1 minute in the butter.

5. Add the tomatoes to the skillet and sauté for 2 to 3 minutes, until softened. Add a pinch of salt and pepper, the cilantro, and the cumin to the pan and stir to combine.

6. Add the drained cauliflower to the skillet and season with a pinch of salt and pepper. Sauté the cauliflower and tomato mixture for 2 more minutes to allow the flavors to meld.

7. In a bowl, beat the eggs with a pinch of salt and pepper. Pour the beaten eggs into the skillet, evenly covering the vegetables, and cook for 1 minute without stirring.

8. Put the skillet in the oven and bake for 7 to 10 minutes, until the eggs are cooked through.

9. Turn the oven to broil to brown the top of the eggs for 1 minute.

10. Remove the skillet from the oven and slice the frittata into wedges. Serve and enjoy.

chef's tip
Any leftovers from this frittata are great to eat on the go. Reheat in a small baking dish in a toaster oven set to 350°F for a few minutes, or just let it warm to room temperature before eating.

nutritionist's note
Cauliflower is a cruciferous vegetable that helps with liver detoxification, which increases our fat-burning ability. Cauliflower also provides vitamin C, which helps support a healthy immune system.

nut-free	Yes
egg-free	No
low FODMAP	Omit the garlic and use garlic-infused olive oil as the cooking fat.
AIP-friendly	No
SCD/GAPS	Yes
lower carb	Yes

92 *mediterranean* PALEO COOKING | *breakfast*

6

nut-free	Yes
egg-free	No
low FODMAP	Omit the garlic and use garlic-infused olive oil as the cooking fat.
AIP-friendly	No
SCD/GAPS	Yes
lower carb	Yes

Paleo FODMAPs Guide

Chart credit: Aglaée Jacob, RD. Radicata Medicine. www.radicatamedicine.com

	Vegetables	Fruits	Starches	Nuts	Dairy
Enjoy	· Alfalfa · Bamboo shoots · Bean sprouts · Bell peppers · Bok choy · Carrots · Cherry tomatoes · Chives · Cucumbers · Eggplant · Endive · Ginger · Green beans · Kale · Lettuce · Olives · Parsnips · Pickles (without sugar) · Scallions (green part only) · Seaweed, nori · Spinach · Swiss chard (silverbeet) · Tomatoes · Zucchini	· Bananas, ripe · Blueberries · Cantaloupe (rock melon) · Grapefruit · Honeydew melon · Kiwifruit · Lemons · Limes · Mandarin oranges · Oranges · Papaya · Passionfruit · Pineapples · Raspberries · Rhubarb · Strawberries	· Plantains (green, verdes) · Rutabagas (swedes) · Taro root · Turnips · White potatoes · White rice · Yuca (cassava)	None	· Butter · Ghee
Limit	· Avocados (polyol) · Beets (fructans) · Broccoli (fructans) · Brussels sprouts (fructans) · Butternut squash (fructans) · Cauliflower (polyol) · Celery (polyol) · Fennel bulbs (fructans) · Green peas (fructans) · Mushrooms (polyol) · Sauerkraut (fructans)	· Bananas, unripe · Grapes (10-15/ serving; fructose) · Longans (polyol) · Lychee (polyol) · Rambutans (polyol)	· Sweet potatoes/ yams (polyol)	· Most nuts and nut butters (cashews, macadamias, pecans, pine nuts, walnuts, pumpkin seeds, sesame seeds, sunflower seeds)	· Aged cheese (lactose) · Cream (only if casein is tolerated)
Avoid	· Artichokes (fructose) · Asparagus (fructose) · Cabbage (fructans) · Garlic (fructans) · Jerusalem artichokes (fructans) · Leeks (fructans) · Okra (fructans) · Onions (fructans) · Shallots (fructans) · Snow peas (fructans, polyols) · Sugar snap peas (fructose) · Radicchio (fructans) · Tomato sauces and paste (fructose and fructans)	· Apples (fructose and polyol) · Apricots (polyol) · Blackberries (polyol) · Cherries (fructose and polyol) · Dried fruits (fructose) · Fruit juices (fructose) · Grapes (>15/serving; fructose) · Mangoes (fructose) · Nectarines (polyol) · Peaches (polyol) · Pears (fructose and polyol) · Persimmons (polyol) · Plums (polyol) · Watermelons (polyol, fructose)	None	· Pistachios (fructans) · Almonds · Hazelnuts	· Fresh cheese (lactose) · Milk (lactose) · Yogurt (lactose and often fructose if sweetened)

	Protein	Fats	Treats	Seasonings	Drinks & Alcohol
Enjoy	· Meat · Poultry · Fish and seafood · Eggs · Bacon (without high fructose corn syrup or fructose)	· Coconut oil · Ghee, butter, cream · Lard · Olive oil · Macadamia oil · Homemade mayo · Olives · Garlic-infused oil	(Best to be avoided for a little while)	· Salt · Pepper · Fresh herbs · Dried herbs · Ginger · Garlic-infused oil · Spices (avoid blends that may contain onion or garlic powder) · Vinegars (balsamic, red wine, apple cider) · Asafetida powder · Seaweed, nori · Olive tapenade · Sun-dried tomatoes	· Water · Tea (green, oolong, black, mate, rooibos) · Homemade bone broth
Limit	None	· Avocados (polyol) · Guacamole (polyol)	· Dried coconut, unsweetened · Coconut sugar · Maple syrup · Coconut milk/cream/butter · Coconut flour · Dark chocolate · Cocoa powder, unsweetened	· Guacamole (polyol)	· Teas with unsafe fruits · Dry wines · Coffee
Avoid	· Any containing breading, gravies, stocks, broth, sauces, or marinades prepared with unsafe ingredients	· Salad dressings, sauces, or marinades prepared with unsafe ingredients	· High fructose corn syrup (fructose) · Agave syrup (fructose) · Honey (fructose) · Sugar-free treats (polyol) · Artificial sweeteners	· Chicory (fructans) · Fructo-oligosaccharide (fructans) · Inulin (fructans) · Prebiotics (fructans) · Onion and garlic powder (fructans) · Gums, carrageenan, and other thickeners or stabilizers · Sugar alcohols (sorbitol, mannitol, xylitol, isomal) · Medicine and supplements	· Sweeter wines · Port wines · Beer (gluten and sometimes mannitol) · Fruit juices · Sodas

low fodmap

The acronym FODMAP stands for "fermentable oligosaccharides, disaccharides, monosaccharides, and polyols." These foods are more likely to be improperly digested, causing gas, bloating, and diarrhea in some people. Often problems digesting fodmap foods are signs of a larger issue, such as small intestinal bacterial overgrowth (SIBO) or a gut infection that needs to be addressed. Avoiding foods high in fodmaps can provide some relief and should be part of a gut-healing protocol.

The chart on pages 54 and 55 gives detailed information on which foods are safe for fodmap sensitivity and which are not. It is important to note that in the recipes, the "low FODMAP" label in the diets key only looks at the foods in the "avoid" column of the chart. Those in the "limit" column should be eaten in moderation, depending on the individual.

If you're sensitive to fodmaps, you may need to avoid some common Paleo foods, including coconut (with the exception of coconut oil), nuts and seeds, and fibrous vegetables such as broccoli, cauliflower, and cabbage. If you're not sure if you're sensitive to a certain fodmap food, keeping your portion size small can help you avoid digestive distress. The "low FODMAP" label will help you select recipes that are lower in fodmaps.

Common Paleo FODMAP Swaps

Onions and garlic	➡	Garlic-infused oil, green part of scallions, chives
Almond flour	➡	Cashew meal (can be used 1:1 in most recipes)
Honey	➡	Stevia extract powder

To make garlic-infused oil:

Pour 4 cups of olive oil into a glass airtight container. Smash 10 to 12 peeled garlic cloves with the side of a knife and add them to the olive oil. Replace the lid and put the container in a cool, dark place. Let it sit for 7 days, then strain out the garlic through a mesh strainer. Using a funnel, transfer the garlic-infused oil into another glass container. Use it as a salad dressing or FODMAP-friendly cooking fat (as indicated in the special diets key for each recipe).

For more information on fodmaps, we recommend these resources:

The Paleo Approach, by Sarah Ballantyne, *Digestive Health with Real Food* by Aglaee Jacob, and SIBOinfo.com (the website of Dr. Allison Siebecker)

scd / gaps

The Specific Carbohydrate Diet, or SCD, is a gut-healing diet created by Dr. Elaine Gottschall in the 1950s. It was later updated by neurologist Dr. Natasha Campbell McBride, who called her variation "the Gut and Psychology Syndrome Diet," or GAPS diet, and who claims the protocol healed her son's autism. These diets eliminate polysaccharides—complex carbohydrates found in grains, starchy veggies, lactose, and glucose—so they have much in common with the standard Paleo template, but they do not allow sweet potatoes or other starches such as tapioca or arrowroot, and unlike Paleo, they do not allow the use of unrefined sweeteners, except honey. Both diets also recommend probiotics to restore balance to gut bacteria, the SCD diet through fermented yogurt and the GAPS diet through raw sauerkraut and beet kvass.

The main difference between the GAPS diet and the SCD is that the GAPS diet places a greater emphasis on food quality, such as grass-fed versus grain-fed animals, and on nutrient-dense foods such as bone broth and organ meats. The "avoid" lists for both of these diets are very similar, however, so they are listed together in the special diets key for each recipe.

Common Paleo SCD / GAPS Swaps

Coconut sugar, maple syrup	➡	Honey
Sweet potatoes	➡	Butternut squash, acorn squash, spaghetti squash
Tapioca flour, arrowroot flour	➡	Almond flour, coconut flour (not 1:1 in recipes, quantities will vary)

For more information on the Specific Carbohydrate Diet and the GAPS protocol, we recommend these resources:

www.breakingtheviciouscycle.info (SCD) and www.gapsdiet.com (GAPS)

aip-friendly

Autoimmune Paleo (AIP), also sometimes known as the Autoimmune (AI) Protocol, is a stricter form of the Paleo diet that eliminates the following foods: eggs, nightshades, nuts, seeds, coffee, chocolate, and seed-based spices. These foods can irritate the gut wall and cause holes to form between the cells of the intestinal lining, allowing undigested food and bacteria into the bloodstream and triggering an immune response that can ultimately cause the immune system to attack healthy tissue.

Please note that while some people also eliminate berry- and fruit-based spices, such as black pepper, cardamom, or vanilla beans, we haven't included these ingredients under the autoimmune Paleo umbrella. Green beans and fresh peas are also gray-area foods that we've allowed in our AIP-friendly recipes and meal plans.

Common Paleo AIP Swaps

Tomatoes	→	Pumpkin, Autoimmune-Friendly No-Mato Sauce (page 187), beets, carrots
Eggplant	→	Zucchini
Eggs	→	Plantains, bananas
Almond flour	→	Coconut flour, tapioca flour, arrowroot flour
Cumin	→	Turmeric, cardamom
Nutmeg	→	Cinnamon
Seed-based spices	→	Garlic, fresh herbs
Cayenne, chili powder, paprika	→	Ginger, black pepper, raw horseradish
Stevia	→	Maple syrup, honey

For more information on the autoimmune Paleo protocol, we recommend these resources:

The Paleo Approach, by Sarah Ballantyne and her website (www. thepaleomom.com); *The Autoimmune Paleo Cookbook,* by Mickey Trescott; *Practical Paleo,* by Diane Sanfilippo.

nightshades

Nightshades are a family of plants that contain alkaloid compounds that can be irritating if you suffer from joint pain or inflammation. Tomatoes, white potatoes, bell peppers, chiles, and eggplants are the most commonly consumed nightshades. Other, less frequently consumed nightshades include tomatillos, tobacco, goji berries, cape gooseberries (not regular gooseberries), ground cherries (not Bing or Rainier cherries), garden huckleberries (not blueberries), and ashwagandha, an herb commonly found in supplements. Paprika is derived from peppers, so it should also be avoided. If a packaged food contains "spices" without listing them individually, paprika is probably one of them.

If you suffer from joint pain, joint inflammation, arthritis, cracking, or any other joint-related issues, eliminate nightshades from your diet for at least thirty days, then add them back in slowly to see how your body responds. See the meal plan on pages 68 to 71 for nightshade-free options, and follow the AIP modification directions for each recipe.

lower carb

Many people initially reduce their carbohydrate intake because they have insulin resistance, metabolic syndrome, or pre-diabetes, but even those without these conditions often feel better, have more energy, and have more stable moods when they reduce carbohydrates.

While we don't emphasize counting calories or carbs, the "lower carb" label will be helpful for anyone who wants to limit their carbohydrates from sweeteners, fruits, and starchy vegetables.

A note on sweeteners: Instead of refined sugar, our dessert recipes use a natural sweetener called stevia extract powder, which is easy to find online, at Whole Foods, or at Trader Joe's. It is a concentrated form of the stevia leaf, which has been used as a sweetener in South America and Asia for hundred of years.

When converting Paleo recipes to fit a lower carb plan, 1 tablespoon of honey is equivalent to 1/4 teaspoon of stevia extract powder. In some of the lower carb modifications we've provided, this conversion may vary a bit, based on our testing results. Feel free to use more or less stevia as desired to suit your palate.

Common Paleo Lower Carb Swaps

Higher carb fruits	➡	Berries
Rice	➡	Cauliflower Couscous (page 332)
Fries, chips	➡	Jicama strips, red pepper strips, endive leaves
Maple syrup, honey	➡	Stevia extract powder (I recommend Sweet Leaf Organic or Trader Joe's brand)
Potatoes, sweet potatoes	➡	Turnips
Grain-free pasta	➡	Spaghetti squash noodles (see page 192), Zucchini Noodles (page 178), sliced cabbage
Grain-free pizza crust	➡	Lower Carb Pizza Crust (page 171)
Tapioca flour, arrowroot	➡	Almond flour, coconut flour (not 1:1 in recipes, quantities will vary)

a word on treats and desserts

Sometimes when you're transitioning to a Paleo lifestyle, it's helpful to have options for sweets and treats—especially at a party or family gathering. Paleo-friendly treats are usually very nutrient-dense compared to store-bought treats because they are made with eggs, nuts, and seeds, and the sweeteners used in Paleo treats are unrefined, so they retain some vitamins and minerals.

But keep in mind that even Paleo treats are best enjoyed on special occasions or holidays and should not be part of an everyday diet. In fact, after following a Paleo diet for a while, most people feel less and less need to have dessert. Be honest with yourself about how many sweets and treats—even if they're Paleo—are too many for your health goals.

meal plans

The following meal plans have been created to provide you with a general idea of how the meals in this book may fit into your everyday life. You may choose to follow them exactly, or they may just give you an idea of how to best balance your intake of a variety of foods.

The plans are written to feed two adults and often make use of leftovers. Since the amount of food that people eat varies widely, you may find that you need a bit more or a bit less food than is planned for here. Keep your own needs in mind when you shop for groceries, and remember that you don't have to eat everything included in these plans to follow the Mediterranean Paleo way of eating for optimal health.

mediterranean paleo meal plan

This meal plan is designed for people following a standard Paleo diet that includes meat, vegetables, fruit, nuts, seeds, and unprocessed fats. It is a good idea to eliminate dairy entirely for thirty days or more and then add it back in slowly to see how you respond. If all goes well, you may want to include high-quality grass-fed dairy on your Paleo plan. During the elimination period, use coconut oil for cooking and omit any cheese that may be an option in the recipes.

Whenever possible, choose organic produce, grass-fed or pastured meat, and wild fish. Remember that you don't have to follow this plan exactly as written, so feel free to mix and match the meals or change the plan to suit your needs.

what about snacks and desserts for this plan?

While you are welcome to snack and enjoy desserts on this meal plan, they aren't listed in the day's meals. Everyone's needs are different, so it's up to you to decide what types of snacks work best for you and whether or not you'll be enjoying desserts while on this plan. In general, though, we recommend snacking on a small handful of nuts with some fruit, leftover protein with some freshly cut vegetables, or even a small portion of leftovers. Although we've included plenty of dessert recipes to tempt your palate later in the book, desserts should be enjoyed sparingly for optimal health. We recommend not making desserts more than once a week or so, or for special occasions or events.

mediterranean paleo meal plan

day	breakfast	lunch	dinner
1 ●●◆	Apricot-Orange Smoothie (94)	Cumin Cauliflower Soup (148), Mediterranean Burgers (252)	Almond-Crusted Cod (280), Golden Raisin Slaw (330)
2 ●●◆	Swiss Chard and Garlic Frittata (86), piece of fruit	*leftover* Almond-Crusted Cod, *leftover* Golden Raisin Slaw	Braised Beef, Artichokes, and Peas (Jelbana) (254)
3 ●◆■	*leftover* Swiss Chard and Garlic Frittata, piece of fruit	*leftover* Braised Beef, Artichokes, and Peas (Jelbana)	Harissa-Spiced Chicken Wings (198), Sautéed Green Beans with Lamb Bacon (318)
4 ●■◆	Gingery Sweet Potato Muffins (106), Savory Breakfast Sausage (88)	*leftover* Harissa-Spiced Chicken Wings, *leftover* Sautéed Green Beans with Lamb Bacon	Creamy Cilantro Salmon (288), Cauliflower Couscous of choice (332)
5 ●◆●	*leftover* Gingery Sweet Potato Muffins, *leftover* Savory Breakfast Sausage	*leftover* Creamy Cilantro Salmon, *leftover* Cauliflower Couscous of choice	Kefta Lamb Kebabs (Persian Version) (244), Minty Cucumber and Tomato Salad (134)
6 ●●■	Strawberry Coffee Cake (108)	*leftover* Kefta Lamb Kebabs (Persian Version), *leftover* Minty Cucumber and Tomato Salad	Za'atar Brick Chicken (216), Nora's Green Bean Soup (156)
7 ●■◆	*leftover* Strawberry Coffee Cake	*leftover* Za'atar Brick Chicken, *leftover* Nora's Green Bean Soup	Shrimp Alfredo (190)
8 ●●◆	Cumin and Cauliflower Frittata (92)	Sardine Salad With Capers And Olives (274)	Harissa Braised Short Ribs (230), Cauliflower Couscous of choice (332)
9 ◆◆◆	*leftover* Harissa Braised Short Ribs, *leftover* Cauliflower Couscous of choice	Cabbage and Meatball Soup (150)	Mediterranean Seafood Salad (266)
10 ◆■■	*leftover* Cabbage and Meatball Soup	*leftover* Mediterranean Seafood Salad	Za'atar and Garlic Roasted Duck (208), Perfect Sweet Potato Fries (320)

key

◆ Beef
● Eggs
● Lamb
● Offal

■ Poultry
◆ Seafood
● Your Choice

Icon denotes the main protein source in the meal and may be altered to your preference.

Printer-friendly shopping lists for this plan can be found at www.MediterraneanPaleoCooking.com. Keep in mind that the plan and shopping lists are designed to feed two people with leftovers.

mediterranean paleo meal plan

day	breakfast	lunch	dinner
11 ●■◆	Fried Sweet Potato Omelet (82)	*leftover* Za'atar and Garlic Roasted Duck over mixed greens with Citrus Dressing (136)	Crispy Fried Sardines (page 276) or Sardine Cakes (270), Mock Potato Salad (326)
12 ●◆●	*leftover* Fried Sweet Potato Omelet	*leftover* Sardine Cakes, *leftover* Mock Potato Salad	Zesty Liver and Beef Meatloaf (306), Easy Sweet Potato Salad (132)
13 ●●◆	Spinach and Olive Scramble (90)	Salmon and Crab Roll-Ups (260)	Siva's Cauliflower and Meatballs (234)
14 ◆◆●	*leftover* Siva's Cauliflower and Meatballs	*leftover* Salmon and Crab Roll-Ups	Allspice Oxtail Soup (310), mixed greens with Citrus Dressing (136)
15 ◆◆●	Cinnamon-Apricot Breakfast Cookies (104), Savory Breakfast Sausage (88)	Lemon Garlic Shrimp (264), Roasted Garlic Cauliflower Hummus (118), Cilantro Crackers (124)	Shish Kebabs (248), Cauliflower Couscous of choice (332)
16 ●●●	Crab Hash with Poached Eggs and Hollandaise (80), Herbes de Provence Biscuits (78)	*leftover* Shish Kebabs, *leftover* Cauliflower Couscous of choice	Sweet Lamb Stew (L'ham Hlou) (238), Cauliflower Couscous of choice (332)
17 ●◆■	*leftover* Sweet Lamb Stew (L'ham Hlou), *leftover* Cauliflower Couscous of choice	Fattoush Shrimp Salad (262) with *leftover* Cilantro Crackers	Chicken and Olive Tajine (196), Cauliflower Couscous of choice (332)
18 ◆●●	Orange Blossom Pancakes (98), Savory Breakfast Sausage (88)	Savory Breakfast Sausage (88), mixed greens with Mint Pesto (186)	Paleo Moussaka (256), mixed greens with Citrus Dressing (136)
19 ●●●	Pomegranate-Blueberry Smoothie (94)	*leftover* Paleo Moussaka, *leftover* mixed greens with Citrus Dressing	Tangy Lamb Stew with Saffron and Ginger (Harira) (146), Tabouli Salad (126)
20 ●◆■	Crêpes with Pomegranate Sauce (102)	Spaghetti and Cumin-Spiced Meatballs (192)	Savory Chicken Kebabs (200), Cauliflower Couscous of choice (332)

key

◆ Beef   ■ Poultry
● Eggs   ◆ Seafood
● Lamb   ● Your Choice
● Offal

Icon denotes the main protein source in the meal and may be altered to your preference.

Printer-friendly shopping lists for this plan can be found at www.MediterraneanPaleoCooking.com. Keep in mind that the plan and shopping lists are designed to feed two people with leftovers.

mediterranean paleo meal plan

day	breakfast	lunch	dinner
21 ◆●○◆	Meatball Chakchouka (76)	protein of choice, Arugula and Artichoke Salad with Citrus Dressing (136)	Easy Paleo Falafel (130), Tahini Dipping Sauce (393), Shish Kebabs (248)
22 ●●○◆	*leftover* Meatball Chakchouka	protein of choice, Shaved Jicama Salad with Citrus Vinaigrette (138)	Peppers and Zucchini Stuffed with Lamb (Lamb Dolmas) (222)
23 ●○●■	*leftover* Peppers and Zucchini Stuffed with Lamb (Lamb Dolmas)	Mediterranean Chicken Liver Pâté (298) with Cilantro Crackers (124) or cut-up raw vegetables	Fig and Ginger Chicken Tajine (204), Cauliflower Couscous of choice (332)
24 ●■◆	Cinnamon Spice Pancakes (96), bacon of choice	*leftover* Fig and Ginger Tajine, *leftover* Cauliflower Couscous of choice	Pistachio-Crusted Sole (284), steamed vegetables of choice
25 ●◆■	Eggs Florentine (84), Herbes de Provence Biscuits (78)	Seared Tuna Salade Niçoise (268)	Lamb-Stuffed Chicken Thighs (212), Charmoula Roasted Vegetables (334)
26 ●●■	Roasted Eggplant Casserole (328)	[make ahead] Algerian Beef Heart Chili (304)	Nacera's Lemon Ginger Chicken Tajine (214)
27 ■○◆	*leftover* Nacera's Lemon Ginger Chicken Tajine	*leftover* Algerian Beef Heart Chili	Paella (292)
28 ●◆◆	Apricot Breakfast Bread (110), bacon of choice	*leftover* Paella	Almond Meatball Soup (M'touam) (160)
29 ●◆●	Mediterranean Paleo Pizza (166), with breakfast toppings (168)	*leftover* Almond Meatball Soup (M'touam)	Spiced Rack of Lamb (242) with Mint Pesto (186), Warm Eggplant and Tomato Salad with Mint (Zaalouk) (324), and Mini Pitas (142)
30 ●●◆	*leftover* Mediterranean Paleo Pizza	*leftover* Spiced Rack of Lamb with Mint Pesto, *leftover* Zaalouk, and Mini Pitas	Cioppino (282)

Key

◆ Beef
● Eggs
● Lamb
○ Offal
■ Poultry
◆ Seafood
○ Your Choice

Icon denotes the main protein source in the meal and may be altered to your preference.

Printer-friendly shopping lists for this plan can be found at www.MediterraneanPaleoCooking.com. Keep in mind that the plan and shopping lists are designed to feed two people with leftovers.

autoimmune meal plan

The autoimmune Paleo protocol is a stricter form of Paleo that eliminates nuts, seeds, eggs, and nightshade vegetables and spices. It is often used for four to eight weeks to significantly reduce inflammation in the body and heal the gut.

If a recipe isn't already AIP-friendly, use the modifications provided for each recipe. Always use either a nondairy cooking fat, such as coconut oil, or an animal fat, such as duck fat or tallow.

Many breakfasts in this plan resemble dishes that are traditionally eaten as dinners. This is primarily because eggs are not included in the plan, and it's a good idea to get used to eating hearty meals for breakfast to ensure your success. Dining out may be a bit of a challenge on this program, so plan ahead and pick a period of time when you can cook at home and take self-prepared meals when traveling.

avoid

- **Eggs** (especially the whites)
- **Nuts and seeds** (including cocoa, coffee, and seed-based spices)
- **Nightshades** (potatoes, tomatoes, eggplants, sweet and hot peppers, cayenne, red pepper, tomatillos, goji berries, and spices derived from peppers, including paprika)
- **Potential gluten cross-reactive foods** (foods that can mimic gluten in the gut, such as coffee, chocolate, dairy, eggs, tapioca, oats, and other grains)
- **Sweeteners,** artificial (such as aspartame and sucralose) and natural (such as stevia)

emphasize

- **Grass-fed meats** (bone-in is best)
- **Wild fish**
- **Organ meats**
- **Organic and local vegetables and fruit** (but limit fruit to 2 servings per day)
- **Coconut oil, pastured animal fats, sustainable palm oil, avocados**
- **Bone broth**
- **Fermented foods,** such as kimchee, kombucha, kefir, kvass, and sauerkraut
- **Fresh and dried herbs and spices,** such as cinnamon, saffron, turmeric, garlic, ginger, and horseradish

what about snacks and desserts for this plan?

You may or may not need snacks on this meal plan. If you do snack, we recommend small servings of fruit, leftover protein with some freshly cut vegetables, or even a small portion of leftovers. Although we've included plenty of dessert recipes to tempt your palate later in the book, along with modifications to fit this plan wherever possible, desserts should be enjoyed sparingly on this plan. We recommend not making desserts more than once a week or so, or for special occasions or events.

autoimmune meal plan

day	breakfast	lunch	dinner
1 ● ◆ ●	Apricot-Orange Smoothie (94)	[make ahead] Seared Tuna Salade Niçoise (268)	Spiced Rack of Lamb (242), Cauliflower Couscous of choice (332)
2 ● ◆ ●	Savory Breakfast Sausage (88), sautéed spinach	*leftover* Seared Tuna Salade Niçoise	Paleo Moussaka (256), mixed greens with Citrus Dressing (136)
3 ● ● ●	*leftover* Savory Breakfast Sausage, Savory Sweet Potato Cakes (page 322)	*leftover* Paleo Moussaka, *leftover* mixed greens with Citrus Dressing	Algerian Beef Heart Chili (304) with *leftover* Savory Sweet Potato Cakes (322)
4 ● ● ■	Autoimmune-Friendly Banana Pancakes (100)	*leftover* Algerian Beef Heart Chili	Kabylie Cinnamon Chicken Tajine (210)
5 ■ ◆ ■	*leftover* Kabylie Cinnamon Chicken Tajine	Sardine Salad With Capers And Olives (274)	Savory Chicken Kebabs (200), Cauliflower Couscous of choice (332)
6 ■ ● ■	*leftover* Savory Chicken Kebabs, *leftover* Cauliflower Couscous of choice	protein of choice, Arugula and Artichoke Salad with Citrus Dressing (136)	Nacera's Lemon Ginger Chicken Tajine (214)
7 ■ ◆ ●	*leftover* Nacera's Lemon Ginger Chicken Tajine	[make ahead] Lemon Garlic Shrimp (264), mixed greens with Mint Pesto (186)	Liver Meatballs with Mushroom Gravy (312)
8 ● ● ◆	Savory Breakfast Sausage (88), Savory Sweet Potato Cakes (322)	*leftover* Liver Meatballs with Mushroom Gravy	Zesty Crab Cakes with Aioli (272), Arugula and Artichoke Salad with Citrus Dressing (136)
9 ◆ ■ ●	*leftover* Zesty Crab Cakes with Aioli, steamed broccoli	[make ahead] Fig and Ginger Chicken Tajine (204)	Allspice Oxtail Soup (310), mixed greens with Citrus Dressing (136)
10 ● ■ ●	Pomegranate-Blueberry Smoothie (94)	*leftover* Fig and Ginger Tajine	Sweet Lamb Stew (L'ham Hlou) (238), Cauliflower Couscous of choice (332)

key

◆ Beef   ■ Poultry
● Lamb   ◆ Seafood
● Offal   ● Your Choice

Icon denotes the main protein source in the meal and may be altered to your preference.

Printer-friendly shopping lists for this plan can be found at www.MediterraneanPaleoCooking.com. Keep in mind that the plan and shopping lists are designed to feed two people with leftovers.

autoimmune meal plan

day	breakfast	lunch	dinner
11 ●○■■	*leftover* Sweet Lamb Stew (L'ham Hlou), Cauliflower Couscous of choice (332)	[make ahead] Beef Tongue with Green Olives (308)	Za'atar Brick Chicken (216), Beet and Carrot Salad (128)
12 ■○●◆	*leftover* Za'atar Brick Chicken, *leftover* Beet and Carrot Salad	*leftover* Beef Tongue with Olives	Lemon-Butter Steamed Mussels (294), mixed greens with Citrus Dressing (136)
13 ●◆●○	Mediterranean Chicken Liver Pâté (298) with cut raw vegetables	*leftover* Lemon-Butter Steamed Mussels, *leftover* mixed greens with Citrus Dressing	Grilled Beef Heart Skewers (314), Minty Cucumber and Tomato Salad (134)
14 ◆○●●	Creamy Cilantro Salmon (288), Cauliflower Couscous of choice (332)	*leftover* Grilled Beef Heart Skewers, *leftover* Minty Cucumber and Tomato Salad	Basil Minestrone Soup (154), Shish Kebabs (248)
15 ●◆●●	*leftover* Basil Minestrone Soup, *leftover* Shish Kebabs	*leftover* Creamy Herb Salmon, *leftover* Cauliflower Couscous of choice	Lamb and Vegetable Tajine (232)
16 ●●○◆	*leftover* Lamb Tajine with Root Vegetables	protein of choice, Shaved Jicama Salad With Citrus Vinaigrette (138)	Fennel and Herb–Stuffed Fish (Hout-Fel-Koucha) (286)
17 ○◆●●	Apricot-Orange Smoothie (94)	*leftover* Fennel and Herb–Stuffed Fish (Hout-Fel-Koucha)	Rosemary Leg of Lamb (240), Golden Raisin Slaw (330)
18 ●●○◆	*leftover* Rosemary Lamb, *leftover* Golden Raisin Slaw	Mediterranean Chicken Liver Pâté (298) with cut raw vegetables	Stuffed Cabbage (Cabbage Dolmas) (246)
19 ◆●○■	*leftover* Stuffed Cabbage (Cabbage Dolmas)	*leftover* Mediterranean Chicken Liver Pâté with cut raw vegetables	Za'atar and Garlic Roasted Duck (208), Easy Sweet Potato Salad (132)
20 ●○■◆	Pomegranate-Blueberry Smoothie (94)	*leftover* Za'tar Roasted Duck, *leftover* Easy Sweet Potato Salad	Siva's Cauliflower and Meatballs (234)

key

◆ Beef   ■ Poultry
● Lamb   ◆ Seafood
○ Offal   ○ Your Choice

Icon denotes the main protein source in the meal and may be altered to your preference.

Printer-friendly shopping lists for this plan can be found at www.MediterraneanPaleoCooking.com. Keep in mind that the plan and shopping lists are designed to feed two people with leftovers.

autoimmune meal plan

day	breakfast	lunch	dinner
21 ◆◆■	*leftover* Siva's Cauliflower and Meatballs	Salmon and Crab Roll-Ups (260)	Lamb-Stuffed Chicken Thighs (212), Charmoula Roasted Vegetables (334)
22 ■◆■	*leftover* Lamb-Stuffed Chicken Thighs, *leftover* Charmoula Roasted Vegetables	Fattoush Shrimp Salad (262)	Basil Minestrone Soup (154), Savory Chicken Kebabs (200)
23 ■◆●	*leftover* Basil Minestrone Soup, *leftover* Savory Chicken Kebabs	canned tuna or protein of choice, Beet and Carrot Salad (128)	Liver Meatballs With Mushroom Gravy (312), Cauliflower Couscous of choice (332)
24 ●●■	*leftover* Liver Meatballs with Mushroom Gravy	[make-ahead] Mediterranean Burgers (252), Tabouli Salad (126)	Saffron Braised Chicken (206), Cauliflower Couscous of choice (332)
25 ■●◆	*leftover* Saffron Braised Chicken, *leftover* Cauliflower Couscous of choice	*leftover* Mediterranean Burgers, *leftover* Tabouli Salad	Paella (292)
26 ●◆◆	Savory Breakfast Sausage (88), Savory Sweet Potato Cakes (322)	*leftover* Paella	Top Sirloin with Mushroom Reduction Sauce (226)
27 ●●■	Apricot-Orange Smoothie (94)	[make ahead] Harira (146), mixed greens and Citrus Dressing (136)	Chicken and Olive Tajine (196), Cauliflower Couscous of choice (332)
28 ■●●	*leftover* Chicken and Olive Tajine, *leftover* Cauliflower Couscous of choice	*leftover* Harira, *leftover* mixed greens and Citrus Dressing	Spiced Rack of Lamb (242) with Mint Pesto (186), Golden Raisin Slaw (330)
29 ●◆●	*leftover* Spiced Rack of Lamb with Mint Pesto, *leftover* Golden Raisin Slaw	[make ahead] Creamy Cilantro Salmon (288), Cauliflower Couscous of choice (332)	Allspice Oxtail Soup (310), mixed greens with Citrus Dressing (136)
30 ●◆●	*leftover* Allspice Oxtail Soup	*leftover* Creamy Cilantro Salmon, *leftover* Cauliflower Couscous of choice	pizza with AIP Crust (171) and toppings of choice

key

◆ Beef   ■ Poultry

● Lamb   ◆ Seafood

● Offal   ● Your Choice

Icon denotes the main protein source in the meal and may be altered to your preference.

Printer-friendly shopping lists for this plan can be found at www.MediterraneanPaleoCooking.con. Keep in mind that the plan and shopping lists are designed to feed two people with leftovers.

recipes

These recipes combine Mediterranean culinary traditions with the health-optimizing guidelines of the Paleo lifestyle. The breakfast recipes are a combination of traditional favorites, such as omelets and pancakes, and outside-the-box egg-free dishes. Easy and tasty salads, appetizers, and sides are full of fresh flavors, while healing soups and odd bits are bursting with nutrients. Pump up your protein with a delectable selection of meat, poultry, and seafood dishes, and finish your meals with sweet, rich desserts. They're all designed to appeal to your palate as well as boost your health.

breakfast

meatball chakchouka

prep time: 15 minutes | *cook time:* 30 minutes | *serves:* 4

In the language of the Berbers, the indigenous people of North Africa, *chakchouka* (also spelled *shakshouka*) means "vegetable ragout," a well-seasoned vegetable mixture cooked in a thick sauce. While it's traditionally enjoyed for dinner, we love to make chakchouka for breakfast, since dishes with eggs are a morning favorite of ours. Chakchouka is a great choice for an elegant breakfast that's not too time-consuming, and it would be perfect to serve to brunch guests.

FOR THE MEATBALLS

1 teaspoon minced garlic

1/4 cup chopped fresh cilantro

1 pound ground beef

2 teaspoons ground cumin

fine sea salt and ground black pepper

FOR THE SAUCE

1 tablespoon unsalted butter, ghee, or coconut oil

1 medium white onion, diced

2 green or red bell peppers, diced

1 teaspoon minced garlic

2 cups diced tomatoes (4 medium)

1 tablespoon tomato paste

fine sea salt and ground black pepper

1 tablespoon ground cumin

1 cup Beef Broth (page 388), Chicken Broth (page 386), or water

4 large eggs

2 tablespoons chopped fresh cilantro, for garnish

1. Make the meatballs: Place the garlic, cilantro, ground beef, and cumin in a bowl. Liberally season the meat with salt and pepper. Mix the ingredients with your hands until thoroughly combined. Form the meat mixture into 1-inch balls, place them on a plate, and set aside.

2. Make the sauce: Melt the fat over medium heat in a large saucepan. Add the onion and peppers to the pan and sauté for 5 minutes. Add the garlic and sauté for 1 to 2 minutes. Add the diced tomatoes and tomato paste to the pan and sauté for 5 more minutes. Season the tomato mixture liberally with salt and pepper and add the cumin.

3. Add the beef broth to the pan and simmer for 10 minutes, uncovered, until the sauce begins to thicken. Add the meatballs to the pan and simmer for 5 to 7 minutes.

4. Make 4 wells for the eggs in the vegetable mixture. Crack the eggs into the wells and cook for 1 minute, covered, until the whites are firm and the yolks are opaque but still runny. Remove the pan from the heat. Sprinkle the cilantro on top and serve.

nut-free	Yes
egg-free	Omit the eggs.
low FODMAP	Omit the garlic and onions. Use garlic-infused olive oil as the cooking fat.
AIP-friendly	No
SCD/GAPS	Yes
lower carb	Yes

herbes de provence biscuits

prep time: 15 minutes | *cook time:* 15 minutes | *yield:* 9 biscuits

Many people who follow a Paleo way of eating miss biscuits and bread. This recipe is a pleasing alternative to wheat-based baked goods, and the biscuits are sturdy enough to be used with eggs for breakfast sandwiches. They're great on their own with butter or honey, and they also go well with soup or slow-cooked meats or stews.

3/4 cup tapioca flour

1/2 teaspoon baking soda

2 1/2 cups blanched almond flour

1/2 teaspoon fine sea salt

1 tablespoon Herbes de Provence (page 401; see Chef's Tip)

5 tablespoons cold unsalted butter, ghee, or coconut oil

3 large eggs, beaten

1. Preheat the oven to 350°F and line a baking sheet with parchment paper. Sift the tapioca flour and the baking soda into a large bowl. Add the almond flour, salt, and herbs and whisk to combine.

2. Slice the butter into 1-tablespoon pats. Add the pats of butter to the bowl with the dry ingredients (or scoop the ghee or coconut oil into the bowl using a tablespoon measuring spoon). Using two knives, cut the fat into the dough until there are pill-sized lumps throughout.

3. Carefully fold the eggs into the dough with a spatula, pouring in about one-third of the beaten eggs at a time.

4. Using a serving spoon, scoop the dough onto the prepared baking sheet in 2-inch mounds, placed 2 to 3 inches apart.

5. Bake for 15 minutes, or until golden brown. Let the biscuits cool on the baking sheet for 10 minutes before serving.

nut-free	No
egg-free	No
low FODMAP	Use cashew meal in place of the almond flour.
AIP-friendly	No
SCD/GAPS	Use the lower carb modification.
lower carb	Use 2 tablespoons sifted coconut flour in place of the tapioca flour.

chef's tip

Herbes de Provence is a blend of dried herbs from the Provence region of France. It can include savory, thyme, basil, oregano, and marjoram, among other herbs. You can make your own with our recipe on page 401, but you can also buy it premade at the grocery store. If you do not have herbes de Provence, you can substitute Italian seasoning in this recipe.

crab hash with poached eggs and hollandaise

prep time: 10 minutes, plus 15 minutes to make the sauce | *cook time:* 20 minutes | *serves:* 4

Caitlin: We love to make this breakfast for a holiday or a special occasion. Nabil taught me how to make poached eggs and hollandaise shortly after he started culinary school, and I was so impressed! He took a technique I'd thought was very difficult and made it easy for me to do on my own. This dish goes well with Herbes de Provence Biscuits (page 78), as pictured.

3 cups sliced sweet potato (about 3 medium)

2 tablespoons apple cider vinegar

1/4 cup unsalted butter, ghee, or coconut oil

fine sea salt and ground black pepper

2 tablespoons finely chopped shallot

2 teaspoons minced garlic

2 tablespoons chopped green onion, plus more for garnish

2 cups tightly packed fresh spinach

1/2 pound cherry tomatoes, halved

12 ounces cooked crabmeat, drained

8 large eggs

1 recipe Hollandaise Sauce (page 383), for serving

1 teaspoon ground paprika, for garnish

1. Heat a few inches of water in the bottom of a steamer pot over medium heat. When the water is boiling, place the sweet potatoes in the steamer basket and cover. Steam the sweet potatoes until slightly soft but not cooked through, about 8 to 10 minutes. Remove the potatoes from the steamer and set aside.

2. Prepare the egg-poaching water: Bring 3 cups of water and the apple cider vinegar to a rolling boil in a large saucepan over medium heat.

3. While the water is coming to a boil, prepare the hash: Melt the fat in a sauté pan over medium heat. Add the partially cooked sweet potatoes and a pinch of salt and pepper and sauté for 1 minute. Add the shallot and cook for 1 more minute, until the shallot is translucent.

4. Add the garlic, green onion, spinach, and tomatoes to the pan and sauté for 2 minutes. Shred the crab meat with your fingers and add it to the pan. Sauté for 1 minute more to heat through. Set the hash aside and cover to keep warm.

5. Crack 1 egg into a small bowl, then gently drop it into the saucepan with the boiling water. Repeat until all the eggs are in the water.

6. Cook the eggs for 1 to 2 minutes, until the whites are firm and opaque and the yolks are starting to firm up but still runny.

7. Portion out the crab hash onto 4 plates. Remove the eggs from the water one by one with a slotted spoon, tap the spoon over a clean towel to remove the excess water, and place 2 eggs over each hash portion.

8. Pour the hollandaise sauce on top of the eggs and hash. Top each plate with chopped green onion, the paprika, and a pinch of salt and pepper.

nut-free	Yes
egg-free	No
low FODMAP	Omit the shallot and garlic. Use garlic-infused olive oil as the cooking fat.
AIP-friendly	No
SCD/GAPS	Use butternut squash in place of the sweet potato.
lower carb	Use cubed pumpkin or spaghetti squash in place of the sweet potatoes.

chef's tip

If you make hollandaise sauce ahead of time, you can reheat it by placing it over simmering water in a double boiler, adding a few teaspoons of water, and whisking a few times until warm.

nutritionist's note

Egg yolks from pastured chickens are some of nature's most nutritious foods. They're full of vitamin D and choline, both of which support the immune system and help us maintain a healthy weight.

fried sweet potato omelet

prep time: 5 minutes, plus 10 to 12 minutes to make the fries |
cook time: 8 to 10 minutes | *serves:* 4

Nabil: This is a dish I grew up eating in Algeria, but we used white potatoes and served it on a French baguette. It was a huge meal, but I was always hungry an hour or two later. Now I make this with sweet potatoes and leave out the bread, and it keeps me full for four or five hours, which helps me keep up my energy during a long day of cooking.

---

1 tablespoon unsalted butter, ghee, or coconut oil

1 recipe freshly cooked Perfect Sweet Potato Fries (page 320)

8 large eggs, beaten

fine sea salt and ground black pepper

1/4 cup chopped fresh cilantro, for garnish

1. Melt the fat in a large skillet over medium heat.

2. Add the sweet potato fries to the skillet and pour the eggs on top. Season the egg mixture liberally with salt and pepper.

3. Lift the edges of the omelet with a spatula and tilt the pan slightly to let the uncooked egg run underneath the omelet and cook on the bottom of the pan. Continue this process until the omelet is fully cooked, 8 to 10 minutes.

4. Sprinkle the cilantro on top of the omelet and slide it onto a plate.

5. Serve the omelet for breakfast or as an appetizing side dish.

nut-free	Yes
egg-free	No
low FODMAP	Yes
AIP-friendly	No
SCD/GAPS	Use the SCD version of Perfect Sweet Potato Fries (page 320).
lower carb	No

nutritionist's note

Cooked sweet potatoes have half the glycemic load of whole wheat bread. They also have a good deal of fiber, which helps blunt their blood sugar impact. Sweet potatoes are also a good source of potassium, which is helpful for regulating blood pressure.

eggs florentine

prep time: 5 minutes, plus 15 minutes to make the sauce |
cook time: 10 minutes | *serves:* 4

This dish reminds us of a trip we took to New York City in 2010. We ate a delicious gluten-free breakfast there in a fancy French café whose dishes had a seasonal focus and were made with organic eggs. This dish goes well with Herbes de Provence Biscuits (page 78), as pictured.

2 tablespoons apple cider vinegar

2 tablespoons unsalted butter, ghee, or coconut oil

8 cups tightly packed fresh spinach

1/4 cup chopped fresh basil

fine sea salt and ground black pepper

2 large tomatoes, sliced into 8 rounds

8 large eggs

1 recipe Hollandaise Sauce (page 383), for serving

1 teaspoon paprika, for garnish

1. Combine 3 cups of water and the vinegar in a saucepan and bring to a rolling boil over medium heat.

2. Meanwhile, prepare the spinach: In a sauté pan, melt the butter over medium heat. Add the spinach and basil with a pinch of salt and pepper and sauté until wilted. Transfer the spinach mixture to a bowl and cover to keep warm. (Do not clean the pan; you'll use it momentarily.)

3. Return the pan to medium heat and add the tomato slices. Sprinkle with salt and pepper and cook for 1 minute on each side, or until slightly browned. Set the tomatoes aside.

4. Crack 1 egg into a small bowl, then gently drop it into the saucepan with the boiling water. Repeat until all the eggs are in the water. Cook for 1 to 2 minutes, until the whites are firm and opaque and the yolks are slightly firm but still runny.

5. Place 2 tomato slices on each plate and top with the spinach. Remove the eggs one by one with a slotted spoon and tap over a dry, clean cloth to remove the excess water. Place 1 egg on top of each spinach and tomato base.

6. Top the eggs with the hollandaise sauce and paprika. Season with a pinch of salt and pepper, serve, and enjoy.

nut-free	Yes
egg-free	No
low FODMAP	Yes
AIP-friendly	No
SCD/GAPS	Yes
lower carb	Yes

nutritionist's note

Spinach has one of the highest amounts of vitamin K1 of any vegetable. Vitamin K1 is great for building bones and maintaining normal blood clotting, but make sure you consume it with healthy fats, as in this recipe, so that it's properly absorbed.

swiss chard and garlic frittata

prep time: 5 minutes | *cook time:* 20 minutes | *serves:* 2 to 3

Nabil: When I was growing up, every week during the summer my mom and I would walk home from the neighborhood farmers market carrying a huge bunch of Swiss chard just to make this frittata. The flavors of the garlic, onion, and paprika combine to enhance the Swiss chard.

1 bunch Swiss chard

2 tablespoons unsalted butter, ghee, or coconut oil, plus more for greasing the dish

1/2 cup diced white onion

1 teaspoon minced garlic

fine sea salt and ground black pepper

1 teaspoon paprika

6 large eggs

1. Preheat the oven to 350°F and grease a 2-quart baking dish.

2. Separate the leaves of the Swiss chard from the stems. Discard the stems or save for another use.

3. Cut the leaves into bite-sized pieces and wash them very well, making sure there is no leftover grit.

4. Heat a few inches of water in a steamer pot over medium-high heat. Steam the Swiss chard for 5 minutes, then remove the steamer from the heat. When it's cool enough to handle, squeeze the excess water out of the Swiss chard and set aside.

5. In a sauté pan, melt the fat over medium heat. Add the onion and cook until soft, about 3 minutes. Add the garlic, a pinch of salt and pepper, and the paprika and sauté the mixture for 1 minute more.

6. Add the steamed Swiss chard to the sauté pan and sauté for 2 minutes, or until wilted.

7. Beat the eggs in a bowl and season them with a pinch of salt and pepper.

8. Transfer the Swiss chard mixture to the prepared baking dish. Pour the eggs over the mixture, making sure they cover the chard evenly.

9. Put the baking dish in the oven and cook for 8 to 10 minutes, until the eggs are firm. Slice and serve.

nut-free	Yes
egg-free	No
low FODMAP	Omit the garlic and use garlic-infused olive oil as the cooking fat. Omit the onion.
AIP-friendly	No
SCD/GAPS	Yes
lower carb	Yes

chef's tip

This dish is similar to a spinach frittata, but the garlic and paprika give it more flavor. It's great to make on the weekend for quick breakfasts on the go during the week. To reheat leftovers, place in a preheated 350°F oven for a few minutes.

savory breakfast sausage

prep time: 5 minutes | *cook time:* 8 minutes | *serves:* 4

We love having sausage for breakfast, but many sausages available at the grocery store have gluten or wheat fillers, or even MSG. We like to make our own sausage at home with pastured or grass-fed meats so that we know exactly what is in it. Another benefit of making sausage at home is that you can flavor it with your favorite seasonings and make it as hot or as mild as you like. This sausage pairs well with Herbes de Provence Biscuits (page 78)

---

1 pound ground meat of choice

2 teaspoons ground cumin

1 teaspoon paprika (use hot paprika if you like spicy sausage)

1/2 teaspoon fine sea salt

1/4 teaspoon ground black pepper

1. Combine the meat and seasonings in a large bowl. Mix well with your hands and form into 2-inch patties.

2. Heat a skillet over medium heat. Place the patties in the skillet, evenly spaced, and cook them for 3 to 4 minutes on each side.

nut-free	Yes
egg-free	Yes
low FODMAP	Yes
AIP-friendly	Use 2 teaspoons ground sage in place of the cumin and paprika.
SCD/GAPS	Yes
lower carb	Yes

chef's tip

Don't press down on sausage while it is cooking—it will dry it out. Also, a cast-iron skillet works perfectly for making sausage and should not require added cooking fat. If you use another type of skillet or a very lean meat, such as ground turkey breast or chicken, melt 1 tablespoon of cooking fat in the pan before placing the patties in to brown.

spinach and olive scramble

prep time: 10 minutes | *cook time:* 10 minutes | *serves:* 2

We often enjoy a quick egg scramble for breakfast—it's a good way to use meat and vegetables left over from dinner. In this scramble, olives are used as a main ingredient; they add a rich, salty flavor that is prevalent in Mediterranean cooking. This dish pairs well with Herbes de Provence Biscuits (page 78).

6 ounces ground meat of choice

1/4 teaspoon fine sea salt

1/4 teaspoon ground black pepper

1 cup cherry tomatoes, halved

4 tightly packed cups spinach

1/4 cup sliced black olives

4 large eggs, beaten

1 avocado, sliced, for serving

2 tablespoons chopped fresh cilantro, for garnish

1/4 cup crumbled feta, for garnish (optional)

1. Heat a skillet over medium heat and add the ground meat. Season the meat with the salt and pepper and cook until browned, about 6 minutes, stirring to break up the meat as it cooks.

2. Add the tomatoes and spinach to the meat in the skillet and cook for 2 minutes, or until the spinach is wilted.

3. Add the olives and eggs to the skillet and keep stirring until the eggs are cooked, 2 to 3 more minutes.

4. Top with the avocado, cilantro, and feta, if desired.

nut-free	Yes
egg-free	No
low FODMAP	Yes
AIP-friendly	Sauté 2 shredded medium sweet potatoes in 1 tablespoon coconut oil for 5 minutes. Add the ground meat to the sweet potatoes and follow the rest of the directions, but omit the eggs, tomatoes, and feta.
SCD/GAPS	Omit the feta.
lower carb	Yes

chef's tip

A cast-iron skillet works perfectly for making sausage and should not require added cooking fat. If you use another type of skillet or a very lean meat, such as ground turkey breast or chicken, melt 1 tablespoon of cooking fat in the pan before placing the patties in to brown.

nutritionist's note

Many people choose to include dairy on a nutrient-dense Paleo diet. When choosing cheese or milk, seek out grass-fed dairy: it is richer in vitamin K2, which has cardiovascular benefits. And if you can find it, choose unpasteurized (raw) milk, which leaves essential enzymes intact for easier digestion. But before making dairy part of your diet, it's a good idea to eliminate it entirely for thirty days and then add it back slowly to see how it affects you.

cumin and cauliflower frittata

prep time: 5 minutes | *cook time:* 30 minutes | *serves:* 4

Caitlin: The cauliflower and cumin used in this frittata give it a unique and distinctive flavor. The first time Nabil made this for me I was so excited because cauliflower is one of my favorite vegetables, and this dish uses it beautifully. The moisture from the cauliflower also helps keep the eggs fluffy.

1 medium head cauliflower

2 tablespoons unsalted butter, ghee, or coconut oil

2 teaspoons minced garlic

1 cup cherry tomatoes, halved

fine sea salt and ground pepper

2 tablespoons chopped fresh cilantro

2 teaspoons ground cumin

6 large eggs

1. Preheat the oven to 350°F.

2. Core the cauliflower and cut it into small florets; discard the core.

3. Place the cauliflower in the top of a steamer pot with a few inches of water in the bottom. Steam the cauliflower over medium heat for about 10 minutes, until it is slightly soft but still firm.

4. Melt the fat in a large oven-safe skillet over medium heat. Sauté the garlic for 1 minute in the butter.

5. Add the tomatoes to the skillet and sauté for 2 to 3 minutes, until softened. Add a pinch of salt and pepper, the cilantro, and the cumin to the pan and stir to combine.

6. Add the drained cauliflower to the skillet and season with a pinch of salt and pepper. Sauté the cauliflower and tomato mixture for 2 more minutes to allow the flavors to meld.

7. In a bowl, beat the eggs with a pinch of salt and pepper. Pour the beaten eggs into the skillet, evenly covering the vegetables, and cook for 1 minute without stirring.

8. Put the skillet in the oven and bake for 7 to 10 minutes, until the eggs are cooked through.

9. Turn the oven to broil to brown the top of the eggs for 1 minute.

10. Remove the skillet from the oven and slice the frittata into wedges. Serve and enjoy.

nut-free	Yes
egg-free	No
low FODMAP	Omit the garlic and use garlic-infused olive oil as the cooking fat.
AIP-friendly	No
SCD/GAPS	Yes
lower carb	Yes

chef's tip

Any leftovers from this frittata are great to eat on the go. Reheat in a small baking dish in a toaster oven set to 350°F for a few minutes, or just let it warm to room temperature before eating.

nutritionist's note

Cauliflower is a cruciferous vegetable that helps with liver detoxification, which increases our fat-burning ability. Cauliflower also provides vitamin C, which helps support a healthy immune system.

pomegranate-blueberry smoothie

prep time: 10 minutes | *cook time:* n/a | *serves:* 2

We often see pomegranates at farmers markets in the fall, when they are in season. When we learned that they are low in carbs and high in antioxidants, we started coming up with new ways to eat them, such as pairing them with blueberries in this delicious smoothie.

2 cups full-fat, canned coconut milk

1 cup pomegranate seeds (about 2 pomegranates; see Chef's Tips)

1 tablespoon rose water (see Chef's Tips) or grated orange zest

2 cups frozen blueberries

1 tablespoon honey

2 tablespoons grass-fed beef gelatin

1. Place the coconut milk and pomegranate seeds in a blender and blend until almost smooth (there will still be small bits of seed).

2. Pour the mixture through a wire-mesh strainer set over a bowl, pressing against the seeds to extract as much liquid as possible. Discard the seeds.

3. Rinse out the blender. Pour the strained coconut and pomegranate mixture back into the blender and add the rose water, blueberries, and honey.

4. Pulse a few more seconds, add the gelatin, and pulse again until smooth. Pour into two 8-ounce glasses and enjoy.

apricot-orange smoothie

prep time: 5 minutes | *cook time:* n/a | *serves:* 2

Apricots, a traditional Mediterranean ingredient, are plentiful and affordable when in season. As a kid, Nabil loved to climb trees and jump over walls to steal a taste of tree-ripened apricots. Luckily, today we can pick up this wonderfully sweet and fragrant fruit at the local farmers market, no wall-climbing necessary.

2 cups full-fat, canned coconut milk

2 medium apricots, pitted

1 large navel orange, peeled

1 tablespoon lemon juice

1 teaspoon rose water (optional; see Chef's Tips)

2 cups ice

2 tablespoons grass-fed beef gelatin

1. Combine the coconut milk, apricots, orange, lemon juice, rose water, if using, and ice in a blender and pulse until smooth.

2. Add the gelatin and pulse again until smooth. Pour into two 8-ounce glasses and enjoy.

for both smoothies

nut-free	Yes
egg-free	Yes
low FODMAP	Use 1/4 teaspoon stevia extract powder in place of the honey. Use 1 banana in place of the apricot.
AIP-friendly	Yes
SCD/GAPS	Yes
lower carb	Use 1/4 teaspoon stevia extract powder in place of the honey.

chef's tips

To extract seeds from a pomegranate, cut the pomegranate crosswise through the middle and, working over a large bowl, bang on the back of the shell to dislodge the seeds. Break open the white shell with your fingers to free the remaining seeds, discarding the white pith.

These recipes use rose water, a steam distillation of rose petals that smells heavenly and tastes great. Rose water is available at Middle Eastern food stores or online at Amazon.com, but if you can't find it, orange or lemon zest can be used for a similar flavor.

nutritionist's note

If, like most of us, you're in a rush in the morning, these are fast and easy recipes to make on the go. Pomegranates and blueberries are full of antioxidants for brain health. Coconut milk is easily digested and converts into fuel in the liver for quick energy. Gelatin has 6 grams of protein per tablespoon and is beneficial for healthy skin, bones, and teeth.

a note on gelatin

I recommend using gelatin from a grass-fed source. Brands I have found include Great Lakes and Vital Proteins. If you choose Great Lakes for smoothies, use the green label as it will dissolve in the liquid. The orange or red label will gel and is useful as an egg replacement to bind ingredients in other recipes.

cinnamon spice pancakes

prep time: 5 minutes | *cook time:* 10 minutes | *serves:* 2 |
yield: 6 (3-inch) pancakes

Caitlin: The scent of these cinnamon pancakes will bring everyone to the kitchen on a Sunday morning. When I made them for my younger brothers, they begged for seconds!

1/4 cup plus 2 tablespoons coconut flour

1/2 teaspoon baking soda

1/4 teaspoon ground nutmeg

1 teaspoon ground cinnamon

4 large eggs, beaten

1/2 cup full-fat, canned coconut milk

1 teaspoon lemon juice

2 teaspoons honey

2 tablespoons unsalted butter, ghee, or coconut oil, for cooking

melted butter or ghee, for serving

1. Sift the coconut flour, baking soda, nutmeg, and cinnamon into a large bowl. Add the eggs, coconut milk, lemon juice, and honey to the bowl. Whisk until smooth.

2. Melt the fat in a medium skillet over medium heat. Pour 1/4 cup of batter into the hot pan for each pancake, leaving room for it to spread. Cook each pancake for 2 minutes, then flip it over and cook for 2 more minutes on the opposite side. Transfer the cooked pancakes to a plate and cover to keep warm while you cook the rest of the pancakes.

3. Top with the melted butter and serve.

nut-free	Yes
egg-free	No
low FODMAP	Use the lower carb modification.
AIP-friendly	No
SCD/GAPS	Yes
lower carb	Use 1/4 teaspoon stevia extract powder in place of the honey.

chef's tip

Nutmeg adds a special dimension to sweet or savory recipes and pairs beautifully with the creamy texture of the coconut milk in these pancakes.

orange blossom pancakes

prep time: 5 minutes | *cook time:* 10 minutes | *serves:* 2 |
yield: 6 (3-inch) pancakes

Caitlin: As a kid, I used to eat pancakes made on a huge griddle right on the table, but they were made from boxed pancake mix, and I used to get a tummy ache and then have to lie down for a while after breakfast. This version will help you avoid any digestive distress and keep you satisfied for hours.

2 tablespoons coconut flour

1/2 teaspoon baking soda

1/4 teaspoon ground nutmeg

2 tablespoons cashew meal or blanched almond flour

4 large eggs

3/4 cup full-fat, canned coconut milk

2 teaspoons orange blossom water (see Chef's Tip) or grated orange zest

1/2 teaspoon apple cider vinegar

2 teaspoons honey (optional)

2 tablespoons unsalted butter, ghee, or coconut oil

sliced fruit of choice, for serving

1. Sift the coconut flour, baking soda, and nutmeg into a large bowl. Add the cashew meal and whisk to combine.

2. In another bowl, whisk together the eggs, coconut milk, orange blossom water, vinegar, and honey, if using. Add the wet mixture to the dry and whisk until smooth.

3. Melt the fat in a large skillet over medium heat. Pour about 1/4 cup of the batter per pancake into the hot pan, leaving room for it to spread. Cook each pancake for 2 minutes, then flip it over and cook for 2 more minutes on the opposite side. Transfer the cooked pancakes to a plate and cover to keep warm while you cook rest of the pancakes.

4. Top with sliced fruit and enjoy.

nut-free	Try Cinnamon Spice Pancakes (page 96) instead.
egg-free	No
low FODMAP	Use 1/4 teaspoon stevia extract powder in place of the honey. Avoid almond flour.
AIP-friendly	No
SCD/GAPS	Yes
lower carb	Use 1/4 teaspoon stevia extract powder in place of the honey.

chef's tip

Orange blossom water is a natural ingredient available at Middle Eastern food stores or online at Amazon.com. It's a steam distillation of Seville orange blossoms, and it adds a unique dimension of flavor to pancakes. If you don't have orange blossom water, grated orange or lemon zest can be used instead.

autoimmune-friendly banana pancakes

prep time: 10 minutes | *cook time:* 25 minutes | *serves:* 3 |
yield: 6 (3-inch) pancakes

Though these baked pancakes can be enjoyed by anyone, we created them especially for those following the autoimmune Paleo protocol. They combine the sweetness of banana with the familiar flavor of cinnamon, and they're delicious with Blueberry Sauce (page 381). They're also especially filling; six pancakes are enough for three people if served with Savory Breakfast Sausage (page 88).

3 medium bananas

1 tablespoon honey

2 tablespoons melted coconut oil

1/2 teaspoon apple cider vinegar

1/3 cup coconut flour

1 teaspoon baking soda

1 tablespoon arrowroot flour

1/4 teaspoon fine sea salt

1 teaspoon ground cinnamon

maple syrup or honey, for serving (optional)

melted butter, ghee, or coconut oil, for serving (optional)

1. Preheat the oven to 350°F. Line a baking sheet with parchment paper.

2. Place all the ingredients in a food processor and pulse until smooth.

3. Spoon a few tablespoons of batter onto the prepared baking sheet and spread into a pancake about 3 inches in diameter and 1/3 inch thick. Repeat until all the batter is used. For a perfectly shaped pancake, use a ring mold.

4. Bake for 15 minutes, then flip the pancakes and bake for 10 more minutes.

5. Let the pancakes cool on the baking sheet for 10 minutes before serving. Top with maple syrup, honey, or melted fat of choice. Serve and enjoy.

nut-free	Yes
egg-free	Yes
low FODMAP	Omit the honey and maple syrup.
AIP-friendly	Yes
SCD/GAPS	Omit the maple syrup.
lower carb	No

crêpes with pomegranate sauce

prep time: 5 minutes, plus 20 minutes to make the sauce |
cook time: 15 minutes | *yield:* 6 (6-inch) crêpes

When we were newlyweds, we frequented a crêperie owned by an Algerian friend of Nabil's in the Castro neighborhood of San Francisco. We often got sweet crêpes with tasty toppings such as fruit and whipped cream, but they also made a delicious savory salmon crêpe that we enjoyed. This grain-free version is our nod to that warm memory. While this recipe doesn't make stuffed crêpes, you can easily roll them up with a jam or filling of your choice. Blueberry Sauce (page 381) would work perfectly.

2 tablespoons tapioca flour

2 tablespoons coconut flour

1/2 teaspoon ground nutmeg (optional)

1/2 teaspoon ground cinnamon (optional)

1/4 teaspoon fine sea salt

3/4 cup full-fat, canned coconut milk

4 large eggs

1 teaspoon vanilla extract (gluten-free)

1 teaspoon orange blossom water (see Chef's Tip, page 98) or grated orange zest

2 tablespoons unsalted butter, ghee, or coconut oil, divided

1 recipe Easy Pomegranate Sauce (page 380)

1. Sift the tapioca and coconut flour into a large mixing bowl. Add the spices, if using, and salt to the flour mixture and whisk to combine.

2. Combine the coconut milk, eggs, vanilla, and orange blossom water in another bowl and whisk until well combined.

3. Slowly whisk the wet ingredients into the dry ingredients until smooth.

4. Melt 1 teaspoon of the fat in a medium skillet over medium heat. Tilt the pan to evenly coat the bottom of the pan with the fat.

5. Pour about 1/4 cup of the batter into the pan. Smooth the batter out with a rubber spatula until it is about 1/8 inch thick.

6. Cook the crêpe for about 1 minute, then carefully flip and cook for 30 seconds more. Place the crêpe on a plate and cover with a towel to keep it warm while you cook the rest of the crêpes. Add the remaining fat, a teaspoon at a time, as needed.

7. Roll the crêpes into cylinders and serve with the pomegranate sauce.

nut-free	Yes
egg-free	No
low FODMAP	Yes
AIP-friendly	No
SCD/GAPS	Use 2 tablespoons cashew meal or blanched almond flour in place of the tapioca flour. Use seeds of 1 scraped vanilla bean in place of the vanilla extract.
lower carb	Use 2 tablespoons cashew meal or blanched almond flour in place of the tapioca flour. Use the lower carb modification for the pomegranate sauce.

chef's tip

Make sure you spread the crêpe thin enough that it gets crispy on the edges. And before you flip it over, run the spatula under the edge all around the crêpe, to make sure it will easily turn over.

nutritionist's note

Many people miss crêpes and pancakes on a Paleo diet, but this recipe gives you the best of both worlds—delicious crêpes without any hard-to-digest wheat or excessive carbs that spike blood sugar.

cinnamon-apricot breakfast cookies

prep time: 10 minutes | *cook time:* 15 to 18 minutes |
serves: 4 | *yield:* 12 cookies

Caitlin: These not-too-sweet cookies are perfect for a quick, portable breakfast when you are on the run in the morning. They also remind me of oatmeal cookies, so if you miss those as much as I do, these are a great replacement.

3 tablespoons ground chia seeds or ground golden flax seeds

2 teaspoons lemon juice

1/2 teaspoon vanilla extract (gluten-free)

1/2 cup plus 1 tablespoon filtered water

1/4 cup coconut flour, sifted

1/2 teaspoon baking soda

1/2 teaspoon fine sea salt

1 teaspoon ground cinnamon

3/4 cup unsweetened shredded coconut

1/2 cup chopped dried apricots

3/4 cup cashew butter or sun butter

2 to 3 tablespoons honey, to taste

1. Preheat the oven to 350°F. Line a baking sheet with parchment paper.

2. In a small bowl, mix the chia seeds with the lemon juice, vanilla, and water. Let the chia mixture sit for about 10 minutes, until it forms a gel.

3. In another bowl, whisk the coconut flour with the baking soda, salt, and cinnamon. Add the shredded coconut and apricots and mix until well combined.

4. Melt the cashew butter and honey in a saucepan over medium heat. Add the cashew butter mixture to the dry ingredients and stir well.

5. Add the chia gel to the dough and mix until a thick, sticky dough forms. Scoop the cookie dough into 2-inch mounds and place on the prepared baking sheet about 2 inches apart. Repeat until all the dough is used.

6. Bake for 15 to 18 minutes, until golden brown. Let the cookies cool on a wire rack. Serve and enjoy.

nut-free	Use sun butter instead of cashew butter.
egg-free	Yes
low FODMAP	Omit the apricots. Use 2 teaspoons stevia extract powder in place of the honey.
AIP-friendly	No
SCD/GAPS	Yes
lower carb	Omit the apricots. Use 2 teaspoons stevia extract powder in place of the honey.

nutritionist's note

Sun butter is made from ground sunflower seeds and can be used as a 1:1 replacement for most nut butters. Look for an organic, unsweetened variety in stores or online.

gingery sweet potato muffins

prep time: 10 minutes | *cook time:* 15 to 20 minutes |
serves: 4 | *yield:* 12 muffins

Ginger is a common Mediterranean ingredient that adds a hint of spice to complement the sweet flavor of these muffins. To make them extra special, frost them with Coconut Icing (page 115).

1/3 cup coconut flour

1/2 teaspoon baking soda

2 teaspoons ground cinnamon

1 teaspoon ground nutmeg

1 teaspoon ground ginger

1/2 cup sweet potato puree
(1 medium sweet potato)

1/2 cup melted coconut oil

6 large eggs

1 teaspoon vanilla extract
(gluten-free)

3 tablespoons honey

1 recipe Coconut Icing
(page 115; optional)

1. Preheat the oven to 350°F. Line 12 muffin cups with paper liners.

2. Sift the coconut flour and baking soda into a large mixing bowl. Add the cinnamon, nutmeg, and ginger and stir the flour mixture together until well combined.

3. In another bowl, combine the sweet potato puree, coconut oil, eggs, vanilla extract, and honey.

4. Slowly add the dry mixture to the wet and whisk until a smooth batter forms.

5. Divide the batter evenly among the muffin cups, filling them two-thirds full.

6. Bake for 15 to 20 minutes, until a toothpick inserted in the center of a muffin comes out clean.

7. Leave the muffins in the pan to cool for 10 minutes before serving. If desired, frost the muffins with the coconut icing when completely cooled and sprinkle additional cinnamon on top.

nut-free	Yes
egg-free	No
low FODMAP	Use 3/4 teaspoon stevia extract powder in place of the honey.
AIP-friendly	No
SCD/GAPS	Use the seeds of 1 scraped vanilla bean in place of the vanilla extract. Use cooked butternut squash in place of the sweet potato.
lower carb	Use 3/4 teaspoon stevia extract powder in place of the honey and 1/2 cup canned pumpkin in place of the sweet potato.

nutritionist's note

Ginger is a pungent and spicy root that helps soothe the digestive system.

strawberry coffee cake

prep time: 10 minutes | *cook time:* 35 minutes | *serves:* 4 to 6

Caitlin: It can be hard to avoid gluten at social events, so I decided to bring this coffee cake to a brunch where I didn't know if there would be Paleo-friendly options. It was a big hit, and no one even knew it was gluten- and grain-free.

1/2 cup coconut flour

1/2 teaspoon baking soda

6 large eggs

1/4 cup ground golden flax seeds

1/2 cup melted coconut oil, plus more for greasing the dish

2 teaspoons orange blossom water (see Chef's Tip, page 98) or grated lemon zest

1/4 cup honey

1 cup sliced strawberries

1. Preheat the oven to 350°F. Grease an 8-by-8-inch baking dish with coconut oil.

2. Sift the coconut flour and baking soda into a medium bowl.

3. In a large bowl, beat the eggs and flax together and let sit for 2 minutes. Then add the coconut oil, orange blossom water, and honey and mix until well combined.

4. Slowly add the dry flour mixture to the egg mixture and stir until thoroughly combined. Gently fold the strawberries into the batter.

5. Pour the batter into the prepared baking dish.

6. Bake for 35 minutes, or until a toothpick inserted in the center comes out clean.

7. Let the cake cool in the pan for 5 to 10 minutes before slicing and serving.

nut-free	Yes
egg-free	No
low FODMAP	Use 1 teaspoon stevia extract powder in place of the honey.
AIP-friendly	No
SCD/GAPS	Yes
lower carb	Use 1 teaspoon stevia extract powder in place of the honey.

chef's tip

This recipe also makes great muffins, which are especially easy to transport if you use paper muffin liners. For muffins, fill 10 lined muffin wells two-thirds full. Don't skip the sifting of the coconut flour—it makes for a fluffier texture. If you do not have a flour sifter, you can use a wire-mesh strainer for the same effect.

nutritionist's note

Buy organic strawberries. Conventionally grown strawberries top the Environmental Working Group's annual list of most contaminated produce, also referred to as the "Dirty Dozen," because their thin skin easily absorbs toxic pesticides.

apricot breakfast bread

prep time: 10 minutes | *cook time:* 15 minutes | *serves:* 6

Caitlin: This bread reminds me of the plentiful selection of breakfast treats we saw on our trip to North Africa. Many people there have sweet rolls and espresso for breakfast at cafés, a habit adopted from continental Europe. This is a healthier version of that breakfast, and it will keep you full and energized until lunchtime.

1/2 cup dried apricots

1/2 cup coconut flour

1/4 teaspoon baking soda

2 tablespoons blanched almond flour

1/2 teaspoon fine sea salt

1/4 cup melted coconut oil, plus more for greasing the pan

2 tablespoons honey

2 teaspoons rose water (see Chef's Tips, page 95) or grated lemon zest

4 large eggs

1. Preheat the oven to 350°F. Grease a 9-inch round cake pan with coconut oil.

2. Dice the apricots and set aside.

3. Sift the coconut flour and baking soda into a large bowl. Add the almond flour and salt and mix well.

4. In another bowl, whisk together the coconut oil, honey, rose water, and eggs.

5. Pour the wet mixture into dry mixture and mix thoroughly.

6. Gently fold the apricots into the dough a little at a time. When all the apricots are fully incorporated in the dough, pour it into the prepared cake pan and spread evenly.

7. Bake for 15 minutes, or until golden brown. Cool in the pan for a few minutes before slicing into triangles. Serve with coffee or tea.

nut-free	Use finely ground sunflower seeds (see page 170) in place of the almond flour.
egg-free	No
low FODMAP	Use cashew meal in place of the almond flour and 1 teaspoon stevia extract powder in place of the honey. Use 1/2 cup sliced bananas in place of the apricots.
AIP-friendly	No
SCD/GAPS	Yes
lower carb	Use 1 cup unsweetened dried cranberries in place of the apricots and 1 teaspoon stevia extract powder in place of the honey.

nutritionist's note

Because dried fruit is high in concentrated fructose, take note of how it affects your blood sugar. It's also important to monitor your portions closely because many people find it hard to stop eating dried fruit. One healthy strategy is to eat it with lots of fat and protein, which will lower its glycemic load. This dish has a good balance of fat and protein to even out the sugar impact of the dried fruit.

easy cinnamon and ginger granola

prep time: 5 minutes | *cook time:* 20 minutes | *serves:* 8

Miss the breakfast cereal of your pre-Paleo days? This granola is a great substitute. The ginger and cinnamon create a wonderful aroma while the granola is baking and add a unique, spicy-sweet flavor to your breakfast bowl.

1 cup raw sunflower seeds

1 cup hulled raw pumpkin seeds

1 cup chopped raw pecans

1 cup chopped raw walnuts

2 cups unsweetened shredded coconut

2 teaspoons ground cinnamon

2 teaspoons ground ginger

1 teaspoon fine sea salt

3 tablespoons coconut sugar

1/4 cup coconut oil, melted

Vanilla Coconut Yogurt (page 114, as pictured) or almond milk, for serving (optional)

1. Preheat the oven to 300°F. Line a rimmed baking sheet with parchment paper.

2. Combine the seeds and nuts, shredded coconut, spices, salt, and coconut sugar in a large bowl.

3. Add the melted coconut oil to the bowl and stir to coat the mixture evenly.

4. Pour the mixture onto the prepared baking sheet and spread it out in a thin layer.

5. Bake for 20 minutes, stirring every 5 minutes to avoid burning.

6. Let the mixture cool completely on the baking sheet, about 45 minutes. Serve with the coconut yogurt or almond milk, if using.

7. Store leftovers in an airtight container in the pantry for 5 to 6 days or in the refrigerator for up to 2 weeks.

nut-free	Omit the walnuts and pecans. Double the pumpkin and sunflower seeds.
egg-free	Yes
low FODMAP	Use 1 teaspoon stevia extract powder in place of the coconut sugar. Omit the almond milk.
AIP-friendly	No
SCD/GAPS	Use 3 tablespoons honey in place of the coconut sugar.
lower carb	Use 1 teaspoon stevia extract powder in place of the coconut sugar.

vanilla coconut yogurt

prep time: 5 minutes, 24 hours to incubate, 3 to 4 hours to chill | *cook time:* n/a | *yield:* 2 cups

Not only is this yogurt a great option if you're sensitive to dairy, it's also an easy way get beneficial bacteria in your diet.

1 (13 1/2-ounce) can full-fat coconut milk

1 probiotic capsule (see Nutritionist's note)

seeds scraped from 1 vanilla bean

1.   Place the coconut milk in a glass container that has a lid. Open the probiotic capsule and pour the contents into the glass container with the milk. Stir to combine; discard the capsule shell.

2.   Place the lid on the container and set it in the oven with the oven light on, leaving the oven off. This will keep the yogurt at 110°F, which helps the beneficial bacteria grow.

3.   Leave the yogurt in the oven for 24 hours. Take the yogurt out of the oven and stir in the vanilla bean seeds. Chill for 3 to 4 hours before serving. The yogurt will keep for 7 days in the refrigerator.

nutritionist's note

Use a probiotic that has about 10 billion bacteria per capsule. The strain Bifidobacterium *is a good one to try. Gut bacteria support the immune system and are necessary for healthy digestive function.*

nut-free	Yes
egg-free	Yes
low FODMAP	Yes
AIP-friendly	Yes
SCD/GAPS	Yes
lower carb	Yes

coconut icing

prep time: 2 minutes | *cook time:* 3 minutes | *yield:* 1 1/2 cups

Use this tasty icing to frost the cooled Gingery Sweet Potato Muffins (page 106).

---

1 cup coconut butter

2 teaspoons ground cinnamon

1/3 cup honey

1 teaspoon vanilla extract (gluten-free)

Mix all the ingredients in a saucepan over medium heat until melted, then let cool for 5 minutes.

nut-free	Yes
egg-free	Yes
low FODMAP	Use 1/2 teaspoon stevia extract powder in place of the honey.
AIP-friendly	Yes
SCD/GAPS	Use the seeds of 1 scraped vanilla bean in place of the vanilla extract.
lower carb	Use 1/2 teaspoon stevia extract powder in place of the honey.

appetizers

roasted garlic cauliflower hummus

prep time: 10 minutes | *cook time:* 45 minutes | *serves:* 4

We made this for our Super Bowl party one year, and no one noticed a difference between it and traditional hummus made from chickpeas. Everyone asked for the recipe! Serve it with Cilantro Crackers (page 124), as pictured, or fresh raw vegetables.

1 head garlic

6 tablespoons extra-virgin olive oil, divided

6 cups cauliflower florets (1 large head)

2 tablespoons tahini (sesame seed paste)

1 tablespoon lemon juice

1 teaspoon ground cumin

1 teaspoon paprika

fine sea salt and ground black pepper

1. Preheat the oven to 350°F.

2. Chop the top off of the head of garlic and coat the head with 2 tablespoons of the olive oil. Place it in a small glass baking dish and roast it in the oven for 35 minutes.

3. Place the cauliflower florets in a steamer pot with several inches of water over medium-high heat. Steam the cauliflower until it's cooked and fork-tender but not mushy, about 10 minutes. Drain the cauliflower and place it in a food processor.

4. Squeeze 4 to 6 of the roasted garlic cloves out of their skins and into the food processor. Save the rest of the roasted garlic for another use, such as a pizza topping.

5. Add the tahini, lemon juice, remaining 4 tablespoons of olive oil, cumin, paprika, and a pinch of salt and pepper to the food processor. Pulse the mixture until smooth. Adjust seasonings to taste and chill for before serving, if desired.

nut-free	Yes
egg-free	Yes
low FODMAP	Omit the garlic and use garlic-infused olive oil in place of the regular olive oil.
AIP-friendly	Omit the tahini, cumin, and paprika and add 2 tablespoons olive oil to the cauliflower.
SCD/GAPS	Yes
lower carb	Yes

chef's tip

The roasted garlic gives the hummus a unique flavor that is rich and earthy. But if you're in a hurry, you can use 1 tablespoon of garlic powder instead.

nutritionist's note

Chickpeas, like all legumes, have hard-to-digest lectins (a type of protein) as well as phytates that can block the absorption of minerals. While legumes can be healthy in moderation if they are soaked first, if you're struggling with health issues, eliminating them entirely for a period of time will help you heal faster. In the meantime, this cauliflower hummus makes a great substitute.

eggplant dip (baba ghanoush)

prep time: 5 minutes | *cook time:* 35 minutes | *serves:* 4

Caitlin: When I was on a low-fat diet, I ate hummus like it was going out of style. I was sad to learn that I would have to give it up because chickpeas can cause digestive problems. But since discovering that baba ghanoush is just as tasty and easy to make as hummus, I haven't given the bean dip a second thought. Serve baba ghanoush with Cilantro Crackers (page 124), as pictured, or your choice of raw vegetables.

2 large purple eggplants

4 cloves garlic

fine sea salt and ground black pepper

1 teaspoon ground cumin

2 tablespoons lemon juice

4 tablespoons tahini (sesame seed paste)

2 tablespoons chopped fresh cilantro, for garnish

2 tablespoons extra-virgin olive oil, for garnish

1. Preheat the oven to 350°F. Line a baking sheet with parchment paper.

2. Place the whole eggplants on the baking sheet. In each eggplant, hollow out 2 holes large enough for a garlic clove. Stick a clove of garlic in each hole. Bake the eggplants for about 30 minutes, until soft.

3. Let the eggplants cool for 5 minutes. Cut the stems off the eggplants and put them in a food processor, skin on. Add a pinch of salt and pepper, the cumin, and the lemon juice to the food processor. Pulse the mixture a few times, until all of the ingredients are combined. Add the tahini and pulse for 10 seconds. Taste the dip and adjust the seasoning to your taste.

4. Transfer the dip to a bowl and top with the cilantro and olive oil. Serve warm.

chef's tip

Eggplants are abundant during the summer in North Africa, where they're cooked in many different ways. They have a high water content, but roasting dries them out and enhances their sweet flavor. After cooking, the eggplant skin becomes soft and undetectable in most dishes.

nutritionist's note

A phytonutrient found in eggplant skin called nasunin is a potent antioxidant and free-radical scavenger—which means it helps protect cell membranes from damage.

nut-free	Yes
egg-free	Yes
low FODMAP	Use 1/2 cup chopped fresh chives in place of the garlic and add in Step 3. Use garlic-infused olive oil in place of the regular olive oil.
AIP-friendly	No
SCD/GAPS	Yes
lower carb	Yes

roasted pepper dip (hmis)

prep time: 10 minutes | *cook time:* 35 minutes | *serves:* 4

Nabil: Hmis is a roasted pepper dish that is traditionally served before a meal to stimulate the appetite. When we were visiting my family in Algeria, we tried many different versions, and it was funny to watch Caitlin's face as she experienced different levels of heat depending on which of my relatives had made it. Hmis is typically served with bread but also works well with Cilantro Crackers (page 124) or crudités for people on a grain-free diet.

4 green, red, or yellow bell peppers, or a combination

1 jalapeño pepper (optional)

1 tablespoon unsalted butter, ghee, or coconut oil

2 teaspoons minced garlic

2 cups diced tomatoes

fine sea salt and black pepper

2 to 4 tablespoons extra-virgin olive oil, for garnish

1/4 cup pitted black olives, for garnish

2 tablespoons chopped fresh cilantro, for garnish

1. Preheat the oven to 400°F. Wash the bell peppers and jalapeño pepper, if using, arrange them whole in a roasting dish, and place it in the oven. Roast for 12 to 15 minutes, until all sides are charred, rotating them with tongs every 4 minutes. (See the detailed tutorial on page 396.)

2. Remove the bell peppers and jalapeño pepper from the oven and place them in an airtight container for 5 minutes. This process will steam off the skins. Once the skins have started to lift away from the peppers, remove the peppers and let them cool. Peel and core the peppers, then cut them lengthwise into thin strips. Discard the core and seeds of the bell peppers. Keep the jalapeño seeds for maximum heat, if desired.

3. Melt the fat over medium heat in a skillet. Add the garlic and sauté for 1 minute.

4. Add the tomatoes and a pinch of salt and pepper. Cook for 5 to 7 minutes, until some of the water from the tomatoes evaporates. Keeping the pan over medium heat, add the sliced peppers and sauté for 5 more minutes. Transfer the cooked mixture to a plate.

5. Garnish with the olive oil, olives, and fresh cilantro. Serve warm or at room temperature.

nut-free	Yes
egg-free	Yes
low FODMAP	Omit the garlic. Use garlic-infused olive oil in place of regular olive oil.
AIP-friendly	No
SCD/GAPS	Yes
lower carb	Yes

chef's tip

Hmis can be mild or very spicy depending on your preference. To make it less spicy, remove the seeds from the jalapeño pepper or omit the jalapeño altogether.

cilantro crackers

prep time: 15 minutes | *cook time:* 15 to 18 minutes |
yield: 8 to 12 crackers | *serves:* 4

If you miss crunchy foods on the Paleo diet, these crisp crackers will bring back the warm memories of wheat crackers without the guilt or digestive upset. They are wonderful with Eggplant Dip (page 120), Roasted Garlic Cauliflower Hummus (page 118), or Roasted Pepper Dip (page 122).

2 cups blanched almond flour

1 tablespoon tapioca flour

fine sea salt and ground black pepper

2 tablespoons chopped fresh cilantro

2 large eggs, beaten

2 tablespoons tahini (sesame seed paste)

1 tablespoon extra-virgin olive oil

1. Preheat the oven to 350°F.

2. Mix together the almond flour, tapioca flour, and a pinch of salt and pepper in a large mixing bowl.

3. Mix the cilantro, eggs, tahini, and olive oil in another bowl. Pour the wet ingredients into the flour mixture and mix thoroughly.

4. Form the dough into a ball with your hands, put the ball on a large piece of parchment paper, and cover with another large sheet of parchment paper.

5. Roll out the dough until it is about 1/8 inch thick.

6. Remove the top parchment paper and cut the dough into 1-inch squares with a sharp knife.

7. Leaving the dough on the parchment paper, transfer it to a baking sheet and bake for 15 to 18 minutes, until golden brown.

8. Let the crackers cool for 5 minutes, then carefully separate the squares. Store in an airtight container for 3 to 5 days.

nut-free	Use finely ground sunflower seeds (see page 170) in place of the almond flour.
egg-free	No
low FODMAP	Use cashew meal in place of the almond flour.
AIP-friendly	No
SCD/GAPS	Use ground flax in place of the tapioca flour.
lower carb	Yes

chef's tip

These crackers do not have preservatives that keep other crackers crispy for many days. Reheat them in a toaster oven to bring back the crunch.

nutritionist's note

Cilantro is full of polyphenols and other antioxidants that help keep us looking and feeling young. This potent herb also helps the body naturally detoxify the heavy metals that we're all exposed to in the environment on a daily basis.

tabouli salad

prep time: 10 minutes | *cook time:* 8 minutes to make the couscous | *serves:* 4

Nabil: I used to work at a Middle Eastern restaurant where I made tabouli every day. It was an adjustment to learn how to make it without wheat, but I think you will love the result. It's just as tasty as the traditional version, and much better for you.

4 Roma tomatoes

1 large cucumber

1 medium red onion, diced

1 recipe Cauliflower Couscous (page 332)

FOR THE DRESSING

1/4 cup chopped fresh mint

1/2 cup chopped fresh parsley

3 tablespoons lemon juice

1/4 cup extra-virgin olive oil

fine sea salt and ground black pepper

1. Cut the tomatoes in half, core them, remove the seeds, and dice them. Peel the cucumber, cut it in half lengthwise, remove the seeds, and dice it.

2. Put the onion, cucumber, tomatoes, and cauliflower couscous in a large bowl.

3. In a small bowl, whisk together the mint, parsley, lemon juice, olive oil, and a pinch of salt and pepper. Pour the dressing over the cauliflower mixture and toss well. Adjust the seasoning to taste.

4. Chill for 30 minutes, if desired, before serving.

chef's tip

Tabouli is usually made with bulgur wheat and is very popular in the Middle East. In this version, we use cauliflower to emulate the texture of the wheat, and the result is delicious.

nutritionist's note

Historically, the wheat in traditional tabouli was soaked, which helped eliminate some of its hard-to-digest properties, but that time-honored practice has fallen out of fashion. Additionally, modern wheat has been hybridized, which increased the gluten content. Modern wheat is also heavily sprayed with strong pesticides, which may be part of the reason so many people are sensitive to it now. The cauliflower couscous used in this recipe is a much safer and healthier alternative.

nut-free	Yes
egg-free	Yes
low FODMAP	Use 1/2 cup chopped scallions in place of the red onion.
AIP-friendly	Use diced, steamed carrots in place of the tomatoes.
SCD/GAPS	Yes
lower carb	Yes

beet and carrot salad

prep time: 10 minutes | *cook time:* 20 to 25 minutes | *serves:* 4

Caitlin: The first time I had this salad was at a big dinner party hosted by an Algerian couple. I had never had a salad made with cooked and chilled vegetables, aside from potato salad. It's light and has a hint of sweetness, and it reminds Nabil of his family and home. It has become a staple in our weeknight menus.

5 medium red beets

5 medium carrots

1/4 cup apple cider vinegar

1/4 cup extra-virgin olive oil

1/2 teaspoon fine sea salt

1/4 teaspoon ground black pepper

1/4 cup chopped fresh cilantro, for garnish

1. Place the unpeeled beets in a large saucepan filled two-thirds of the way with water. Bring to a boil over medium-high heat and boil the beets for 20 to 25 minutes, until fork-tender.

2. Meanwhile, peel and slice the carrots into 1/2-inch circles, then boil them until slightly soft but still firm, about 5 minutes. Drain the cooked carrots and set them aside.

3. Rinse the boiled beets under cold running water, allowing the peels to slip off easily in your hands. Cut the beets into bite-sized pieces.

4. Arrange the carrots around the edge of a serving platter, then place the beets in the center.

5. Mix the vinegar, olive oil, salt, and pepper in a small bowl and pour the dressing over the vegetables. Sprinkle the cilantro on top.

6. Serve warm, at room temperature, or chilled.

chef's tip

Boiling the beets whole saves time, since there is no need to peel them—once the beets cool, their skins easily slip off under running water. Use gloves while peeling to avoid staining your hands.

nutritionist's note

Beets are teeming with nutrients. They have phytonutrients called betalains that help support the liver detox pathways. Also, beets have been studied a great deal for their cancer-protective properties. What's more, just 1 cup of cooked beets contains 35 percent of the recommended dietary intake of folate, which is very important for reproductive health.

nut-free	Yes
egg-free	Yes
low FODMAP	Yes
AIP-friendly	Yes
SCD/GAPS	Yes
lower carb	No

easy paleo falafel

prep time: 10 minutes | *cook time:* 10 minutes |
serves: 4 | *yield:* 12 balls

Falafel is a Middle Eastern street food that's thought to have originated in Egypt during times when meat was scarce. It's usually made with chickpeas or fava beans and wheat flour, but we made this recipe Paleo-friendly, without beans or gluten.

1 medium head cauliflower

2 large eggs, beaten

1/2 cup blanched almond flour

fine sea salt and ground black pepper

2 tablespoons chopped fresh parsley

2 teaspoons ground cumin

2 cups sustainable palm shortening or coconut oil

1 recipe Tahini Dipping Sauce (page 393), for serving

1. Core the cauliflower and cut it into florets, discarding the core. Using the shredder blade on a food processor, shred the florets.

2. Place the shredded cauliflower in a steamer pot with a few cups of water over medium heat. Steam the cauliflower for about 5 minutes, until cooked but not mushy. Squeeze the cooked cauliflower in a clean towel over the sink to drain the excess water.

3. Place the cauliflower in a bowl and stir in the eggs, almond flour, a pinch of salt and pepper, the parsley, and the cumin. Mix the ingredients until well combined.

4. Melt the fat in a medium skillet over medium-high heat. The oil should be about 2 inches deep.

5. Form the cauliflower mixture into 2-inch balls and set them on a plate. Stick the end of wooden spoon into the fat; if you see bubbles form around the handle, the fat is hot enough. Carefully lower the balls into the fat with a slotted spoon.

6. Cook the falafel balls for 1 to 2 minutes, until golden brown, and then flip them and cook for another 1 to 2 minutes, until golden brown.

7. Remove the balls from the fat and let them cool on paper towels for 2 minutes. Serve the falafel with the dipping sauce and enjoy.

nut-free	Use 1/3 cup coconut flour in place of the almond flour.
egg-free	Use AIP-friendly modification.
low FODMAP	Use cashew meal in place of the almond flour.
AIP-friendly	Use 1 cup mashed ripe plantains and 1/4 cup coconut flour in place of the eggs and almond flour. Use 1 teaspoon ground ginger in place of the cumin. Use Tzatziki Sauce (page 392) in place of the Tahini Dipping Sauce.
SCD/GAPS	Yes
lower carb	Yes

chef's tip

It may be hard to believe, but I think this dish tastes even better than the original. The dough may seem a little wet before frying, but the egg cooks quickly, creating a firm, satisfying texture.

nutritionist's note

One benefit of making falafel at home is that you can control the quality of oil or fat used. Most restaurants use poor-quality industrial seed oils, which in some people can lead to digestive distress and advanced aging of the skin.

easy sweet potato salad

prep time: 10 minutes | *cook time:* 10 minutes | *serves:* 4

Potato salad is always a favorite for holidays and picnics. This version uses sweet potatoes, which are higher in antioxidants than white potatoes. It also adds the Mediterranean flavors of ginger and cilantro for a change of pace.

---

4 medium sweet potatoes

1/2 teaspoon fine sea salt

1/2 teaspoon ground black pepper

1/2 cup minced red onion

1 teaspoon ground ginger

1/4 cup extra-virgin olive oil

2 tablespoons apple cider vinegar

1/4 cup chopped fresh cilantro

1. Peel the sweet potatoes and cut them into bite-sized pieces.

2. Place the sweet potatoes in a steamer pot with 3 cups of water over medium heat. Cook until slightly soft or fork-tender but not mushy, about 10 minutes.

3. Place the sweet potatoes in a glass bowl and let cool for 5 minutes.

4. Make the dressing: In a small bowl, mix together the salt, pepper, onion, ginger, olive oil, vinegar, and cilantro. Pour the dressing over the sweet potatoes and toss.

5. Serve warm or chill for 1 hour before serving.

nut-free	Yes
egg-free	Yes
low FODMAP	Use 1/2 cup chopped scallions in place of the red onion.
AIP-friendly	Yes
SCD/GAPS	Use 6 cups cubed butternut squash in place of the sweet potatoes.
lower carb	No. Try the Mock Potato Salad (page 326) instead.

chef's tip

Look for sweet potatoes that are firm and free of cuts or scrapes. Avoid stringy potatoes by choosing ones that are medium-sized. Store them in a cool, dark cabinet or pantry.

nutritionist's note

Some people have a reaction to the skins of white potatoes because they have glycoalkaloids that can irritate the digestive tract. Sweet potatoes are from a different plant family and do not cause the same problems for people with sensitive digestive systems.

minty cucumber and tomato salad

prep time: 5 minutes | *cook time:* n/a | *serves:* 4

Dressed simply with olive oil and lemon juice and seasoned with a touch of fresh mint and garlic, this cucumber and tomato salad has a light, fresh flavor. In North Africa and the Middle East, it's traditionally served as an accompaniment to grilled meats and is made with plain, full-fat yogurt. We've made the yogurt optional here—it's just as good without it!

2 medium cucumbers

2 Roma tomatoes

1/2 cup plain yogurt (optional)

2 tablespoons extra-virgin olive oil

1 teaspoon minced garlic

2 tablespoons chopped fresh mint

fine sea salt and black pepper to taste

2 tablespoons lemon juice

1. Peel the cucumbers, cut them in half lengthwise, and then scoop out the seeds with a spoon. Discard the seeds. Cut the tomatoes in half and scoop out the seeds and discard.

2. Dice the cucumbers and tomatoes.

3. Combine all of the ingredients in a salad bowl and toss.

4. If desired, chill the salad for 1 hour before serving.

nut-free	Yes
egg-free	Yes
low FODMAP	Omit the yogurt. Use 1/4 cup chopped scallions in place of the garlic.
AIP-friendly	Use diced, steamed carrots in place of the tomatoes and omit the yogurt.
SCD/GAPS	Yes
lower carb	Yes

chef's tip

Removing the seeds from the tomatoes makes the salad taste less acidic. Removing the cucumber seeds makes it less watery.

nutritionist's note

If you make this salad with yogurt, make sure to buy grass-fed, organic, full-fat yogurt for the most nutrients. Crucial immune-supporting vitamins A and D cannot be absorbed without fat.

arugula and artichoke salad with citrus dressing

prep time: 10 minutes | *cook time:* n/a | *serves:* 4

Artichoke hearts are a favorite at our house for adding texture and flavor to salads. They go wonderfully with bright citrus flavors, as in this easy-to-throw-together but still entirely impressive salad. If you like, you can add meat or fish to make this salad a full meal.

10 ounces arugula (about 8 cups)

1/2 red onion, sliced into 1-inch pieces

1 cup cherry tomatoes, halved

1/2 cup pomegranate seeds (see Chef's Tip)

1 1/2 cups canned, quartered artichoke hearts, drained (one 14-ounce can)

FOR THE DRESSING

2 tablespoons orange juice

2 teaspoons lemon juice

2 teaspoons lime juice

6 tablespoons extra-virgin olive oil

fine sea salt and ground black pepper to taste

1. Combine the arugula, onion, tomatoes, pomegranate seeds, and artichoke hearts in a large bowl.

2. In a small bowl, whisk together the dressing ingredients.

3. Pour the dressing over the salad ingredients and toss to coat thoroughly.

chef's tip

Arugula is a bitter green with a spicy flavor. It can be served cooked or fresh, as it is in this flavorful summer salad.

Pomegranates are in season in the United States from September through February; if you are making this salad at another time of year, you can substitute berries. Almonds or walnuts will also add crunch to this salad.

To easily extract the pomegranate seeds, follow Step 1 in the recipe for Easy Pomegranate Sauce (page 380). You will need about 1 pomegranate to get the 1/2 cup of seeds used in this recipe.

nutritionist's note

Arugula is a cruciferous vegetable that has been shown to have cancer-protective properties. Cruciferous vegetables also support the liver as it filters out toxins.

nut-free	Yes
egg-free	Yes
low FODMAP	Use hearts of palm in place of the artichoke hearts.
AIP-friendly	Omit the tomatoes.
SCD/GAPS	Yes
lower carb	Yes

shaved jicama salad with citrus vinaigrette

prep time: 10 minutes | *cook time:* n/a | *serves:* 2

Caitlin: This salad is similar to one Nabil made while working in a trendy San Francisco restaurant. Combining Mediterranean flavors with the cuisine of California, it's just the right light bite for a summer evening. It's also perfect topped with grilled shrimp or roasted chicken for a full meal.

1 head butter lettuce

6 ounces jicama (1 small)

1 mandarin orange

1/2 cup pomegranate seeds (see Chef's Tip)

FOR THE DRESSING

2 tablespoons extra-virgin olive oil

1/4 cup orange juice

fine sea salt and ground black pepper to taste

1. Wash and dry the lettuce, then chop it into bite-sized pieces.

2. Whisk the dressing ingredients in a large bowl and toss the lettuce in the dressing.

3. Pile the lettuce on two plates, with the largest pieces on the bottom.

4. Peel the hard skin off the jicama with a vegetable peeler and slice it very thin with a sharp knife, mandoline, or vegetable peeler.

5. Peel the mandarin and separate it into segments.

6. Arrange the sliced jicama, pomegranate seeds, and mandarin segments on top of the dressed lettuce.

nut-free	Yes
egg-free	Yes
low FODMAP	Use carrots in place of the jicama.
AIP-friendly	Yes
SCD/GAPS	Yes
lower carb	Omit the orange and use lemon juice in place of the orange juice in the dressing.

chef's tip

Jicama is a nonstarchy root vegetable from Central America that's common in California. If you don't see it at your everyday market, look for it at a Latino grocery store. It's crunchy and very versatile— try cutting it into fries or using it as a crudité with dips.

To easily extract pomegranate seeds, follow Step 1 in the recipe for Easy Pomegranate Sauce (page 380). You will need about 1 pomegranate to get the 1/2 cup of seeds used in this recipe.

caprese salad with basil dressing

prep time: 15 minutes | *cook time:* n/a | *serves:* 4

Caprese salad always brings back warm memories of eating in North Beach, an Italian neighborhood in San Francisco. In Italian this salad is called *insalata caprese*, which means "salad of Capri." It is usually made with tomatoes, fresh mozzarella, basil, and olive oil—the red, white, and green echo the colors of the Italian flag. If you don't eat dairy, simply replace the mozzarella with avocado, as we've done here.

2 cups cherry tomatoes

1 medium red onion

2 ripe medium avocados or 8 ounces fresh mozzarella balls

1/4 cup tightly packed fresh basil leaves

FOR THE DRESSING

1 cup tightly packed fresh basil leaves

1 teaspoon grated lemon zest

juice of 1 lemon

1/2 cup extra-virgin olive oil

fine sea salt and ground black pepper to taste

1. Rinse and dry the tomatoes.

2. Slice the red onion into small, bite-sized pieces.

3. If using the avocado, cut it in half lengthwise, slice into the pit to lodge the edge of the knife, and pull to remove the pit.

4. Use a melon baller to scoop the avocado into small balls.

5. Build the salad by placing a ball of avocado, basil leaf, piece of red onion, tomato, and a second basil leaf on a toothpick or small skewer. Repeat the process until all the ingredients are used.

6. Place the dressing ingredients in a food processor and pulse until smooth. Pour the dressing on a serving dish and place the skewers on top for dipping.

chef's tip

To store fresh basil, cut off the very end of the stems and place the leaves in a jar. Keep the jar in the refrigerator to extend the life of the basil several days.

nutritionist's note

Adding a handful of fresh basil to your Italian dishes can benefit your heart: basil is rich in beta-carotene, which protects the epithelial cells that line the heart. Basil is also rich in flavanoids, which help protect against excess environmental radiation.

nut-free	Yes
egg-free	Yes
low FODMAP	Omit the onion and cheese. For the dressing, add 1/4 cup chopped scallions.
AIP-friendly	Use cucumber slices in place of the tomato.
SCD/GAPS	Yes
lower carb	Yes

mini pitas

prep time: 10 minutes | *cook time:* 15 to 18 minutes | *yield:* 5 to 6 mini pitas

Pita is an unleavened bread that's common in the Mediterranean region, where it's often served with meat and vegetables stuffed inside. Our Paleo version is a great replacement for the original, which uses wheat flour. We've provided instructions for three slightly different variations, so you can impress your guests when you're entertaining or just add variety to your everyday meals.

FOR PLAIN PITA

1 large egg

1 tablespoon extra-virgin olive oil

1/4 teaspoon apple cider vinegar

1 tablespoon coconut flour

1/4 cup plus 2 tablespoons blanched almond flour

2 tablespoons ground golden flax seeds

1/2 teaspoon baking soda

1/4 teaspoon fine sea salt

1 teaspoon garlic powder

1/4 teaspoon ground black pepper

FOR GARLIC & HERB PITA

(add to plain pita recipe)

1 teaspoon garlic powder

1 tablespoon chopped fresh cilantro

FOR CHILI & PAPRIKA PITA

(add to plain pita recipe)

1 teaspoon paprika

1/4 teaspoon chili powder

1. Preheat the oven to 350°F. Line a baking sheet with parchment paper.

2. Whisk the egg, olive oil, vinegar, and 1/4 cup of water in a small bowl.

3. In another bowl, combine the coconut flour, almond flour, flax, baking soda, salt, and spices and/or herbs. Pour the egg mixture into the dry mixture and stir to combine.

4. Scoop a spoonful of the batter onto the parchment and spread it into a 3-inch circle that's about 1/2 inch thick. Repeat until all the batter is used.

5. Bake the pitas for 15 to 18 minutes, until firm to the touch. Cool on the baking sheet for 5 minutes, then serve and enjoy.

FOR A CASHEW VERSION

Use cashew meal instead of almond flour and increase the water to 1/2 cup.

nut-free	Use finely ground sunflower seeds (see page 170) in place of the blanched almond flour.
egg-free	No
low FODMAP	Omit the garlic powder. Use garlic-infused olive oil, if desired. Use the cashew version.
AIP-friendly	No
SCD/GAPS	Yes
lower carb	Yes

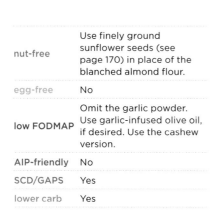

soups

tangy lamb stew with saffron and ginger (harira)

prep time: 10 minutes | *cook time:* 65 minutes | *serves:* 4

This soup gets its bold flavor from not just one but two acidic ingredients—lemon and vinegar—and the exotic pairing of fresh mint with turmeric, ginger, and saffron. Harira is made during religious festivals in North Africa and Middle East and is usually enjoyed as a first course. It traditionally contains lentils, but we've omitted them to be Paleo-compliant. We don't think you will miss them in this flavorful, meaty soup.

3 tablespoons unsalted butter, ghee, or coconut oil

1 pound lamb or beef stew meat

1/2 teaspoon saffron threads

1 teaspoon ground turmeric

1 teaspoon ground ginger

fine sea salt and ground black pepper

1 cup diced celery

1 medium onion, diced

4 medium tomatoes, cored, or 1 (14 1/2-ounce) can diced tomatoes

4 cups Beef Broth (page 388)

1/4 cup chopped fresh mint, divided

2 tablespoons apple cider vinegar

2 tablespoons lemon juice

1 lemon, sliced, for garnish

1. In a stockpot, melt the fat over medium heat. Add the meat, saffron, turmeric, ginger, and a pinch of salt and pepper. Sauté the meat for 5 minutes, then add the celery and onion and sauté for another 5 minutes, until the onion is translucent.

2. Place the tomatoes in a food processor and pulse until they are pureed. Add them to the pot. Add the beef broth and cook the mixture, uncovered, for about 45 minutes.

3. With a slotted spoon, remove the meat and set aside in a bowl.

4. Use an immersion blender to puree the soup. If you do not have an immersion blender, you can puree it in batches in a stand blender instead (see Chef's Tip).

5. Add the meat back to the pot and simmer the soup over medium heat, uncovered, until it thickens, about 10 minutes.

6. Add half of the mint, the vinegar, and the lemon juice to the soup and stir. Adjust the seasoning to taste and ladle into bowls. Garnish with remaining mint and the lemon slices.

nut-free	Yes
egg-free	Yes
low FODMAP	Omit the onion and garlic. Use garlic-infused olive oil as the cooking fat.
AIP-friendly	Use 2 cups canned pumpkin in place of the tomatoes.
SCD/GAPS	Yes
lower carb	Yes

chef's tip

When pureeing soup in a blender, take care not to overfill it—hot liquids will expand in the blender. It's best to puree the soup in batches. To avoid dangerous and messy accidents, put the blender lid firmly in place on top of the pitcher, but remove the center valve from the lid. Hold a thick kitchen towel over the lid, covering the valve opening, as you puree each batch.

nutritionist's note

Turmeric is one of the most potent anti-inflammatory spices. It has been shown to reduce pain and inflammation as well as many prescription medications.

cumin cauliflower soup

prep time: 5 minutes | *cook time:* 15 to 20 minutes | *serves:* 4

Nabil: In my family, cauliflower is a favorite, and I am always experimenting with new ways to prepare it, particularly when it's in season. This soup combines cauliflower with cumin and chili peppers—two of my other loves—to create a truly delicious and unique flavor.

---

1 large head cauliflower (about 2 pounds), cored and cut into florets (see Chef's Tip)

4 tablespoons unsalted butter, ghee, or coconut oil, divided

1 medium white onion, minced

2 teaspoons minced garlic

2 teaspoons ground cumin, plus more for garnish

1 teaspoon chili powder

fine sea salt and ground black pepper

4 cups Chicken Broth (page 386)

extra-virgin olive oil, for garnish

1. Rinse the cauliflower florets, drain, and set aside.

2. Melt 2 tablespoons of the fat in a large saucepan over medium heat. Add the onion and sauté it for 2 to 3 minutes. Add the garlic, cumin, chili powder, and a pinch of salt and pepper, and sauté for about 1 minute, until onion is translucent.

3. Add the chicken broth and cauliflower to the saucepan and simmer until tender, about 10 minutes. Stir in the remaining 2 tablespoons of fat.

4. Puree the soup with an immersion blender until creamy, or puree in a blender or food processor in batches. Adjust the seasonings to taste.

5. Ladle the soup into 4 bowls and top each with a sprinkle of cumin and a drizzle of olive oil.

nut-free	Yes
egg-free	Yes
low FODMAP	Use 1/2 cup chopped scallions in place of the onion and reduce cooking time to 1 minute. Omit the garlic and use garlic-infused olive oil as the cooking fat.
AIP-friendly	Omit the cumin and chili powder. Add 1/4 cup chopped fresh cilantro as a garnish.
SCD/GAPS	Yes
lower carb	Yes

chef's tip

Cauliflower is easily prepped in just a few seconds. First, remove the hard base and leaves with a knife, cutting straight across just under the florets. Then turn the cauliflower core to face upwards and insert a paring knife between the core and the florets. Cut in a circular motion around the core to extract it, much as you would core an apple. Discard the core. You are left with perfect florets.

nutritionist's note

Cauliflower and onions are rich sources of quercetin, a potent antioxidant that regulates blood sugar, lowers inflammation, and provides cardiovascular benefits.

cabbage and meatball soup

prep time: 10 minutes | *cook time:* 40 minutes | *serves:* 4

Nabil: This is a simpler version of a soup my mom makes at home. I streamlined her method to make it easier for people with busy schedules. This version takes less time but has just as much flavor and love.

FOR THE SOUP

1 large head cabbage (about 2 pounds)

3 tablespoons unsalted butter, ghee, or coconut oil

2 medium white onions, diced

2 teaspoons minced garlic

1 to 2 teaspoons chili powder

1 tablespoon ground cumin

1 teaspoon paprika

fine sea salt and ground black pepper

4 cups Beef Broth (page 388)

1/4 cup chopped fresh cilantro, for garnish

FOR THE MEATBALLS

2 pounds ground beef

fine sea salt and ground black pepper

1 tablespoon garlic powder

2 tablespoons chopped fresh cilantro

2 teaspoons ground cumin

1. Cut the cabbage into thin strips and set aside.

2. Make the meatballs: Combine the beef, a pinch of salt and pepper, the garlic powder, cilantro, and cumin in a large bowl and mix well with your hands. Form the meat mixture into 1-inch balls and set aside.

3. Make the soup: Melt the fat in a stockpot over medium heat. Add the onions and garlic and cook for 2 minutes. Add the chili powder, cumin, paprika, and a pinch of salt and pepper.

4. Sauté the onion mixture for about 2 minutes, then add the sliced cabbage. Continue to cook until the cabbage starts to soften, about 5 minutes.

5. Add the broth and meatballs to the pot and cook, uncovered, over medium heat for 30 minutes. Adjust seasoning to taste.

6. Ladle the soup into 4 bowls and top with the cilantro.

nut-free	Yes
egg-free	Yes
low FODMAP	Use sliced kale in place of the cabbage. Omit the garlic and onion. Use garlic-infused olive oil as the cooking fat.
AIP-friendly	Omit the chili powder, cumin, and paprika. Use 1 teaspoon ground turmeric and 1 teaspoon ground ginger instead.
SCD/GAPS	Yes
lower carb	Yes

nutritionist's note

Grass-fed ground beef is full of anti-inflammatory omega-3 fatty acids. It also has a special fat called conjugated linoleic acid (CLA), which has been shown in many studies to have cancer-fighting properties. The level of CLA in beef decreases significantly when cattle are grain-fed, even if just for a few weeks.

cilantro pumpkin soup

prep time: 5 minutes | *cook time:* 15 minutes | *serves:* 4

Caitlin: Knowing how much I love pumpkin soup—it's one of my favorite foods—Nabil made this great version with cilantro and nutmeg for me. We know your family will enjoy it as much as we do.

1 tablespoon unsalted butter, ghee, or coconut oil

1 medium white onion, diced

1 teaspoon ground nutmeg

1 teaspoon paprika

fine sea salt and ground black pepper

2 cups full-fat, canned coconut milk

3 cups homemade cooked pumpkin or canned pumpkin (about two 15-ounce cans)

4 cups Chicken Broth (page 386)

1/4 cup minced fresh cilantro, divided

1/4 cup chopped pine nuts, for garnish

1. Melt the fat in a stockpot over medium heat. Add the onion and sauté for 2 minutes, until translucent. Add the nutmeg, paprika, and a pinch of salt and pepper and cook for 1 more minute.

2. Add the coconut milk, pumpkin, and broth to the pot and stir to combine. Bring the mixture to a simmer over medium heat, uncovered. Keep simmering for about 10 minutes, stirring often.

3. Remove the soup from the heat. Use an immersion blender to puree, or puree in a blender or food processor in batches. Adjust the seasonings to taste.

4. Add half of the cilantro and stir. Divide the soup between bowls and garnish with the remaining cilantro and the pine nuts before serving.

nut-free	Use chopped sunflower seeds in place of the pine nuts.
egg-free	Yes
low FODMAP	Use 1/4 cup chopped scallions in place of the onion and reduce cooking time to 1 minute.
AIP-friendly	Omit the nutmeg, paprika, and pine nuts. Substitute 1 teaspoon ground turmeric and 1 teaspoon ground ginger.
SCD/GAPS	Yes
lower carb	Yes

nutritionist's note

Pumpkin is high in soluble fiber, which supports beneficial bacteria in the gut, which in turn support healthy digestion. It's also loaded with beta-carotene and vitamin C.

basil minestrone soup

prep time: 10 minutes | *cook time:* 30 minutes | *serves:* 6

Minestrone soup is usually made with beans and pasta, which are not suitable for people following a Paleo lifestyle. Our version, based on a minestrone soup served at one of our favorite Italian restaurants, omits the beans and pasta and is a wonderful starter or side dish.

1 tablespoon unsalted butter, ghee, or coconut oil

1 medium white onion, diced

2 stalks celery, chopped

3 medium carrots, diced

3 cloves garlic, minced

fine sea salt and ground black pepper

6 cups Chicken Broth (page 386)

1 tablespoon dried oregano leaves

3 cups cauliflower florets

2 cups cubed butternut squash

3 medium zucchini, sliced

1 cup tightly packed basil, plus more for garnish

1/2 cup extra-virgin olive oil

1. Melt the fat in a stockpot over medium heat. Add the onion, celery, carrots, and garlic to the pot. Season with a pinch of salt and pepper. Sauté the vegetables until they are soft, about 5 minutes.

2. Add the broth and oregano to the pot. Bring the mixture to a simmer over medium heat. Add the cauliflower, squash, and zucchini to the pot and cook, uncovered, for an additional 15 minutes, until the vegetables are tender. Remove the soup from the heat.

3. Place the basil in a food processor with the olive oil and a pinch of salt and pepper. Pulse the mixture until smooth. Pour the basil puree into the soup and stir. Adjust the seasonings to taste, garnish with basil leaves, and serve.

chef's tip

Adding the basil mixture at the very end preserves its color and freshness. Fresh herbs are usually best added at the end of the cooking process for this reason.

nutritionist's note

Many minestrone soups are made with a tomato base, which can be a problem if you have autoimmune issues. Nightshades like tomatoes can exacerbate gut inflammation in some people, which in turn can cause autoimmune symptoms such as joint pain and stiffness.

nut-free	Yes
egg-free	Yes
low FODMAP	Omit the garlic and onion. Use garlic-infused olive oil as the cooking fat.
AIP-friendly	Yes
SCD/GAPS	Yes
lower carb	Yes

nora's green bean soup

prep time: 15 minutes | *cook time:* 40 minutes | *serves:* 6

Nabil: My sister Nora made this soup several times while visiting us in San Francisco on an extended trip. Caitlin always asked for it after she left, so we started calling it "Nora's soup." It uses cinnamon to accentuate the flavors of the vegetables.

1 tablespoon unsalted butter, ghee, or coconut oil

1 medium white onion, diced

1 tablespoon minced garlic

fine sea salt and ground black pepper

1 stick cinnamon

2 bay leaves

1 cup diced celery

4 large carrots, diced

5 cups Chicken Broth (page 386)

3 medium zucchini

1 pound green beans, trimmed

3 tablespoons tomato paste

1/4 cup chopped fresh parsley, for garnish

1. Melt the fat in a stockpot over medium heat.

2. Add the onion to the pot and sauté for 1 minute.

3. Add the garlic, a pinch of salt and pepper, the cinnamon, and the bay leaves while stirring for 2 minutes. Add the celery and carrots and sauté the mixture for 2 more minutes.

4. Add the chicken broth and bring the soup to a boil. Reduce the heat, cover, and let simmer for 20 minutes.

5. Slice the zucchini into quarters lengthwise, then in half crosswise. Add the zucchini, green beans, and tomato paste and stir to incorporate the paste. Simmer the soup, uncovered, until the green beans are soft, about 10 minutes.

6. Remove from heat and adjust the seasonings to taste. Remove the cinnamon stick and bay leaves, ladle into bowls, top with parsley, and enjoy.

nut-free	Yes
egg-free	Yes
low FODMAP	Omit the onion and garlic. Use garlic-infused olive oil as the cooking fat. Use 1 cup chopped tomatoes in place of the tomato paste.
AIP-friendly	Use 1/2 cup canned pumpkin in place of the tomato paste.
SCD/GAPS	Yes
lower carb	Yes

chef's tip

The cinnamon stick infuses a unique sweet and pungent flavor in the broth while this vegetable soup is cooking.

caramelized onion soup

prep time: 15 minutes | *cook time:* 50 to 60 minutes | *serves:* 4

Nabil: I learned to make this quick version of the classic soup in culinary school. It brings together the sweetness of onions with the complex flavor of thyme for an unforgettable taste combination. If you want to avoid dairy, try serving it with Cilantro Crackers (page 124) instead of the cheese wafers.

10 medium white onions (about 2 pounds)

2 tablespoons unsalted butter, ghee, or coconut oil

fine sea salt and ground black pepper

1/2 teaspoon dried thyme leaves

4 cups Beef Broth (page 388)

2 bay leaves

1/4 cup apple cider vinegar

4 ounces grated Parmesan cheese, for garnish (optional)

1. Slice the onions into rings.

2. Melt the fat over medium heat in a stockpot.

3. Add the onions, a pinch of salt and pepper, and the thyme. Cook the onions until golden brown, about 20 to 22 minutes, stirring frequently.

4. Add the beef broth and bay leaves and bring the liquid to a simmer over medium heat. Scrape the bottom of the pot to release any browned bits of onion.

5. Cook the onion broth for an additional 20 minutes, uncovered.

6. Add the vinegar and another of pinch of salt and pepper. Let the soup simmer until all the flavors combine, about 10 more minutes.

7. If using the Parmesan cheese, turn on the broiler to high and line a baking sheet with parchment paper. Place the cheese on the lined baking sheet in 2-inch mounds. Broil the cheese in the oven for 2 to 3 minutes, until golden brown.

8. Remove the crisped cheese mounds from the parchment paper and let them cool for 5 minutes on a wire rack.

9. Divide the soup among 4 serving bowls. Place the crispy cheese wafers on top, if desired.

chef's tip

Onions release sugar when browned slowly, which gives the soup an earthy flavor. It is important to scrape the brown bits off the bottom of the pan to increase the rich taste of this soup. If the onions look like they are drying out or burning, simply reduce the heat to medium-low and add a few tablespoons of water until they are cooked down enough to add the broth.

nutritionist's note

Onions boost the immune system to help you fight off colds and flus. They are also high in sulfur, which supports detoxification processes.

nut-free	Yes
egg-free	Yes
low FODMAP	No
AIP-friendly	Omit the cheese.
SCD/GAPS	Yes
lower carb	Yes

almond meatball soup (m'touam)

prep time: 15 minutes | *cook time:* 1 hour | *serves:* 6

Nabil: This hearty soup is a traditional Algerian dish that my mother makes during holidays. It uses two cuts of meat, a feature of many Mediterranean slow-cooked dishes, and it's very comforting to me because it has two ingredients that I associate with home: meatballs and turnips. .

---

1 tablespoon unsalted butter, ghee, or coconut oil

1 pound stew beef (preferably on the bone)

fine sea salt and ground black pepper

1 medium white onion, minced

2 teaspoons minced garlic

4 cups Beef Broth (page 388)

2 turnips, peeled and diced

1 cup blanched whole almonds (see Chef's Tip)

1/4 cup chopped fresh cilantro, for garnish

FOR THE MEATBALLS

1 pound ground beef

2 teaspoons minced garlic

1 tablespoon ground cumin

1 tablespoon ground cinnamon

fine sea salt and ground black pepper

1. Melt the fat in a stockpot over medium heat. Add the beef cubes and brown on all sides, about 5 minutes.

2. Add a pinch of salt and pepper and the onion and sauté for 3 minutes, until the onion is translucent. Add the garlic and cook for 1 minute.

3. Add the broth to the pot, cover, and bring it to a simmer. Remove the lid and continue to simmer the meat mixture for 30 minutes.

4. Meanwhile, make the meatballs: Combine the ground beef, garlic, cumin, cinnamon, and a pinch of salt and pepper in a bowl. Mix thoroughly and form the meat into 1-inch balls. Set aside.

5. Add the turnips and blanched almonds to the stockpot and cook for 5 minutes. Add the meatballs to the soup and continue to cook for 15 to 20 minutes. Add salt and pepper to taste and ladle the soup into bowls. Garnish with the cilantro.

nut-free	Omit the almonds.
egg-free	Yes
low FODMAP	Omit the onion and garlic and use garlic-infused olive oil as the cooking fat. Use cashews in place of the almonds.
AIP-friendly	Omit the almonds and cumin.
SCD/GAPS	Yes
lower carb	Yes

chef's tip

Blanching your own almonds saves money and is really easy: Just pour boiling water in a bowl with the almonds. Repeat this one or two times until the almond skins steam off and are easy to remove with your fingers.

nutritionist's note

Almonds are a great source of B vitamins, magnesium, potassium, and vitamin E.

pizza & pasta

nut-free

low-carb

almond flour

cashew flour

mediterranean paleo pizza

prep time: 20 minutes | *cook time:* 25 minutes | *yield:* 1 (9-inch) pizza

Nabil: I started making pizza at age sixteen at the restaurant where I worked, and it has always been one of my favorite foods. I missed it when I started a Paleo lifestyle and began looking for a way to get it back into my diet. My brother-in-law Micah makes a great pizza crust that's otherwise Paleo-friendly but has Parmesan cheese, so we were inspired to create one for those of us who don't eat dairy. This thin-crust pizza is perfect for satisfying those junk food cravings while sticking to your Paleo diet.

1/3 cup almond meal

1 cup tapioca flour

1/2 teaspoon fine sea salt

1 egg

6 tablespoons extra-virgin olive oil

1/2 to 1 cup Basic Tomato Sauce (page 182) or other sauce of choice

pizza toppings of choice

1. Place a pizza stone on the middle rack of the oven, and preheat the oven to 400°F. (See the Chef's Tip if you don't have a pizza stone.)

2. In a medium bowl, mix together the almond meal, tapioca flour, and salt.

3. In another medium bowl, beat together the egg and olive oil until well combined. Pour the wet mixture into the dry mixture and stir until well combined, forming a dough.

4. Place a large piece of parchment paper on the counter or tabletop. Place the dough on the parchment paper and roll it out with a rolling pin until it is about 9 inches in diameter and 1/4 to 1/3 inch thick. (If the rolling pin is sticking to the dough, place a second piece of parchment paper on top of the dough.) Use your fingers to form a thicker edge around the outside.

5. Add the desired amount of sauce and cover with toppings of choice. Keep in mind that a very wet sauce, such as tomato sauce, should be used sparingly.

6. Place the parchment paper with the pizza dough onto the stone that is inside the oven. Bake for 20 minutes, or until the edges of the crust are slightly browned.

7. Slowly and carefully pull out the parchment paper and turn the oven to broil. Broil the pizza directly on the stone for 2 to 3 more minutes. This step will make the crust light and crispy.

8. Remove the pizza from the oven, slice, and enjoy.

nut-free	Use Sunflower Pizza Crust (page 170).
egg-free	Use AIP Pizza Crust (page 171).
low FODMAP	Use Cashew Pizza Crust (page 170).
AIP-friendly	Use AIP Pizza Crust (page 171).
SCD/GAPS	Use Lower Carb Pizza Crust (page 171).
lower carb	Use Lower Carb Pizza Crust (page 171).

chef's tip

The effect of a pizza stone is crucial for this recipe to work: without it, the crust will not become crispy. Pizza stones can be found at discount stores such as Target or Walmart, but we've also found that a large cast-iron skillet lined with parchment paper has a similar effect.

We've used almond meal, which is made by grinding almonds with the skins on, to give the crust a little more texture. Almond meal tends to be less expensive than blanched almond flour and can be found at natural grocery stores.

mediterranean paleo pizza, cont.

Below are just a few of the pizza toppings we've used. Try them in any combination, or in the combinations listed at the bottom of the page. Or use your imagination—the sky is the limit!

PIZZA TOPPINGS

Basic Tomato Sauce (page 182)

Basil pesto (see page 186)

Alfredo Clam Sauce (page 184)

Mushroom Sauce (page 185)

Puttanesca Sauce (page 183)

Cooked diced or shredded chicken

Fried eggs (crack a raw egg on top of the pizza 10 minutes before the pizza is done and continue to bake)

Crumbled feta

Sliced fresh mozzarella

Grated Parmesan cheese

Sun-dried tomatoes

Browned ground beef or lamb

Beef bresaola or other cured meats, such as pepperoni

Sautéed thinly sliced or diced red bell peppers

Sautéed thinly sliced or diced green bell peppers

Sautéed sliced mushrooms

Sautéed sliced red or white onion

Fresh cilantro, basil, or parsley

Pineapple

Pomegranate seeds

Sliced olives

COMBINATIONS

Green Olive and Red Pepper Pizza: olives, mushrooms, red peppers, and Basic Tomato Sauce (page 182)

Clam Pizza: Alfredo Clam Sauce (page 184) and fresh cilantro

Black Olive and Caramelized Onion Pizza: Mint Pesto (page 186), cherry tomatoes, mushrooms, green and black olives, and caramelized onions

Breakfast Pizza: caramelized onions, bresaola or other cured meats, eggs, and fresh mozzarella

Mushroom and Cilantro Pizza: olives, tomatoes, mushrooms, and fresh cilantro

Pesto Pizza: Mint Pesto (page 186), mozzarella, black olives, and red onions

Pepperoni Pizza: pepperoni and fresh basil

cashew pizza crust

prep time: 10 minutes | *cook time:* 25 minutes | *yield:* 1 (12-inch) pizza crust

2 1/4 cups cashew meal

1/4 cup ground golden flax seeds

2 tablespoons extra-virgin olive oil

1 teaspoon fine sea salt

1/2 teaspoon ground black pepper

2 large eggs, beaten

nut-free	No
egg-free	No
low FODMAP	Yes
AIP-friendly	No
SCD/GAPS	Yes
lower carb	Yes

1. Preheat the oven to 400°F. If using a pizza stone, place it on the middle rack of the oven.

2. Place the cashew meal, flax, olive oil, salt, pepper, and eggs in a large bowl. Mix until the ingredients are well combined.

3. Set the dough on a large sheet of parchment paper and press it into a circle that's about 1/4 to 1/3 inch thick. Place it on a baking sheet or pizza stone, still on the parchment paper.

4. Bake the crust for 15 minutes and remove from the oven. Add toppings of choice and bake for 10 more minutes, until golden brown.

sunflower pizza crust

prep time: 10 minutes | *cook time:* 25 minutes | *yield:* 1 (12-inch) pizza crust

2 cups unsalted sunflower seeds

1/4 cup ground golden flax seeds

2 tablespoons extra-virgin olive oil

1 tablespoon Italian seasoning

1 teaspoon fine sea salt

1/2 teaspoon ground black pepper

2 large eggs, beaten

nut-free	Yes
egg-free	No
low FODMAP	Yes
AIP-friendly	No
SCD/GAPS	Yes
lower carb	Yes

1. Preheat the oven to 400°F. If using a pizza stone, place it on the middle rack of the oven.

2. Place the sunflower seeds in a food processor and pulse until they are a fine powder. Transfer the sunflower seed flour to a large bowl.

3. To the bowl, add the flax, olive oil, Italian seasoning, salt, pepper, and eggs. Mix until the ingredients are well combined.

4. Set the dough on a large sheet of parchment paper and press it into a circle that's about 1/4 to 1/3 inch thick. Place it on a baking sheet or pizza stone, still on the parchment paper.

5. Bake the crust for 15 minutes and remove from the oven. Add toppings of choice and bake for 10 more minutes, until golden brown.

nutritionist's note

Sunflower seeds are one of the few foods that are high in selenium, which is very important for thyroid health.

lower carb pizza crust

prep time: 10 minutes | *cook time:* 25 minutes | *yield:* 1 (12-inch) pizza crust

---

2 1/4 cups blanched almond flour

1/4 cup ground golden flax seeds

2 tablespoons extra-virgin olive oil

1 teaspoon fine sea salt

1/2 teaspoon ground black pepper

2 large eggs, beaten

nut-free	No
egg-free	No
low FODMAP	No
AIP-friendly	No
SCD/GAPS	Yes
lower carb	Yes

1. Preheat the oven to 400°F. If using a pizza stone, place it on the middle rack of the oven.

2. Place the almond flour, flax seeds, olive oil, salt, pepper, and eggs in a large bowl. Mix until the ingredients are well combined.

3. Set the dough on a large sheet of parchment paper and press it into a circle that's about 1/4 to 1/3 inch thick. Place it on a baking sheet or pizza stone, still on the parchment paper.

4. Bake the crust for 15 minutes and remove from the oven. Add toppings of choice and bake for 10 more minutes, until golden brown.

aip pizza crust

prep time: 10 minutes | *cook time:* 30 minutes | *yield:* 1 (10-inch) pizza crust

---

3/4 cup boiling hot water

2 tablespoons grass-fed beef gelatin (see Chef's Tip)

1 1/2 cups tapioca flour

1/2 cup coconut flour, sifted

1/2 teaspoon fine sea salt

1/2 teaspoon baking soda

1/2 cup sustainable palm shortening or coconut oil, room temperature

1 teaspoon apple cider vinegar

nut-free	Yes
egg-free	Yes
low FODMAP	Yes
AIP-friendly	Yes
SCD/GAPS	No
lower carb	No

1. Preheat the oven to 400°F. Line a baking sheet with parchment paper.

2. Combine the hot water and gelatin in a small, heatproof bowl. Stir until the gelatin is dissolved. Set aside.

3. In another bowl, mix together the tapioca, coconut flour, salt, and baking soda.

4. Add the fat to the flour mixture and mix well. Add the vinegar and gelatin water to the flour mixture and stir to combine.

5. Set the dough on the lined baking sheet and press it into a circle that's about 1/4 to 1/3 inch thick.

6. Bake the crust for 15 minutes and remove from the oven. Add toppings of choice and bake for 15 more minutes, until golden brown.

chef's tip

Gelatin can work as a binder in certain recipes when eggs are not wanted. It is important to dissolve the gelatin in boiling water to remove clumps and increase usability. Avoid the non-gelling collagen hydrosolate gelatin, which won't give the dough the proper consistency. See "A Note on Gelatin" on page 95.

paleo pasta

prep time: 20 minutes | *cook time:* 5 minutes | *serves:* 4 to 6

This recipe is perfect if you're craving pasta but don't want to eat gut-irritating gluten. While this pasta is starchy, it's made from nutritious ingredients that should not cause digestive distress or upset the way wheat can. Tapioca and flax give the versatile dough the elasticity of wheat pasta, so it can be used for any kind of pasta noodles or cut into squares for ravioli (see page 176). If you don't have a pasta machine, it can be made by hand with a knife and rolling pin.

1 1/2 cups tapioca flour, plus more for rolling

1 cup blanched almond flour

fine sea salt

3 large eggs, beaten

2 tablespoons ground golden flax seeds

1 tablespoon extra-virgin olive oil

1. In a large bowl, mix together the tapioca flour, almond flour, and a pinch of salt. Pour the flour mixture onto a clean, flat surface, such as a countertop or table. Make a well in the center of the mixture.

2. Mix the eggs and flax in a separate bowl and let sit for 5 minutes.

3. Pour the egg mixture in the well in the flour mixture. Use a fork to slowly incorporate the flour mixture into the eggs little by little until the dough is thoroughly mixed.

4. Knead the dough for 3 to 5 minutes. Split the dough into 3 balls and put them in a bowl to rest for 5 minutes.

5. If using a pasta machine, roll out the dough and form the noodles following the detailed photo tutorial on page 175. If forming noodles by hand, roll the dough out to 1/4 inch thick and cut it into noodles with a knife.

6. Bring a pot of water to a boil and add the olive oil and a pinch of salt. Add the pasta to the water and boil for 3 to 5 minutes, until cooked but not mushy. Drain the pasta and serve with your choice of sauce.

nut-free	No
egg-free	No
low FODMAP	Use 1 cup cashew meal in place of the almond flour.
AIP-friendly	No
SCD/GAPS	No
lower carb	No. Use Zucchini Noodles (page 178) or spaghetti squash noodles (see page 192) instead.

nutritionist's note

Tapioca flour comes from the cassava plant, a root vegetable and staple crop grown in equatorial regions. Ancestral cultures ate this plant for thousands of years without experiencing the chronic health problems we see today, so it should be fine on occasion for most people. Make sure to eat it with fat and protein to lower its glycemic impact.

Pour the flour mixture onto a clean, flat surface such as a countertop or smooth tabletop.

Mix the flour well with your hands, getting any clumps out with your fingers.

Make a well to allow space to pour your beaten eggs into the center of the flour mixture.

Slowly and carefully pour the beaten eggs into the center of the flour well.

With a fork, slowly begin to incorporate the flour mixture a little bit at a time.

The slow mixing of the flour allows you to coat all of the dry ingredients evenly with the egg.

Continue mixing, using your fork to fold the flour over from the edges into the middle.

Fold with the fork until the egg is no longer soft at all before switching to hand mixing.

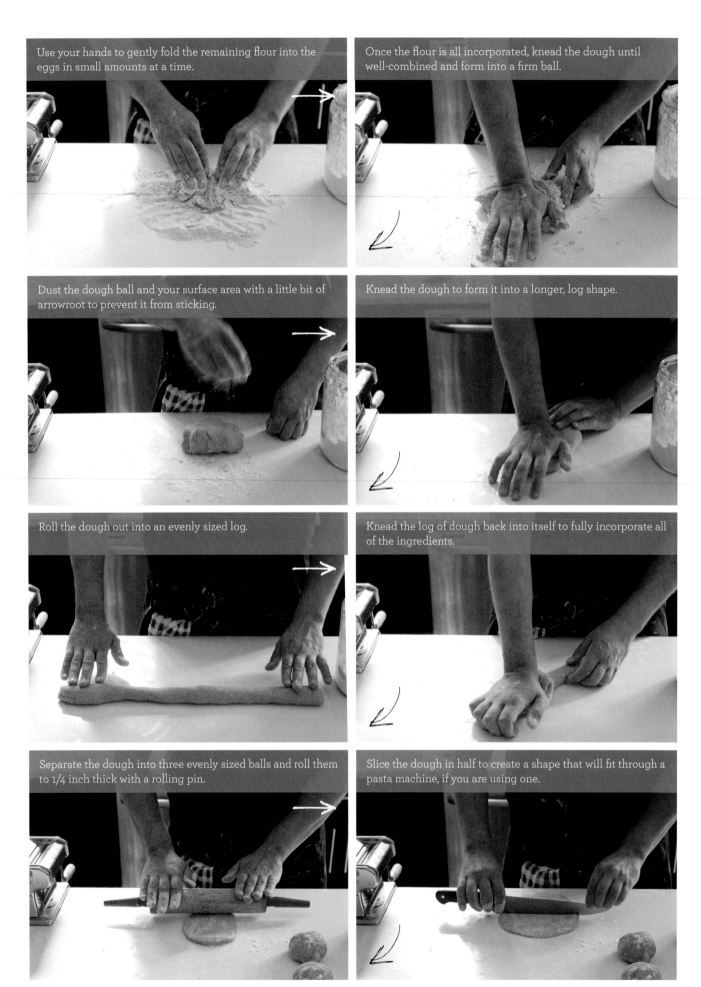

Use your hands to gently fold the remaining flour into the eggs in small amounts at a time.

Once the flour is all incorporated, knead the dough until well-combined and form into a firm ball.

Dust the dough ball and your surface area with a little bit of arrowroot to prevent it from sticking.

Knead the dough to form it into a longer, log shape.

Roll the dough out into an evenly sized log.

Knead the log of dough back into itself to fully incorporate all of the ingredients.

Separate the dough into three evenly sized balls and roll them to 1/4 inch thick with a rolling pin.

Slice the dough in half to create a shape that will fit through a pasta machine, if you are using one.

Pass the dough gently through the pasta machine on the first, loosest setting. (You may use a rolling pin if you do not have a pasta machine.)

Pass the dough through the pasta machine several more times, each time adjusting the setting down incrementally.

The dough should be about 1/8 inch thick when you complete the process. (Note the difference below.)

Continue the process until all of the dough is flattened.

For a clean-edged pasta, trim off any excess dough to make a rectangle.

Slice the dough into 1/4-inch-wide strips, or to any width you prefer.

To make shorter noodles, fold the rectangle of dough back onto it self a few times before cutting.

Then, slice the folded dough into thin strips, 1/4 inch or smaller.

ravioli

prep time: 10 minutes, plus 10 minutes to make the dough | *cook time:* 5 minutes | *serves:* 4

This dish uses the Paleo Pasta recipe on page 172. It has a great texture and bite that is similar to wheat ravioli.

tapioca flour, for rolling out the dough

1 recipe Paleo Pasta, uncut (page 172)

filling of choice: sautéed spinach, cooked ground meat, sautéed mushrooms, cooked sweet potato, goat cheese, or ricotta

2 large eggs, beaten

pasta sauce of choice (pages 182–187)

1. Sprinkle a handful of tapioca flour on a clean, dry surface. Place the dough on the surface and roll it out to 1/8 inch thick. Cut the pasta into 4-by-12-inch strips.

2. Place a tablespoon of filling on the flat pasta and repeat until there are 4 or 5 mounds in a row, spaced 2 1/2 to 3 inches apart. Use a pastry brush to spread the egg wash around the filling.

3. Place a second sheet of pasta over the filling and press down around each filling mound. Cut round circles or squares around each mound with a pasta tool or a sharp knife. Use your fingers to pinch the edges of each ravioli to make sure they are tightly sealed. Repeat the process until all the pasta is made into ravioli.

4. Boil 6 cups of water in a saucepan. Gently drop the ravioli in and cook for 2 to 3 minutes, until they're cooked but not soft and float to the top. Drain and serve with your sauce of choice.

nut-free	No
egg-free	No
low FODMAP	Use the low FODMAP pasta variation and FODMAP-friendly fillings.
AIP-friendly	No
SCD/GAPS	No
lower carb	No. Use Zucchini Noodles (page 178) instead.

Place tablespoons of filling on the flat pasta, spaced 2 1/2 to 3 inches apart.

Repeat until you run out of space.

Use a pastry brush to spread the egg wash around the filling.

Place a second sheet of pasta over the filling.

Press down around each filling mound.

Repeat until the filling mounds are all sealed.

Cut round circles around each mound with a pasta tool or a sharp knife.

Use your fingers to pinch the edges of each ravioli to make sure they are tightly sealed. Repeat the process until all the pasta is made into ravioli.

zucchini noodles

prep time: 5 minutes | *cook time:* 1 minute | *yield:* 2 1/2 cups

Zucchini noodles are a great pasta substitute when you want to avoid grains. They're low in carbohydrates and easy to eat raw or lightly cooked, and they take on the flavor of whatever sauce is used.

4 large or 8 small zucchini

1. Using a julienne vegetable peeler, slice the zucchini lengthwise into noodles, rotating slightly after each slice, until nearly all of the zucchini is used. Alternatively, to make fettuccine-shaped noodles (pictured on page 191), use a standard vegetable peeler. Discard the middle, seedy portion.

2. The noodles may be eaten raw or cooked. To cook, boil or steam them for 1 minute, then drain well. Alternatively, place the noodles on 2 parchment-lined baking sheets and bake in a 350°F oven for 5 to 10 minutes. Serve with about 2 cups of your favorite sauce.

nut-free	Yes
egg-free	Yes
low FODMAP	Yes
AIP-friendly	Yes
SCD/GAPS	Yes
lower carb	Yes

chef's tip

Creating vegetable noodles is even easier with a spiral slicer, known commonly by the brand name Spiralizer. If you have a spiral slicer, follow the manufacturer's instructions.

mushroom sauce

puttanesca sauce

mint pesto

bolognese meat sauce

basic tomato sauce

basic tomato sauce

prep time: 10 minutes | *cook time:* 30 minutes | *yield:* 3 to 4 cups | *serves:* 4

Keep this basic tomato sauce on hand for topping Zucchini Noodles (page 178), spaghetti squash noodles (see page 192), Paleo Pasta (page 172), or Ravioli (page 176).

---

6 ripe medium tomatoes

1 tablespoon unsalted butter, ghee, or coconut oil

1 cup diced onion

2 teaspoons minced garlic

1 tablespoon dried basil

1 tablespoon dried oregano leaves

2 bay leaves

fine sea salt and ground black pepper

1 tablespoon tomato paste

1. Puree the tomatoes in a food processor and set aside.

2. In a saucepan, melt the fat over medium heat. Add the onion and sauté until translucent. Add the garlic, basil, oregano, bay leaves, and a pinch of salt and pepper, and cook for 2 minutes. Add the tomato puree, tomato paste, and 3 cups of water to the pan.

3. Cook the mixture, uncovered, over low heat for 25 to 30 minutes, until thickened. Adjust the seasonings to taste. Remove the bay leaves before serving.

nut-free	Yes
egg-free	Yes
low FODMAP	Use 1/2 cup chopped scallions in place of the onion and cook for just 1 minute. Omit the garlic and use garlic-infused olive oil as the cooking fat. Use 7 tomatoes instead of 6 and omit the tomato paste.
AIP-friendly	No. Use the Autoimmune-Friendly No-Mato Sauce (page 187) instead.
SCD/GAPS	Yes
lower carb	Yes

nutritionist's note

Tomatoes are a rich source of the antioxidant lycopene, which helps reduce inflammation for better bone and cardiovascular health. Another great benefit of tomatoes is that just 1 cup of raw tomatoes provides nearly 40 percent of the recommended daily allowance of vitamin C.

puttanesca sauce

prep time: 5 minutes | *cook time:* 8 minutes | *yield:* 2 to 3 cups | *serves:* 4

This savory, salty, and slightly spicy sauce goes well with Zucchini Noodles (page 178) or Paleo Pasta (page 172).

1 (3-ounce) can anchovies

1 tablespoon unsalted butter, ghee, or coconut oil

1 tablespoon minced garlic

1/2 teaspoon crushed red pepper

4 medium tomatoes, finely diced, or 1 (28-ounce) can crushed tomatoes

1 cup sliced cherry tomatoes

1/2 cup sliced black olives

2 tablespoons capers, rinsed and drained

1. Rinse the anchovies and cut them into small pieces.

2. Heat a skillet over medium heat and melt the fat. Add the garlic and sauté for 2 minutes. Add the anchovies and crushed red pepper to the skillet and sauté for 1 minute. Add the diced or crushed tomatoes, cherry tomatoes, olives, and capers and cook, stirring continuously, for 5 minutes to allow the flavors to combine.

nut-free	Yes
egg-free	Yes
low FODMAP	Omit the garlic and use garlic-infused olive oil as the cooking fat.
AIP-friendly	Use 1 teaspoon ground ginger in place of the crushed red pepper. Use 2 cups canned pumpkin and 2 cups water in place of the tomatoes.
SCD/GAPS	Yes
lower carb	Yes

alfredo clam sauce

prep time: 5 minutes | *cook time:* 25 minutes | *yield:* 2 cups | *serves:* 4

This sauce makes an excellent topping for any of our pizza crusts (pages 166, 170–171) and for Paleo Pasta (page 172).

1 tablespoon unsalted butter, ghee or coconut oil

1/2 cup diced onion

2 teaspoons minced garlic

2 cups full-fat, canned coconut milk

1 (6 1/2-ounce) can chopped clams, drained

2 tablespoons capers, rinsed and drained

1/2 cup chopped fresh cilantro

1. In a medium saucepan, melt the fat over medium heat. Add the onion and garlic and sauté until translucent, about 5 minutes.

2. Pour in the coconut milk and simmer for about 15 minutes, until the sauce reduces and thickens, stirring every 2 minutes.

3. Pat the clams dry in a paper towel. Add the clams and capers to the saucepan and simmer for 5 more minutes, then stir in the cilantro. Serve over pasta or use as a topping for pizza.

nut-free	Yes
egg-free	Yes
low FODMAP	Omit the onion and garlic and use garlic-infused olive oil as the cooking fat.
AIP-friendly	Yes
SCD/GAPS	Yes
lower carb	Yes

nutritionist's note

Clams are a great source of iron, providing more than half the daily recommend amount. They are also high in phosphorus and potassium, which are crucial for cell function and strong bones and teeth.

mushroom sauce

prep time: 5 minutes | *cook time:* 20 minutes | *yield:* 2 cups | *serves:* 4

This creamy sauce is a great substitute for Alfredo sauce, which is usually thickened with flour or cheese, two ingredients that are not Paleo-friendly. It makes an excellent topping for any of our pizza crusts (pages 166, 170–171) and for Paleo Pasta (page 172).

1 tablespoon unsalted butter, ghee, or coconut oil

1 medium white onion, diced

2 teaspoons minced garlic

fine sea salt and ground black pepper

8 ounces mushrooms, sliced

2 cups full-fat, canned coconut milk

1. Melt the fat in a saucepan over medium heat. Add the onion and sauté for 2 minutes.

2. Add the garlic and a pinch of salt and pepper and sauté for 2 minutes. Add the mushrooms and sauté for 2 minutes, or until soft.

3. Add the coconut milk and simmer until the sauce thickens, about 15 minutes, stirring every 2 minutes.

nut-free	Yes
egg-free	Yes
low FODMAP	Omit the onion and garlic. Use garlic-infused olive oil as the cooking fat.
AIP-friendly	Yes
SCD/GAPS	Yes
lower carb	Yes

mint pesto

prep time: 5 minutes | *cook time:* n/a | *yield:* 2 cups | *serves:* 6

Pesto is so versatile. It can be used as a pasta sauce, meat marinade, salad dressing, or dip for vegetables. It has hundreds of variations, and there is no right or wrong way to make it. Three possible variations are given below; use your imagination and invent other variations of your own. This mint pesto pairs perfectly with Spiced Rack of Lamb (page 242).

3 cups tightly packed fresh mint leaves

1/2 teaspoon fine sea salt

1/2 teaspoon ground black pepper

1/2 cup pine nuts

2 cloves garlic, peeled

1/2 cup chopped scallions (optional)

1 tablespoon lemon juice

1 cup extra-virgin olive oil

1. Place all of the ingredients except the oil in a food processor and pulse until a paste forms, about 10 seconds.

2. While the machine is running, slowly add the oil (this should take about 30 seconds). You may need to stop the food processor once or twice to scrape down the sides with a spatula.

BASIL PESTO
Use basil leaves in place of the mint leaves.

CILANTRO PESTO
Use cilantro leaves in place of the mint leaves.

PARSLEY PESTO
Use parsley leaves in place of the mint leaves.

nut-free	Use 1/2 cup hulled sunflower seeds in place of the pine nuts.
egg-free	Yes
low FODMAP	Omit the garlic and use garlic-infused olive in place of the regular olive oil.
AIP-friendly	Use 1/2 cup frozen and defrosted artichoke hearts in place of the pine nuts.
SCD/GAPS	Yes
lower carb	Yes

autoimmune-friendly no-mato sauce

prep time: 10 minutes | *cook time:* 30 to 40 minutes | *yield:* 4 cups | *serves:* 4

This sauce is designed for people who are sensitive to nightshade vegetables such as tomatoes. It looks like a traditional red sauce and has just enough Italian flavor to help people on an elimination diet enjoy comfort foods such as pasta and pizza.

4 large raw beets, peeled and shredded

4 medium carrots, peeled and shredded

4 cups Beef Broth (page 388)

2 teaspoons minced garlic

1/2 teaspoon fine sea salt

1/2 teaspoon ground black pepper

1/2 cup chopped fresh basil, for garnish

1. Place all the ingredients except the basil in a large saucepan and bring to a simmer over medium heat. Cover and simmer for 30 minutes, or until the vegetables are tender.

2. Use an immersion blender to puree the mixture. If the sauce seems too thin, simmer it for 5 to 10 more minutes, uncovered. Adjust the seasonings to taste, top with fresh basil, serve, and enjoy.

nut-free	Yes
egg-free	Yes
low FODMAP	Use 1/4 cup chopped scallions in place of the garlic.
AIP-friendly	Yes
SCD/GAPS	No
lower carb	No

bolognese meat sauce

prep time: 10 minutes | *cook time:* 30 minutes | *serves:* 4

Cumin gives this traditional northern Italian sauce a Mediterranean flavor that is accentuated by the cilantro. This sauce pairs well with Zucchini Noodles (page 178), spaghetti squash noodles (see page 192), or Paleo Pasta (page 172).

---

1 pound ground beef

1/2 cup diced onion

2 teaspoons minced garlic

1 teaspoon ground cumin

1 teaspoon fine sea salt

1/2 teaspoon ground black pepper

4 cups diced fresh tomatoes or 1 (28-ounce) can crushed tomatoes

2 tablespoons tomato paste

4 cups Beef Broth (page 388) or water

1/4 cup chopped fresh cilantro, for garnish

1. Heat a skillet over medium heat. Add the meat and cook for 5 minutes, stirring with a spatula to break it up.

2. Add the onion to the pan and cook for 5 minutes, until translucent. Add the garlic and cook for 1 to 2 minutes, until fragrant. Add the cumin, salt, and pepper and stir until absorbed.

3. Add the tomatoes, tomato paste, and broth and simmer, uncovered, for 15 minutes. Remove from the heat, top with the cilantro, and serve.

nut-free	Yes
egg-free	Yes
low FODMAP	Omit the garlic and onions. Use garlic-infused olive oil as the cooking fat. Omit the tomato paste.
AIP-friendly	Use 1 cup canned pumpkin in place of the tomatoes. Alternatively, add cooked meat to Autoimmune-Friendly No-Mato Sauce (page 187).
SCD/GAPS	Yes
lower carb	Yes

shrimp alfredo

prep time: 20 minutes | *cook time:* 10 minutes | *serves:* 4

Located in the middle of the Mediterranean Sea, Italy has contributed many popular dishes to the cuisine of the region. This classic Italian dish is usually made with heavy cream and Parmesan cheese, but we've used coconut milk to make it more Paleo-friendly. We eat this sauce all the time on weeknights over Zucchini Noodles (page 178), Paleo Pasta (page 172), or spaghetti squash noodles (see page 192). But it's so good and filling that sometimes we just eat it right out the bowl with a spoon.

1 pound medium shrimp

1 tablespoon butter, ghee, or coconut oil

2 tablespoons diced shallot (1 medium)

2 teaspoons paprika

2 teaspoons minced garlic

fine sea salt and ground black pepper

2 cups full-fat, canned coconut milk

1 cup frozen peas, defrosted and drained

1 tablespoon arrowroot flour

1/4 cup chopped fresh parsley, for garnish

1. Peel, devein, and rinse the shrimp and set aside.

2. Melt the fat over medium heat in a sauté pan. Add the shrimp and shallot and sauté for 1 minute. Add the paprika, garlic, and a pinch of salt and pepper and stir for 2 minutes, until the shrimp are pink. Add the coconut milk and peas and stir to combine. Simmer for 5 to 7 minutes, uncovered, stirring frequently.

3. Mix the arrowroot with 1 tablespoon of water in small bowl. Add the arrowroot mixture to the shrimp sauce and stir until the sauce thickens.

4. Serve the sauce over pasta or zucchini noodles, top with fresh parsley, and enjoy.

nut-free	Yes
egg-free	Yes
low FODMAP	Omit the shallot and garlic. Use garlic-infused olive oil as the cooking fat.
AIP-friendly	Use 1 teaspoon ground ginger in place of the paprika.
SCD/GAPS	Omit the arrowroot and simmer the sauce a few minutes longer, until it reduces.
lower carb	Use sautéed mushrooms in place of the peas.

chef's tip

When purchasing fresh or defrosted, previously frozen shrimp, make sure the flesh looks translucent and they smell like the sea; if they smell like ammonia, they are old and should be discarded. To prevent frozen shrimp from becoming rubbery during cooking, defrost them in cool water first. While you're cooking, look for the shrimp to form a C shape, which indicates perfect doneness. If they have twisted into an O shape, they are overcooked.

nutritionist's note

Always choose wild shrimp from coastal areas as close to home as possible. Farmed shrimp from Asia are often contaminated with pesticides and heavy metals.

spaghetti and cumin-spiced meatballs

prep time: 20 minutes | *cook time:* 40 minutes | *serves:* 4

The texture of spaghetti squash mimics that of wheat-based pasta noodles, making it a great way to add variety to a Paleo diet. It's also versatile and will absorb the flavors of any sauce you pair it with. Spaghetti squash is low in starch, so it's a good choice if you're reducing carbs.

---

1 large spaghetti squash (about 2 pounds)

1 pound ground beef

1 tablespoon cumin

fine sea salt and ground black pepper

1 tablespoon unsalted butter, ghee, or coconut oil

1 medium white onion, diced

2 green bell peppers, diced

2 teaspoons minced garlic

1 bay leaf

1 tablespoon dried oregano leaves

2 medium tomatoes, diced

1/4 cup tomato paste

3 cups Beef Broth (page 388)

1/4 cup chopped fresh parsley, for garnish

1/4 cup chopped fresh basil, for garnish

1. Preheat the oven to 350°F.

2. Cut the spaghetti squash in half lengthwise and remove the seeds. Place the squash cut side down on a baking dish in an inch of water. Place in the oven and cook for 30 to 35 minutes, or until tender.

3. While the squash is cooking, make the meatballs and sauce. Place the beef in a large bowl, add the cumin, and season generously with salt and pepper. Mix the seasoning into the beef with your hands. Roll the meat into 1-inch balls and set aside.

4. In a large sauté pan, melt the fat over medium heat. Cook the onion, bell peppers, and garlic with a pinch of salt and pepper until the onion is translucent, about 5 minutes.

5. Add the bay leaf, oregano, tomatoes, tomato paste, and broth to the pan and bring to a slow boil. Add the meatballs and let the mixture simmer, uncovered, for 20 to 25 minutes, until it starts to thicken. Taste to check the seasoning and add another pinch of salt and pepper if desired.

6. Remove the squash from the oven and scoop the flesh out of the shells. Let it drain in a colander for a few minutes to remove the excess water. Arrange the squash noodles on plates and add the desired amount of sauce and meatballs on top. Garnish with the fresh parsley and basil before serving.

nut-free	Yes
egg-free	Yes
low FODMAP	Omit the onion and garlic. Use garlic-infused olive oil as the cooking fat. Double the tomatoes and omit the tomato paste.
AIP-friendly	Use Autoimmune-Friendly No-Mato Sauce (page 187), then add the meatballs and continue in Step 4.
SCD/GAPS	Yes
lower carb	Yes

chef's tip

Placing raw meatballs right into the sauce ensures that they are moist and tender after simmering, and the rich flavor of the meat enhances the sauce.

nutritionist's note

Spaghetti squash is high in potassium, which helps us maintain normal blood pressure. It also makes the perfect base for spaghetti sauce, instead of hard-to-digest wheat noodles. These squash noodles have a low glycemic load, meaning that, unlike conventional noodles, they help keep blood sugar stable for hours after eating.

poultry

chicken and olive tajine

prep time: 15 minutes | *cook time:* 1 hour 10 minutes | *serves:* 4

This is one of our very favorite dishes because it is so simple and flavorful. The combination of olives, saffron, and cumin will make you feel like you are on a Mediterranean getaway.

1 tablespoon butter, ghee, or coconut oil

1 whole (5-pound) chicken, cut into 8 to 10 pieces

fine sea salt and ground black pepper

1 pinch saffron

1 tablespoon ground cumin

1 medium white onion, diced

1 teaspoon minced garlic

4 cups Chicken Broth (page 386)

2 cups pitted green olives

3 medium carrots, cut into 1/4-inch circles

1 lemon (optional)

1/4 cup chopped fresh cilantro, for garnish

1. In a large stockpot, melt the fat over medium heat. Add the chicken and a pinch of salt and pepper and cook for 10 minutes. Season the chicken with the saffron and cumin and continue to sauté for 2 minutes. Add the onion and garlic and sauté for another 2 minutes, or until the chicken is browned and the onions are translucent.

2. Add the broth to the pot and cover. Bring the mixture to a boil and reduce the heat to medium-low.

3. Remove the lid and simmer for 30 minutes.

4. While the chicken simmers, bring a saucepan of 4 cups of water to a boil. Put the olives in the water and boil for about 5 minutes, then drain.

5. Add the olives and carrots to the chicken and cook for another 20 minutes, or until the carrots are tender.

6. Halve the lemon, if using, and squeeze it over the finished dish before serving. Slice the other half thinly. Serve the chicken with the sauce, lemon slices (as pictured on the front cover), and cilantro.

SLOW COOKER INSTRUCTIONS
Boil the olives for 7 to 10 minutes to remove bitterness and drain. Place all of the ingredients except the cilantro in a slow cooker and cook for 6 hours on low. Garnish with the cilantro and serve.

make it a meal
This dish pairs perfectly with any of the Cauliflower Couscous recipes on page 332.

chef's tip
Make sure you don't skip boiling the olives. This step removes their bitterness and makes a big difference in the flavor of the dish.

nutritionist's note
Using a whole chicken on the bone allows the bones to infuse the sauce with healing gelatin, which is helpful for supple skin and strong nails and teeth.

nut-free	Yes
egg-free	Yes
low FODMAP	Omit the onion and garlic. Use garlic-infused olive oil as the cooking fat.
AIP-friendly	Use 1 teaspoon ground turmeric in place of the cumin.
SCD/GAPS	Yes
lower carb	Yes

harissa-spiced chicken wings

prep time: 5 minutes, plus up to 8 hours to marinate |
cook time: 45 minutes | *serves:* 4

Nabil: Harissa is a Tunisian hot sauce that is commonly used in savory dishes in my home country. It's made from dried chili peppers, garlic, and coriander, and it gives these wings a Mediterranean-flavored kick. They're perfect for an easy dinner or Paleo meet-up.

---

3 cloves garlic, peeled

1/2 cup chopped onion

2 tablespoons Harissa (page 394)

1 tablespoon ground cumin

2 tablespoons dried ground thyme

1/4 cup chopped fresh cilantro

fine sea salt and ground black pepper

1/4 cup extra-virgin olive oil

2 pounds chicken wings

1. In a food processor, pulse together the garlic, onion, harissa, cumin, thyme, cilantro, a pinch of salt and pepper, and the olive oil.

2. Place the chicken wings in a bowl, add the spice mixture, and stir to coat. For maximum flavor, marinate the chicken, covered, in the refrigerator for up to 8 hours.

3. Preheat the oven to 350°F. Line a rimmed baking sheet with parchment paper.

4. Place the chicken wings on the prepared baking sheet, spreading them out evenly, and discard the excess marinade.

5. Bake the chicken for 45 minutes, or until the juices running out of the chicken are clear.

6. If desired, broil the chicken wings for 2 to 3 minutes before serving for crispier skin.

nut-free	Yes
egg-free	Yes
low FODMAP	Use 1/2 cup chopped scallions in place of the onion. Use garlic-infused olive oil in place of the regular olive oil.
AIP-friendly	Use 2 teaspoons turmeric in place of the cumin and 1 tablespoon ground ginger in place of the harissa.
SCD/GAPS	Yes
lower carb	Yes

nutritionist's tip

Our harissa recipe on page 394 is all natural, with no artificial ingredients. If you're not using homemade harissa, it is important to find one that is organic to avoid artificial and processed ingredients.

savory chicken kebabs

prep time: 15 minutes, plus up to 8 hours to marinate | *cook time:* 10 minutes | *serves:* 2 to 3

These kebabs can be cooked outside or inside, depending on your preference and what's most convenient. In our apartment in San Francisco we are prohibited from outdoor grilling, so we make them on a grill pan and they turn out great. These kebabs go well with Easy Sweet Potato Salad (page 132) or Cauliflower Couscous (page 332, pictured).

1/4 cup extra-virgin olive oil

1 medium white onion, finely diced

2 teaspoons minced garlic

2 tablespoons lemon juice

1 teaspoon paprika

1 pinch saffron

fine sea salt and ground black pepper

1/4 cup chopped fresh cilantro

2 red or green bell peppers, seeded and cut into chunks

1 medium red onion, cut into chunks

1 pound boneless chicken breast or thighs, cubed

1 tablespoon butter, ghee, or coconut oil, melted

1. In a large bowl, mix the olive oil, white onion, garlic, lemon juice, paprika, saffron, a pinch of salt and pepper, and the cilantro and stir to combine. Add the bell peppers, red onion, and chicken to the bowl and coat well with the marinade. For maximum flavor, marinate the chicken, covered, in the refrigerator for up to 8 hours.

2. Preheat a grill pan or outside grill to medium-high heat. If using wooden skewers, soak them for 10 minutes in water to prevent burning.

3. Remove the chicken mixture from the refrigerator. Put the chicken pieces on wooden or metal skewers, alternating with the peppers and red onion.

4. Brush the grill or grill pan with the melted fat.

5. Cook the kebabs for 5 minutes on one side, then turn and repeat for another 5 minutes, or until browned and the chicken is cooked through (no pink remains).

make it a meal

This dish pairs perfectly with any of the Cauliflower Couscous recipes on page 332.

nut-free	Yes
egg-free	Yes
low FODMAP	Omit the garlic and use garlic-infused olive oil in place of the regular olive oil. Use 1/4 cup minced chives in place of the onion.
AIP-friendly	Use ground turmeric in place of the paprika. Use 8 ounces whole white mushrooms in place of the peppers.
SCD/GAPS	Yes
lower carb	Yes

chef's tip

The key to flavorful kebabs is to marinate the meat as long as possible. Lemon juice helps break down the meat, so that it's more tender when cooked.

nutritionist's note

Grilling meat can create toxic carcinogens called heterocyclic amines. Marinating the meat reduces the amount of toxins produced by as much as 96 percent.

spicy chicken tajine

prep time: 10 minutes | *cook time:* 50 minutes | *serves:* 4

Caitlin: This dish has a little more kick than our other tajines. Nabil likes his food spicier than I do, so usually we meet in the middle. I think you'll find this has the just right level of heat.

---

3 tablespoons butter, ghee, or coconut oil

1 whole (5-pound) chicken, cut into 8 pieces

1 medium white onion, diced

2 teaspoons minced garlic

2 teaspoons ground cinnamon

1 tablespoon ground chili powder

fine sea salt and ground black pepper

1 jalapeño or other hot pepper, sliced, seeded if desired for less heat

4 cups Chicken Broth (page 386)

1/4 cup chopped fresh cilantro, for garnish

1. Melt the fat in a stockpot over medium heat. Add the chicken and sauté for 5 minutes, or until browned.

2. Add the onion, garlic, cinnamon, chili powder, a pinch of salt and pepper, and the jalapeño to the pot. Sauté for 5 more minutes, or until the onion is translucent.

3. Add the chicken broth to the pot, cover, and bring to a boil. Remove the lid and simmer for 40 minutes. Serve the chicken with the sauce, topped with the cilantro.

SLOW COOKER INSTRUCTIONS

Place all of the ingredients except the cilantro in a slow cooker and cook for 6 hours on low. Garnish with the cilantro and serve.

make it a meal

This dish pairs perfectly with any of the Cauliflower Couscous recipes on page 332.

nut-free	Yes
egg-free	Yes
low FODMAP	Use 2 teaspoons freshly grated ginger or 1 tablespoon ground ginger in place of the chili powder and hot peppers. Omit the onion and garlic. Use garlic-infused olive oil as the cooking fat.
AIP-friendly	Use 2 teaspoons freshly grated ginger or 1 tablespoon ground ginger in place of the chili powder and hot peppers.
SCD/GAPS	Yes
lower carb	Yes

chef's tip

When making a slow-cooked tajine, it is important to season the meat before adding the broth. If the seasonings are added at the same time as the broth, the meat will not absorb the flavor and the dish will be bland.

nutritionist's note

Capsaicin is an antioxidant in hot peppers that can combat the cell destruction caused by free radicals.

fig and ginger chicken tajine

prep time: 10 minutes | *cook time:* 1 hour | *serves:* 4 to 6

Nabil: Figs are in season in July and August in Algeria, and we enjoyed them fresh from the tree when I was a little boy. I used to eat so many I would get a stomachache. Sometimes I would climb trees and pick figs where I was not supposed to, which made it all the more fun. The flavor of this tajine takes me right back to those childhood summers in Algeria.

---

1 tablespoon butter, ghee, or coconut oil

1 whole (5-pound) chicken, cut into 8 pieces

1 medium white onion, diced

2 teaspoons minced garlic

1 teaspoon ground cumin

1 teaspoon ground coriander

1 teaspoon ground cinnamon

2 tablespoons grated fresh ginger

fine sea salt and ground black pepper

4 cups Chicken Broth (page 386)

1 1/2 cups dried figs, halved (about 12 whole figs)

1/4 cup chopped fresh cilantro, for garnish

1. Melt the fat in a large stockpot over medium heat, then add the chicken and sauté for 10 minutes, or until browned.

2. Add the onion, garlic, cumin, coriander, cinnamon, ginger, and a pinch of salt and pepper and sauté the mixture for 5 minutes, or until the onion is translucent.

3. Add the broth, cover, and bring to a boil. Remove the lid and simmer, uncovered, for 20 minutes. Add the dried figs and continue to simmer the mixture for another 20 minutes, uncovered.

4. Serve the chicken with the sauce, topped with the cilantro.

SLOW COOKER INSTRUCTIONS
Place all of the ingredients except the cilantro in a slow cooker and cook for 5 to 6 hours on low. Garnish with the cilantro and serve.

make it a meal
This dish pairs perfectly with any of the Cauliflower Couscous recipes on page 332.

nut-free	Yes
egg-free	Yes
low FODMAP	Omit the garlic and onion. Use garlic-infused olive oil as the cooking fat. Use 2 cups cubed sweet potato instead of figs.
AIP-friendly	Use 1 teaspoon ground turmeric and 1 teaspoon ground cardamom in place of the ground cumin and coriander.
SCD/GAPS	Yes
lower carb	Yes

chef's tip
To have all-natural dried figs at a fraction of the cost of store-bought, try dehydrating your own when they're in season.

nutritionist's note
Look for dried figs without added sulfur to avoid unnecessary chemicals, and choose figs that have no added oil coating or sweetener.

saffron braised chicken

prep time: 10 to 15 minutes | *cook time:* 1 hour | *serves:* 4

Nabil: Saffron is abundant and affordable in the southern Mediterranean region; I usually bring some home with me after I visit my family. If you don't have any saffron, a good alternative is ground turmeric.

1 tablespoon butter, ghee, or coconut oil

1 whole (5-pound) chicken, cut into 8 pieces

fine sea salt and ground black pepper

1 tablespoon paprika

1 pinch saffron

2 teaspoons ground ginger

2 teaspoons ground cumin

1 medium white onion, diced

2 teaspoons minced garlic

4 cups Chicken Broth (page 386)

2 tablespoons chopped fresh cilantro

2 tablespoons chopped fresh parsley

1. Melt the fat in a large stockpot over medium heat. Season the chicken liberally with salt and pepper, add it to the pan, and brown it completely on all sides, about 10 minutes. Sprinkle the paprika, saffron, ginger, and cumin over the chicken. Add the onion and garlic and sauté until the onion is translucent, about 5 minutes.

2. Add the broth, cover, and bring to a boil. Remove the lid and simmer for 40 minutes.

3. Turn the broiler on high and place a rack in the top position. Use tongs to remove the chicken from the pot and place it in a 9-by-13-inch baking dish. Broil the chicken in the oven for 5 minutes to crisp the skin.

4. Stir the cilantro and parsley into the sauce. Plate the chicken and cover with the sauce.

SLOW COOKER INSTRUCTIONS

Place all of the ingredients except the cilantro and parsley in a slow cooker and cook for 6 hours on low. Stir in the cilantro and parsley and serve.

make it a meal

This dish pairs perfectly with any of the Cauliflower Couscous recipes on page 332.

nut-free	Yes
egg-free	Yes
low FODMAP	Omit the garlic and onion. Use garlic-infused olive oil as the cooking fat.
AIP-friendly	Use 2 teaspoons turmeric in place of the cumin.
SCD/GAPS	Yes
lower carb	Yes

chef's tip

Just a tiny pinch of saffron turns this whole dish a beautiful orange color and imparts a deep and exotic flavor.

nutritionist's note

Saffron has been studied for its ability to suppress the appetite—it has compounds that can reduce the urge to overeat. In historical accounts it was used as an aphrodisiac.

za'atar and garlic roasted duck

prep time: 10 minutes | *cook time:* 1 1/2 hours | *serves:* 4

Caitlin: Where we live in San Francisco, we have an amazing community-supported agriculture (CSA) service that delivers pastured duck to our door. This wonderfully fatty bird is nicely complemented by the preparation given here. Cauliflower Couscous (page 332) is a great side for this dish.

---

1 whole (5-pound) duck

fine sea salt and ground black pepper

3 tablespoons Za'atar Spice Blend (page 401)

1 tablespoon ground paprika

1 tablespoon ground cumin

1 tablespoon garlic powder

3 bay leaves, crushed

3 cloves garlic, peeled

1/2 cup chopped fresh cilantro

1 lemon, sliced

1. Preheat the oven to 350°F. Have on hand a roasting pan with a rack inserted in place. (Ideally, the rack will keep the duck an inch or so above the bottom of the pan.)

2. Remove the giblets package from the duck and save it for another use.

3. Place a pinch of salt and pepper, the za'atar, paprika, cumin, and garlic powder in a small bowl and stir to combine. Thoroughly rub the outside of the duck with the spice mix.

4. Stuff the bay leaves, garlic cloves, cilantro, and lemon slices into the cavity of the duck. Place the duck on the rack in the roasting pan, breast side up. Cook the duck for 1 1/2 hours, or until the internal temperature is 175°F and the juices running out are clear.

5. Broil the duck for an additional 4 to 5 minutes to crisp the skin. Serve on a platter and slice as desired.

nut-free	Yes
egg-free	Yes
low FODMAP	Omit the garlic. Rub the duck with garlic-infused olive oil if desired.
AIP-friendly	Use ground cardamom and turmeric in place of the paprika and cumin. Omit the za'atar (see Nutritionist's Note).
SCD/GAPS	Yes
lower carb	Yes

chef's tip

Duck release a lot of luscious fat when cooked. Make sure to save this healthy fat for use in other recipes, such as Perfect Sweet Potato Fries (page 320).

nutritionist's note

If you have autoimmune issues, you can make your own za'atar at home and leave out the red pepper spices—it will still have the flavor of the authentic herb blend. See the recipe for za'atar on page 401, which includes autoimmune modifications.

Kabylie cinnamon chicken tajine

prep time: 15 minutes | *cook time:* 1 hour 15 minutes | *serves:* 4

Nabil: Kabylie is a region of northern Algeria where the indigenous people prepare this dish, and when I was growing up, we often had it during large family dinners. It's stewed in a delicate tomato sauce that captures the flavors of the vegetables and chicken. Feel free to serve it with as much or as little sauce as desired.

1 tablespoon butter, ghee, or coconut oil

1 whole (5-pound) chicken, cut into 8 pieces

fine sea salt and ground black pepper

1 tablespoon ground cinnamon

1 medium white onion, diced

4 cups Chicken Broth (page 386)

3 large carrots, cut lengthwise into quarters and then halved

3 medium turnips, peeled and cut into wedges

2 tablespoons tomato paste

3 medium zucchini, cut lengthwise into quarters

1/4 cup chopped fresh cilantro, for garnish

1. Melt the fat in a stockpot over medium heat.

2. Add the chicken, a pinch of salt and pepper, and the cinnamon and brown for 10 minutes. Add the onion and sauté for 5 more minutes, or until the onion is translucent.

3. Add the chicken broth, cover, and bring to a boil. Remove the lid and simmer for 40 minutes.

4. Add the carrots, turnips, and tomato paste to the broth. Let the carrots and turnips simmer for 12 to 15 minutes, until fork-tender. Add the zucchini and cook for another 5 minutes.

5. Adjust the seasoning to taste. Remove the pot from the heat, garnish with the cilantro, and serve.

SLOW COOKER INSTRUCTIONS
Place the fat, chicken, spices, onion, and broth in a slow cooker and cook for 5 hours on low. Add the carrots, turnips, tomato paste, and zucchini and cook for 1 more hour, or until the vegetables are tender. Garnish with the cilantro and serve.

make it a meal
This dish pairs perfectly with any of the Cauliflower Couscous recipes on page 332.

chef's tip
Turnips are underutilized in the United States. I grew up eating them, and the key to improving the flavor is slow-cooking them. They absorb the flavor of the other foods they are cooked with, and they keep their shape and texture even after many hours of cooking.

nutritionist's note
This tajine is usually served with wheat couscous. Our healthier version of couscous uses cauliflower, which gives the texture of couscous without the gut-irritating effects of wheat.

nut-free	Yes
egg-free	Yes
low FODMAP	Use 1/2 cup chopped scallions in place of the onion and reduce sauté time to 1 minute.
AIP-friendly	Use 1/2 cup canned pumpkin in place of the tomato paste.
SCD/GAPS	Yes
lower carb	Reduce the amount of carrots, if desired.

lamb-stuffed chicken thighs

prep time: 20 minutes | *cook time:* 35 minutes | *serves:* 4

Nabil: Not only are chicken thighs usually less expensive than breast meat, I find that they have more flavor and are easier to work with. This recipe makes chicken thighs even more delicious with ground lamb stuffing, which adds more fat and dimension to the flavors. It pairs well with Charmoula Roasted Vegetables (page 334), as pictured.

FOR THE STUFFING

1 pound ground lamb or beef

2 teaspoons minced garlic

1 teaspoon ground cumin

1 teaspoon paprika

1/4 cup chopped fresh cilantro

1 large egg, beaten

fine sea salt and ground black pepper

FOR THE CHICKEN

1 teaspoon ground cumin

1 teaspoon paprika

fine sea salt and ground black pepper

1 pound boneless chicken thighs

1 tablespoon butter, ghee, or coconut oil

1. Preheat the oven to 350°F.

2. Mix all of the stuffing ingredients together in a large bowl until well combined. Let the stuffing sit for 10 minutes to allow the flavors to combine.

3. Prepare the chicken: In a small bowl, mix together the cumin, paprika, and a pinch of salt and pepper. Season the chicken thighs on both sides with the spice mixture. Put the chicken thighs between two pieces of parchment and pound them out with a meat mallet or rolling pin until they are 1/4 inch thick and uniform. Place about 1/4 cup of the stuffing mixture in the middle of each piece of chicken.

4. Roll the chicken around the stuffing until it creates a cylinder. Wrap cotton cooking string around the roll several times and tie to secure.

5. In an oven-safe skillet, melt the fat over medium-high heat. Sear the chicken for 30 seconds on each side. Place the skillet into the oven and bake for 30 minutes, or until golden brown.

chef's tip

To increase the depth of flavor even more, place the chicken over the raw charmoula vegetables and bake them together. They'll cook in about the same amount of time, and the flavors complement each other well.

nutritionist's note

Look for chicken that's labeled "air-chilled." It means that the chicken is slowly cooled down to safe temperatures after processing, rather than being rushed through a cold water bath, which can make chicken unnaturally heavier and can affect flavor. And of course, look for pastured and organic chicken, which has more vitamins and minerals than conventionally raised chicken.

nut-free	Yes
egg-free	Yes
low FODMAP	Use 1/4 cup minced chives in place of the garlic.
AIP-friendly	Use ground turmeric in place of the paprika and cardamom in place of the cumin.
SCD/GAPS	Yes
lower carb	Yes

nacera's lemon ginger chicken tajine

prep time: 15 minutes | *cook time:* 1 hour | *serves:* 4

Nabil: We named this recipe after my sister Nacera, who used to make this dish for our family. The lemons and ginger cook down to create a broth with a beautiful balance of acid and spice that will make your family beg for seconds.

---

1 tablespoon butter, ghee, or coconut oil

1 whole (5-pound) chicken, cut into 8 pieces

fine sea salt and ground black pepper

1 medium white onion, diced

2 teaspoons minced garlic

1/2 cup chopped fresh parsley

2 tablespoons chopped fresh cilantro

1 pinch saffron

4 cups Chicken Broth (page 386)

2 lemons, thinly sliced

3 ounces fresh ginger, thinly sliced

1/4 cup chopped fresh cilantro, for garnish

1. In a large stockpot, melt the fat over medium heat. Season the chicken liberally with salt and pepper, then brown it in the fat, about 10 minutes. Add the onion, garlic, parsley, cilantro, a pinch of salt and pepper, and the saffron and sauté for 5 more minutes, until the onion is translucent.

2. Add the chicken broth to the pot and cover until the mixture comes to a boil. Remove the lid and simmer for 20 minutes.

3. Add the sliced lemons and ginger to the pot and continue to cook for another 20 minutes, uncovered. Garnish with the cilantro and serve.

SLOW COOKER INSTRUCTIONS
Place all of the ingredients except the cilantro in a slow cooker and cook for 6 hours on low. Garnish with the cilantro and serve.

make it a meal
This dish pairs perfectly with any of the Cauliflower Couscous recipes on page 332.

nut-free	Yes
egg-free	Yes
low FODMAP	Omit the garlic and onion. Use garlic-infused olive oil as the cooking fat.
AIP-friendly	Yes
SCD/GAPS	Yes
lower carb	Yes

nutritionist's note
Ginger is well known for supporting digestion and soothing nausea and other common digestive ailments. It also reduces inflammation, which helps with joint pain and stiffness.

za'atar brick chicken

prep time: 15 minutes, plus up to 1 hour to marinate | *cook time:* 1 hour | *serves:* 4

This rustic method for cooking chicken, popular in California restaurants, creates a crispy skin that everyone loves. Using bricks also ensures that the skin is kept in close contact with the cooking surface, which helps the seasoning adhere to the skin and makes it more flavorful.

---

2 tablespoons Za'atar Spice Blend (page 401)

2 tablespoons ground cumin

2 tablespoons dried basil

1 tablespoon paprika

2 to 3 bay leaves, crushed

fine sea salt and ground black pepper

1/4 cup lemon juice

2 tablespoons extra-virgin olive oil

1 whole (5-pound) chicken

1 tablespoon butter, ghee, or coconut oil

1. Mix all the spices and a pinch of salt and pepper in a small bowl with the lemon juice and olive oil.

2. Using a sharp knife, cut the chicken in half along each side of the backbone. Remove the backbone and save it for making broth. Completely coat the outside of the chicken with the marinade and let it sit in the fridge for up to 1 hour.

3. Preheat the oven to 350°F. Cover 2 fire bricks with aluminum foil and put them in the oven for 15 minutes to warm up.

4. In a large cast-iron skillet, melt the fat over medium-high heat. Place the chicken halves in the pan skin side down. Put the bricks on top of the chicken to weigh it down.

5. Sear the chicken without moving it for 3 to 5 minutes, until the skin is browned. Keeping the bricks in place, transfer the chicken to the oven and bake for 50 to 60 minutes, until the juices run clear.

6. Remove the chicken from the oven and let it rest in the pan for 10 minutes before serving.

chef's tip

Many chefs cook the chicken all in one piece when using this brick method, but Caitlin found that cutting it in half both made it easier for her to handle and made the prospect of cooking a whole chicken less intimidating.

nutritionist's note

The healthiest chickens forage on green grass in the sunshine with access to bugs and worms. These pastured chickens have more vitamin D and a healthier ratio of essential fats than factory-farmed chickens, which are fed a diet of primarily corn and soy. Look for a local farmer in your area who raises pastured chickens and buy direct to get the best price. For more information, visit www.eatwild.com.

nut-free	Yes
egg-free	Yes
low FODMAP	Yes
AIP-friendly	Use turmeric in place of the cumin. Omit the paprika. Use dried marjoram leaves in place of the Za'atar Spice Blend (page 401).
SCD/GAPS	Yes
lower carb	Yes

crispy fried chicken tenders

prep time: 10 minutes | *cook time:* 10 minutes | *serves:* 4

Many people transitioning to a Paleo diet find that they miss fried chicken. This version of the comforting American classic, which adds cumin and cilantro for a Mediterranean twist and is perfectly Paleo-friendly, will fulfill your cravings. It pairs well with Harissa Dipping Sauce (page 395) and Mock Potato Salad (page 326), as pictured.

2 cups blanched almond flour

1/2 cup minced fresh cilantro

1 tablespoon paprika

fine sea salt and ground black pepper

4 boneless, skinless chicken breasts (1 1/2 pounds)

3 large eggs

1 cup sustainable palm shortening or coconut oil

1. In a shallow bowl, combine the almond flour with the cilantro, paprika, and a pinch of salt and pepper.

2. Cut the chicken breasts lengthwise into 2-inch-wide strips, about 3 per breast. Season the chicken strips liberally with salt and pepper on all sides.

3. Break the eggs into a separate shallow bowl and beat them with a fork. Coat each chicken strip thoroughly with the beaten eggs. Dredge the chicken in the flour mixture, coating both sides, and shake off the excess. Place the coated chicken on a plate and set aside. Repeat the process until all of the chicken is coated with the flour mixture.

4. Heat the palm shortening in a large skillet over high heat. To test the heat, insert the end of wooden spoon handle into the fat. If the fat bubbles around the handle, it's sufficiently hot.

5. Carefully place the chicken strips into the fat. Fry the chicken strips for 5 minutes, then flip them and cook for another 5 minutes, or until the chicken is golden brown on the outside and no pink remains on the inside.

6. Let the chicken drain on a paper towel for 1 minute before serving.

chef's tip

Flavorful fried chicken needs the proper seasoning. This recipe uses seasoning in the flour mixture as well as on the raw chicken, which makes a big difference. It's also key to get the oil very hot before adding the chicken in order to give it a crispy crust.

nutritionist's note

Fried chicken can be a healthy food when it is not coated in white flour and fried in oxidized vegetable oil. Grain-free flour, such as almond or coconut flour, is a great alternative that gives a breaded texture and taste but won't cause the gut irritation associated with wheat flour. The fats suggested in this recipe, coconut oil and sustainable palm shortening, are full of healthy lauric acid, which is found in breast milk, nature's perfect food.

nut-free	Use finely ground sunflower seeds (see page 170) in place of the almond flour.
egg-free	No
low FODMAP	Use cashew meal in place of the almond flour. Omit the dipping sauce.
AIP-friendly	No
SCD/GAPS	Yes
lower carb	Yes

red meat

peppers and zucchini stuffed with lamb (lamb dolmas)

prep time: 10 minutes | **cook time:** 40 minutes | **serves:** 4

Caitlin: I first had this dish when my sister-in-law visited from Algeria and stayed with us for two weeks. I could not believe how tasty this simple, one-pot meal was and how beautiful all the colors looked while it was cooking. The broth and cinnamon simmer together with the beef and vegetables to create a rich, unforgettable flavor.

---

4 bell peppers, any color

2 large zucchini

1 tablespoon unsalted butter, ghee, or coconut oil

1 medium white onion, diced

fine sea salt and ground black pepper

1 stick cinnamon

2 teaspoons minced garlic

4 cups Beef Broth (page 388)

2 tablespoons tomato paste

1 pound ground lamb

1 tablespoon ground cinnamon

1/2 cup chopped fresh cilantro, divided

1. Cut the tops off the bell peppers and remove the cores and seeds. Cut the zucchini in half crosswise and hollow out the middle. Set aside.

2. Melt the fat in a large sauté pan over medium heat. Add the onion, a pinch of salt and pepper, and the cinnamon stick and sauté for 2 minutes. Add the garlic and sauté for 2 more minutes. Add the beef broth and tomato paste to the pot and stir. Let the sauce simmer for 5 minutes.

3. In a bowl, mix the meat with a few pinches of salt and pepper, the ground cinnamon, and half of the cilantro. Stuff the peppers and zucchini with the meat mixture. Arrange the peppers and zucchini in the pan of sauce with the meat stuffing facing up.

4. Cook the stuffed vegetables, covered, over medium heat for about 30 minutes. Top with the remaining fresh cilantro and serve.

nut-free	Yes
egg-free	Yes
low FODMAP	Omit the onion and garlic. Use garlic-infused olive oil as the cooking fat. Use 1/2 cup chopped tomatoes in place of the tomato paste.
AIP-friendly	Omit the peppers and use 6 large zucchini. Use 1/2 cup canned pumpkin in place of the tomato paste.
SCD/GAPS	Yes
lower carb	Yes

chef's tip

In France and Algeria, zucchini, also known as courgettes, are a staple vegetable during the spring and summer. It's a very versatile and mild vegetable that takes on the flavor of the spices in the dish in which it is used.

nutritionist's note

Zucchini is mostly water and has very few carbohydrates and calories. It is high in fiber and full of vitamin C and beta-carotene, which helps protect cells from free-radical damage.

cinnamon braised beef tajine

prep time: 10 minutes | *cook time:* 50 minutes | *serves:* 4

Nabil: This is one of my all-time favorite dishes. It's incredibly simple, but the flavors are unbelievably rich. In my country, cinnamon is essentially the national spice; it's used in many savory dishes that my family eats regularly. The cinnamon adds a sweet and spicy taste that makes for a truly memorable dish.

1 tablespoon unsalted butter, ghee, coconut oil

1 medium white onion, diced

2 pounds beef or lamb stew meat (preferably on the bone)

fine sea salt and ground black pepper

3 sticks cinnamon

4 cups Beef Broth (page 388)

1/4 cup chopped fresh cilantro, for garnish

1. Melt the fat in a stockpot over medium heat. Add the diced onion and sauté for 3 minutes. Add the stew meat and sauté until browned, about 5 minutes. Add a pinch of salt and pepper and the cinnamon sticks and cook for 2 more minutes.

2. Add the broth to the pot, cover, and bring to a simmer over medium-low heat. Remove the lid and simmer for 40 minutes, or until the meat is very tender.

3. Adjust the seasonings to taste, remove the cinnamon sticks, garnish with cilantro, and serve.

SLOW COOKER INSTRUCTIONS
Place all of the ingredients in a slow cooker and cook for 6 hours on low.

make it a meal
This dish pairs perfectly with any of the Cauliflower Couscous recipes on page 332.

nut-free	Yes
egg-free	Yes
low FODMAP	Omit the onion and garnish with 1/4 cup chopped chives when serving.
AIP-friendly	Yes
SCD/GAPS	Yes
lower carb	Yes

chef's tip
When braising meat, it is important to scrape the brown bits of cooked onion or meat from the bottom of the pan with a wooden spatula. These bits are full of flavor that will enhance the dish when the broth is added.

top sirloin with mushroom reduction sauce

prep time: 15 minutes | *cook time:* 45 minutes | *serves:* 4

This is similar to a French dish called *tournedos vert-pre.* "Tournedos" refers to small pieces of beef cut from a tenderloin. We used a less expensive cut of meat to make this recipe more affordable, but it's just as tasty. The mushroom reduction sauce is also delicious over any cut of steak or chicken.

FOR THE SAUCE

2 tablespoons unsalted butter, ghee, or coconut oil

2 tablespoons minced shallot (1 medium shallot)

2 teaspoons minced garlic

1 pound mushrooms, sliced

1 tablespoon tomato paste

1 teaspoon ground cumin

3 cups Beef Broth (page 388)

FOR THE STEAKS

4 (6-ounce) top sirloin steaks, room temperature

fine sea salt and ground black pepper

1 tablespoon unsalted butter, ghee, or coconut oil

1/4 cup chopped fresh parsley, for garnish

1. Make the sauce: Melt the fat in a saucepan over medium heat. Add the shallot and garlic to the saucepan and sauté for 2 to 3 minutes, stirring continuously. Add the mushrooms and keep stirring until they are soft, about 3 minutes.

2. Add the tomato paste, cumin, and beef broth. Turn the heat to medium-low and let it simmer, uncovered, for 30 minutes to reduce, until it coats the back of a spoon when stirred. Remove the saucepan from the heat and cover to keep warm.

3. When the sauce is nearly done, preheat the oven to 350°F.

4. Prepare the steaks: Season the steaks liberally with salt and pepper and preheat a large cast-iron skillet or oven-safe grill pan over medium-high heat until it is very hot, about 2 minutes. Drop in the cooking fat and briefly tilt the pan to make sure it is covered in grease. Add the steaks to the pan and sear the meat on one side for 30 seconds, then flip and sear the other side.

5. Transfer the pan to the oven for 3 to 5 minutes for medium doneness, or until the steak is cooked to your preferred temperature. Let the steaks rest on a plate for 5 minutes before serving.

6. Top the steaks with the mushroom sauce and garnish with the parsley to serve.

nut-free	Yes
egg-free	Yes
low FODMAP	Use garlic-infused oil as the cooking fat. Omit the shallot and garlic. Use 1/2 cup chopped tomatoes in place of the tomato paste.
AIP-friendly	Use 1/4 cup canned pumpkin in place of the tomato paste. Omit the cumin.
SCD/GAPS	Yes
lower carb	Yes

chef's tip

For a perfectly seared steak, always make sure the pan is very hot before adding the meat. Use an oven-safe pan that can go from the stovetop to the oven, such as a cast-iron skillet, and be sure to preheat the oven so it is hot when you are ready to transfer the steak. For the best flavor, let the steak rest for a few minutes before slicing.

nutritionist's tip

Mushrooms are one of the few vegetables with vitamin D, but they have to be eaten with fat for it to be absorbed. Many mushroom growers expose the mushrooms to sunlight during growth, which increases the vitamin D content.

marinated filet mignon with béarnaise sauce

prep time: 5 minutes, plus up to 2 hours to marinate and 15 minutes to make the sauce | *cook time:* 10 minutes | *serves:* 4

Nabil: Béarnaise sauce always impresses people and elevates eggs, fish, or steak. This simple preparation for filet mignon highlights the rich flavor of the meat, which is complemented by the creamy sauce.

---

2 tablespoons lemon juice

1/2 cup extra-virgin olive oil

2 tablespoons fresh thyme

fine sea salt and ground black pepper

1 tablespoon butter, ghee, or coconut oil

4 (6-ounce) filet mignons

1 recipe Béarnaise Sauce (page 382)

2 tablespoons chopped fresh parsley, for garnish

1. Mix together the lemon juice, olive oil, thyme, and a pinch of salt and pepper, then pour the mixture over the steaks. Marinate the steaks for up to 2 hours in the refrigerator.

2. About 20 minutes before you cook the steaks, remove them from the marinade, pat them dry, and allow them to come to room temperature. Discard the marinade.

3. Preheat a grill pan or cast-iron skillet over medium-high heat until very hot, 3 to 5 minutes. Add the fat and melt it.

4. Place the steaks in the pan and cook for 3 to 4 minutes on each side for medium doneness, or until the steak is cooked to your preferred temperature.

5. Transfer the steaks to a serving plate and let them rest for 2 minutes before cutting. Serve with the béarnaise sauce and garnish with the parsley.

nut-free	Yes
egg-free	No. Use Mint Pesto (page 186) in place of the béarnaise sauce.
low FODMAP	Yes
AIP-friendly	No. Use Mint Pesto (page 186) in place of the béarnaise sauce.
SCD/GAPS	Yes
lower carb	Yes

chef's tip

Marinating a steak in lemon juice will break down some of its fibers to make it more tender when sliced. Another way to make a filet mignon more tender is to slice it against the grain.

nutritionist's note

Grass-fed beef is high in B vitamins, which are crucial for steady energy. Also, just 4 ounces has 40 percent of the recommended amount of zinc and selenium, which support a healthy thyroid.

harissa braised short ribs

prep time: 15 minutes | *cook time:* 2 hours 40 minutes | *serves:* 4

Caitlin: When Nabil first made these for me, I thought I'd died and gone to heaven. The meat falls off the bone, and the sauce is finger-licking good. Braised short ribs are served at upscale restaurants all over San Francisco, but now you can feel like a chef without spending the big bucks. We've added harissa to give it a touch of spice and North African flair.

---

2 1/2 pounds short ribs

fine sea salt and ground black pepper

5 cups Beef Broth (page 388)

3 medium carrots, sliced

2 medium white onions, chopped

4 stalks celery, sliced

2 tablespoons tomato paste

1 tablespoon Harissa (page 394)

1/4 cup apple cider vinegar

2 tablespoon minced garlic

1/2 cup chopped fresh parsley, divided

1. Place a rack in the middle of the oven. Turn the oven to the broil setting on high.

2. Place the meat in a large Dutch oven or other deep baking dish with a lid (such as a covered casserole or gratin dish) and season on all sides with salt and pepper. Set the dish in the oven and broil for 5 minutes. Flip the meat with tongs and broil on the other side for 5 minutes. Take the Dutch oven out of the oven and set aside. Turn off the broiler and preheat the oven to 350°F.

3. Cover the meat, still in the Dutch oven, with the broth until it's submerged. Add the vegetables, tomato paste, harissa, vinegar, garlic, half of the parsley, and a pinch of salt and pepper to the broth. Stir slightly until the tomato paste and harissa are dissolved.

4. Cover the Dutch oven or baking dish with aluminum foil and a lid. Make sure the dish is sealed tightly, so that no moisture escapes. Return the Dutch oven to the oven and cook for 2 1/2 hours, or until the meat is tender.

5. Remove the meat from the pan, set it on a serving plate, and cover to keep warm. Use an immersion blender to blend the sauce, or transfer it to a stand blender to blend. If the sauce is too thin, transfer it to a saucepan and reduce it over medium heat, uncovered, for 10 minutes, or until thickened.

6. Spoon the sauce over the meat and garnish with the rest of the parsley to serve.

SLOW COOKER INSTRUCTIONS

Place all the ingredients, reserving half of the parsley, in the slow cooker for 6 hours on low. Carefully remove the meat with tongs, transfer to a serving plate, and cover to keep warm. Puree the sauce with an immersion blender. Pour the sauce over the meat and top with the remaining parsley.

nut-free	Yes
egg-free	Yes
low FODMAP	Use 1/2 cup chopped scallions in place of the onion and garlic. Use 1 cup chopped tomatoes in place of the tomato paste. Use 1 teaspoon chili flakes in place of the harissa.
AIP-friendly	Use 1 cup canned pumpkin in place of the tomato paste. Use 1 tablespoon ground ginger in place of the harissa.
SCD/GAPS	Yes
lower carb	Yes

chef's tip

When I make this dish at home, I use a Dutch oven because it has a lid, which keeps the ribs from drying out. I also cover the dish with aluminum foil before placing the lid on top. Do not skip this step! The worst thing that can happen is that the ribs dry out. If there is too much liquid left at the end, you can reduce the sauce over medium heat after pureeing, until the sauce thickens.

lamb and vegetable tajine

prep time: 10 minutes | *cook time:* 1 hour | *serves:* 4

Though this recipe is very similar to the Kabylie tajine on page 210, which is made with chicken, the flavor of the lamb makes this version distinct and unique. The villagers in the mountains of Algeria, Morocco, and Tunisia have made this type of tajine for thousands of years.

---

1 tablespoon unsalted butter, ghee, or coconut oil

2 to 2 1/2 pounds lamb or beef stew meat (preferably on the bone)

fine sea salt and ground black pepper

1 medium white onion, diced

2 teaspoons ground cinnamon

6 cups Beef Broth (page 388)

1 tablespoon tomato paste

2 medium turnips, peeled and cut into bite-sized pieces

2 medium carrots, cut into bite-sized pieces

2 medium zucchini, cut into bite-sized pieces

1/4 cup finely chopped fresh cilantro, for garnish

1. Melt the fat in a stockpot over medium heat. Season the lamb liberally with salt and pepper, then brown it for 3 to 4 minutes. Add the onion, a pinch of salt and pepper, and the cinnamon and cook for 3 to 4 minutes, until the onion is translucent. Add the broth and tomato paste, cover, and bring to a simmer. Remove the lid and simmer for 30 minutes.

2. Add the turnips and carrots to the pot and cook for 5 minutes.

3. Add the zucchini and cook for another 10 minutes, or until all the vegetables are soft.

4. Garnish with the cilantro to serve.

SLOW COOKER INSTRUCTIONS

Place all of the ingredients except the zucchini in a slow cooker and cook for 5 hours on low. Add the zucchini, cook for 1 more hour, and serve.

make it a meal

This dish pairs perfectly with any of the Cauliflower Couscous recipes on page 332.

chef's tip

I was not crazy about coconut oil when Caitlin first convinced me to go Paleo, even though I do like coconut treats. I eventually discovered that expeller-pressed coconut oil has no flavor or smell, so it works well with all types of cuisine. I have cooked this tajine with expeller-pressed coconut oil and didn't taste it at all.

nutritionist's note

Cinnamon is commonly used in Mediterranean recipes. It is known for balancing blood sugar, and when eaten several times a day it may reduce cravings for sweets.

nut-free	Yes
egg-free	Yes
low FODMAP	Omit the onion and add 1/4 cup chopped chives as garnish.
AIP-friendly	Use 1/4 cup canned pumpkin in place of the tomato paste.
SCD/GAPS	Yes
lower carb	Yes

siva's cauliflower and meatballs

prep time: 10 minutes | *cook time:* 30 minutes | *serves:* 4

Caitlin: When I was in Algeria for two weeks in April 2013, Nabil's family made me feel at home because they made food that fit with my Paleo plan. It seemed like every mouthwatering dish was so simple, spiced and seasoned with just cumin or cinnamon and salt and pepper. Siva, Nabil's youngest sister, made this wonderful dish for me because she knew how much I love cauliflower.

---

1 pound ground beef

1 teaspoon ground cinnamon

fine sea salt and ground black pepper

1 medium head cauliflower, cored and cut into florets

1 tablespoon butter, ghee, or coconut oil

1 cup diced white onion

4 cups Beef Broth (page 388)

2 tablespoons tomato paste

3 medium turnips, peeled and quartered

2 medium carrots, cut into 1/4-inch rounds

1/4 cup chopped fresh cilantro, for garnish

1. Place the ground beef in a large bowl with the cinnamon and a pinch of salt and pepper and mix well. Roll the meat into 1-inch balls and set on a plate.

2. In a medium saucepan, boil the cauliflower florets for 5 to 7 minutes, until partially cooked, then drain and set aside.

3. Melt the fat in a stockpot over medium heat. Add the onion and cook for 3 to 4 minutes, until translucent. Season the onion with a pinch of salt and pepper.

4. Add the broth and tomato paste to the pot and bring to a simmer for 2 minutes. Drop the meatballs into the sauce and cook them for 5 minutes.

5. Add the turnips and carrots to the sauce and cook, uncovered, until tender, about 7 minutes.

6. Add the partially cooked cauliflower florets and let them simmer until tender, about 5 minutes. Adjust the salt and pepper to taste. Serve in bowls and top with the cilantro.

nut-free	Yes
egg-free	Yes
low FODMAP	Omit the onion. Use garlic-infused olive oil as the cooking fat.
AIP-friendly	Use 1/2 cup canned pumpkin in place of the tomato paste.
SCD/GAPS	Yes
lower carb	Yes

lamb kebabs

prep time: 15 minutes, plus up to 8 hours to marinate | *cook time:* 10 minutes | *serves:* 4

One of the great things about these kebabs is how easy they are to transport and cook away from home. We frequently put them together at home and take them to get-togethers with friends for a crowd-pleasing meal, or we take them down to a park by the bay in San Francisco and grill them there. These kebabs pair well with Cauliflower Couscous (page 332), as pictured.

FOR THE MARINADE

3 tablespoons extra-virgin olive oil

2 tablespoons lemon juice

1 teaspoon minced garlic

1 teaspoon paprika

1 teaspoon dried ground oregano

1 pinch saffron

1 pinch fine sea salt

1 pinch ground black pepper

FOR THE KEBABS

1 1/2 pounds lamb or beef stew meat, cubed

1 medium red onion, cut into 1-inch pieces

1 yellow bell pepper, cut into 1-inch pieces

1 red bell pepper, cut into 1-inch pieces

2 tablespoons unsalted butter, ghee, or coconut oil, melted

1. Combine the ingredients for the marinade in a large nonreactive bowl and stir thoroughly.

2. Add the meat and the vegetables to the marinade and mix well. Set the bowl in the refrigerator, cover, and allow the meat and vegetables to marinate for up to 8 hours.

3. If using wooden skewers, soak them in water for 10 minutes. Put the meat and vegetables on the soaked wooden skewers or stainless-steel skewers, alternating the peppers, onion, and meat.

4. Preheat a grill pan over medium heat or an outdoor grill to medium-high heat. Brush the grill with the melted fat. Grill the skewers for 5 minutes on one side, then flip and grill for 5 minutes on the other side for medium doneness, or a few minutes longer for well done.

nut-free	Yes
egg-free	Yes
low FODMAP	Use 1/2 pound whole mushrooms in place of the onion. Use garlic-infused olive oil for the marinade and omit the garlic.
AIP-friendly	Use 1 teaspoon ground ginger in place of the paprika. Use 3 medium zucchini, sliced into circles, in place of the bell peppers.
SCD/GAPS	Yes
lower carb	Yes

chef's tip

Marinating these kebabs overnight makes a big difference in the flavor. If you are short on time, let them sit in the marinade for at least an hour before grilling to maximize the impact of the seasoning.

sweet lamb stew (l'ham hlou)

prep time: 30 minutes | *cook time:* 1 hour | *serves:* 4

Nabil: This is a traditional North African dish that I grew up eating. It features fruits that are plentiful and affordable in my country. As the dish cooks, the sweetness from the fruit concentrates, which, in combination with the cinnamon, creates an unforgettable flavor.

1 cup prunes

1 cup raisins

1 cup dried apricots

1 tablespoon unsalted butter, ghee, or coconut oil

2 1/2 pounds lamb stew meat (preferably on the bone)

fine sea salt and ground black pepper

1 medium white onion, diced

3 sticks cinnamon

6 cups Beef Broth (page 388)

1 tablespoon orange blossom water (see Chef's Tip, page 98) or grated orange zest

1/4 cup chopped fresh parsley, for garnish

1.   Put the prunes, raisins, and apricots in a bowl of hot water for about 30 minutes to rehydrate.

2.   In a stockpot, melt the fat over medium heat. Season the meat liberally with salt and pepper, then brown it for 5 minutes. Add the onion, a pinch of salt and pepper, and the cinnamon sticks. Continue to sauté the mixture for 5 minutes, or until the onion is translucent.

3.   Add the broth and bring to a simmer with the lid on.

4.   Remove the lid and continue to cook for 30 minutes.

5.   Drain the excess water from the soaking prunes, raisins, and apricots. Add the fruit and orange blossom water to the meat mixture. Cook for 20 more minutes, uncovered.

6.   Remove the cinnamon sticks and transfer the stew to a serving dish. Top with the fresh parsley and serve.

SLOW COOKER INSTRUCTIONS

Place everything except the parsley in the slow cooker and cook for 6 hours on low. Garnish with the parsley and serve.

make it a meal

This dish pairs perfectly with any of the Cauliflower Couscous recipes on page 332.

chef's tip

Using cinnamon sticks instead of ground cinnamon creates a slightly different flavor. Cinnamon sticks are more subtle and infuse a deeper, richer cinnamon flavor than ground cinnamon.

nutritionist's tip

Ceylon cinnamon is easier on the liver than cassia cinnamon, but it's also harder to find. Cassia cinnamon tends to be less expensive and is commonly available in supermarkets. It's usually dried and ground, which makes its nutrients less bioavailable.

nut-free	Yes
egg-free	Yes
low FODMAP	No. Use Cinnamon Braised Beef Tajine (page 224) instead.
AIP-friendly	Yes
SCD/GAPS	Yes
lower carb	Yes

rosemary leg of lamb

prep time: 5 minutes, plus up to 8 hours to marinate | *cook time:* 1 hour 10 minutes | *serves:* 6

Caitlin: Leg of lamb is a wonderful dish for a special occasion or family holiday—because it's not common in the US, your guests will feel spoiled. Nabil likes lamb best when it's prepared one of two ways: barbecued or coated in a flavorful marinade, as in this recipe. This dish goes well with Golden Raisin Slaw (page 330), as pictured.

1/2 cup dried rosemary

fine sea salt and ground black pepper

1 cup Dijon mustard (gluten-free)

1 (5-pound) bone-in leg of lamb (see Chef's Tip)

1. Put the dried rosemary in a spice or coffee grinder and pulse until it is a fine powder.

2. Mix the rosemary, a big pinch of salt and pepper, and the mustard in a small bowl to make a marinade. Place the lamb in a large baking dish. Spread the marinade all over the outside of the lamb, coating it evenly.

3. Let the lamb marinate in the refrigerator for up to 8 hours.

4. Turn the oven to broil. Place the lamb in the oven to sear the top for 5 minutes, then flip over and repeat. Reduce the temperature to 350°F and cook the lamb for 1 hour, or until the internal temperature reaches 160°F, for well-done meat.

5. Let the lamb rest for 10 minutes before slicing.

SLOW COOKER INSTRUCTIONS

Place the marinated lamb in a slow cooker. Add 6 cups of beef broth (page 388) and cook on low for 6 hours. Serve and enjoy.

nut-free	Yes
egg-free	Yes
low FODMAP	Yes
AIP-friendly	Use 1/2 cup lemon juice and 1/2 cup extra-virgin olive oil in place of the mustard.
SCD/GAPS	Use 1/4 cup dry mustard powder and 1/2 cup extra-virgin olive oil in place of the mustard.
lower carb	Yes

chef's tip

This recipe can be made with a 4-pound, boneless leg of lamb. If using a boneless leg, make sure to ask your butcher to tie it up for you. If you buy it at a wholesale club, it will already have a netting on the outside and will be ready to cover in the rub.

nutritionist's note

Many store-bought brands of mustard have processed ingredients listed as "natural flavors," which can be hidden forms of monosodium glutamate (MSG). MSG can cause reactions such as bloating and rashes in some people, and it has been shown to have detrimental long-term effects on the brain. Mustard may also contain gluten, so look for a brand labeled "gluten-free."

spiced rack of lamb

prep time: 5 minutes, plus up to 1 hour to marinate and 5 minutes to make the pesto | *cook time:* 15 minutes | *serves:* 4

A rack of lamb is very easy to cook, but many people in North America are intimidated by it because lamb is not as common here as beef. But cooking a rack of lamb is actually similar to cooking a steak: sear the outside, then finish it in the oven. Searing the meat crisps the fat on the outside and seals in the flavor. This lamb pairs perfectly with Warm Eggplant and Tomato Salad with Mint (page 324) and Cauliflower Couscous (page 332), as pictured.

1 teaspoon chili powder

1 teaspoon paprika

1 tablespoon dried oregano leaves

1 teaspoon ground coriander

2 tablespoon dried thyme leaves

1 tablespoon ground cumin

fine sea salt and ground black pepper

2 tablespoons extra-virgin olive oil

1 (2-pound) rack of lamb

1 tablespoon unsalted butter, ghee, or coconut oil

1 recipe Mint Pesto (page 186), for serving

1. Mix together the chili powder, paprika, oregano, coriander, thyme, cumin, a pinch of salt and pepper, and the olive oil in a small bowl. Rub the mixture onto the lamb evenly and let it sit for up to 1 hour in the refrigerator.

2. Preheat the oven to 350°F. Melt the fat in an oven-safe skillet over medium-high heat. Sear the rack of lamb for 1 minute on each side, pressing down firmly.

3. Transfer the pan with the lamb to the oven for 10 minutes for medium doneness or 12 minutes for well-done. Take the lamb out of the oven and let it rest for 2 minutes before slicing. Top with the pesto and serve.

nut-free	Use the nut-free modification for the pesto.
egg-free	Yes
low FODMAP	Yes
AIP-friendly	Omit the chili powder, paprika, coriander, and cumin. Add 1 tablespoon ground ginger. Use the AIP-friendly modification for the pesto.
SCD/GAPS	Yes
lower carb	Yes

nutritionist's note

Lamb is very high in B vitamins, which help give us energy. When eating meat-based meals, it's important to be in a relaxed state and chew very well to increase digestibility.

kefta lamb kebabs (persian version)

prep time: 10 minutes, plus up to 2 hours to marinate |
cook time: 10 minutes | *serves:* 4

This version of a kebab uses spices common in Persia (modern-day Iran), a cradle of ancient civilization where many Mediterranean dishes originated. At one time the Persian Empire spread all the way to Turkey and Egypt. The variety of fresh herbs in this dish results in amazing flavor that will make you feel like you're eating restaurant food at home. It pairs well with Minty Cucumber and Tomato Salad (page 134), as pictured.

---

1 medium white onion, peeled

2 pounds ground lamb

2 teaspoons ground cumin

2 teaspoons ground cinnamon

2 teaspoons ground nutmeg

2 teaspoons paprika

1 teaspoon fine sea salt

1 teaspoon ground black pepper

1/2 cup loosely packed fresh parsley leaves

1/2 cup loosely packed fresh cilantro leaves

1/2 cup loosely packed mint leaves

1 tablespoon unsalted butter, ghee, or coconut oil, melted

1.   In a food processor, pulse the onion until it is finely chopped. Add the ground lamb, spices, and herbs to the food processor.

2.   Pulse the lamb mixture several times until well mixed, and place in the refrigerator for up to 2 hours. If using wooden skewers, soak them in water for 10 minutes.

3.   Split the lamb mixture into 3-ounce pieces. Form each piece into the shape of a sausage, then place it on a metal or wooden skewer.

4.   Heat a grill pan on the stovetop or an outdoor grill to medium-high heat. Brush the grill pan or grill grate with the melted fat.

5.   Place the skewers on the grill pan or grill and cook for 3 to 5 minutes on each side for medium doneness, or until cooked to your preferred temperature.

chef's tip

If the skewers are turned too much, the meat will become chewy and overcooked. Cook them on one side for 3 to 5 minutes and then turn, and do not cook the same side again.

nutritionist's note

Look for lamb that is 100 percent grass-fed, as it will have an ideal anti-inflammatory ratio of fatty acids. Lamb is also very high in tryptophan, an amino acid that helps balance the brain for good sleep and a happy mood. If you do not have access to organic, 100 percent grass-fed meat, choose leaner conventional meat to avoid the toxins and hormones that are stored in fat. Then, during cooking, add your own fat from clean sources, such as ghee, grass-fed butter, or coconut oil.

nut-free	Yes
egg-free	Yes
low FODMAP	Use 1/2 cup chopped scallions in place of the onion.
AIP-friendly	Use 1 teaspoon ground turmeric in place of the cumin. Use 1 teaspoon ground ginger in place of the nutmeg and paprika.
SCD/GAPS	Yes
lower carb	Yes

stuffed cabbage (cabbage dolmas)

prep time: 10 to 15 minutes | *cook time:* 1 hour | *serves:* 4 to 6

Nabil: In the Middle East, *dolma* refers to a grape leaf stuffed with meat and rice, but in North Africa, it refers to a vegetable stuffed with beef and then slowly simmered in broth. Cabbage dolmas are a common savory dish in Algeria, as are dolmas made with zucchini and bell peppers (page 222).

---

12 large cabbage leaves

1 tablespoon unsalted butter, ghee, or coconut oil

1 pound beef stew meat

1 medium white onion

2 sticks cinnamon

fine sea salt and ground black pepper

4 cups Beef Broth (page 388)

1/4 cup chopped fresh cilantro, for garnish

FOR THE STUFFING

1 pound ground beef

1/4 cup chopped fresh parsley

2 teaspoons ground cumin

2 tablespoons ground cinnamon

1. Boil 3 cups of water in a steamer pot over medium heat. Steam the cabbage leaves for 3 to 5 minutes, until soft, and set them aside.

2. In a large sauté pan, melt the fat over medium heat. Add the stew meat to the pan and brown on all sides, about 5 minutes. Add the onion, cinnamon sticks, and a pinch of salt and pepper and cook another 3 minutes, or until the onion is translucent.

3. Cover the mixture with the beef broth and bring to a boil with the lid on. Remove the lid and simmer for 30 minutes.

4. While the stew meat is cooking, mix the stuffing ingredients together in a large bowl. Place 1/4 cup of the stuffing mixture in the middle of a steamed cabbage leaf. Roll the leaf halfway, then tuck in the sides and finish rolling. Place the rolled leaf aside on a plate, seam side down. Repeat until all of the stuffing is used up.

5. Using tongs, carefully add the stuffed cabbage leaves to the sauté pan. Cover and simmer the cabbage rolls for 15 to 20 minutes. Remove the cinnamon sticks and top the dish with the fresh cilantro to serve.

nut-free	Yes
egg-free	Yes
low FODMAP	No. Try Peppers and Zucchini Stuffed with Lamb (page 222) instead.
AIP-friendly	Use 1 teaspoon ground ginger in place of the cumin.
SCD/GAPS	Yes
lower carb	Yes

nutritionist's note

Raw vegetables such as cabbage, kale, and broccoli have goitrogenic properties that can disrupt thyroid function if overconsumed. The best thing to do is to cook these vegetables thoroughly. Doing so lowers the levels of goitrogens so that you can enjoy the many health benefits of these vegetables.

shish kebabs

prep time: 10 minutes, plus up to 3 hours to marinate |
cook time: 10 minutes | *serves:* 4

The term *shish kebab* means "skewered roasted meat." This tradition originated in Turkey, where nomadic tribes used to marinate meat to reduce the flavor of particularly gamey animals and then cook the marinated meat on skewers over an open flame. It pairs well with Cauliflower Couscous (page 332), as pictured.

---

1 medium white onion, peeled

1 1/2 pounds ground lamb

2 cloves garlic, peeled

1 pinch saffron

1 tablespoon ground cinnamon

2 teaspoons ground cumin

1/2 cup tightly packed fresh cilantro leaves

1/4 cup tightly packed fresh mint leaves

fine sea salt and ground black pepper

1 tablespoon unsalted butter, ghee, or coconut oil, melted

1. If using wooden skewers, soak them in water for 10 minutes.

2. Pulse the onion in a food processor until finely chopped. Add the lamb, garlic, saffron, cinnamon, cumin, cilantro, mint, and a pinch of salt and pepper.

3. Pulse a few times, until the mixture is thoroughly combined.

4. Chill the meat mixture in the refrigerator for up to 3 hours. Split the mixture into 3-ounce pieces. Using your hands, form each 3-ounce portion of meat into a long sausage shape around a skewer.

5. Heat a grill pan on the stovetop or an outdoor grill to medium-high heat. Brush the grill pan or grate with the melted fat. Cook the skewers for 8 to 10 minutes, rotating every 2 minutes, until all sides are cooked.

nut-free	Yes
egg-free	Yes
low FODMAP	Use 1/2 cup chopped scallions in place of the onion and garlic.
AIP-friendly	Use 1 teaspoon ground turmeric in place of the cumin.
SCD/GAPS	Yes
lower carb	Yes

chef's tip

Combining all the ingredients in the food processor and then chilling allows the meat to absorb the aromatics from the chopped herbs, creating a new dimension of taste and flavor. Chilling also solidifies the fat to create a moist and tender finished product.

beef and artichokes

prep time: 10 minutes | *cook time:* 1 hour 10 minutes | *serves:* 4 to 6

Nabil: My mom makes this recipe the traditional way, with fresh artichoke hearts. Working with fresh artichoke hearts is very labor intensive, however, and can be intimidating to the uninitiated. Caitlin had the idea to use frozen artichoke hearts to make it easier for busy cooks, and the result is still very close to my mom's version.

---

1 tablespoon unsalted butter, ghee, or coconut oil

1 pound beef stew meat (preferably on the bone)

fine sea salt and ground black pepper

1 medium white onion, diced

2 bay leaves

2 sticks cinnamon

4 cups Beef Broth (page 388)

1 pound ground beef

1/4 cup chopped fresh parsley

4 cups frozen artichoke hearts, defrosted and drained

2 tablespoons chopped fresh cilantro, for garnish

1. Melt the fat in a stockpot over medium heat. Season the beef stew meat with salt and pepper and sear on each side for 3 minutes. Season the meat with a pinch of salt and pepper. Add the onion and cook for 2 minutes. Add the bay leaves and cinnamon sticks to the pot and sauté for 1 minute longer.

2. Add the broth to the pot, cover, and bring to a simmer. Remove the lid and simmer for 35 minutes.

3. In a large bowl, mix the ground beef with a few generous pinches of salt and pepper and the parsley. Form the mixture into 1-inch meatballs and place them in the pot. Cook for 5 minutes.

4. Add the artichoke hearts to the pot and simmer for 20 more minutes. Remove the bay leaves and cinnamon sticks, garnish with the cilantro, and serve.

SLOW COOKER INSTRUCTIONS

Add all the ingredients except the artichoke hearts to a slow cooker and cook for 5 hours on low. Add the artichoke hearts and cook for 1 more hour. Garnish with the cilantro and serve.

nut-free	Yes
egg-free	Yes
low FODMAP	Omit the onion and use 1/2 cup sliced scallions as a garnish. Use 3 medium zucchini, cut into 1/2-inch slices, in place of the artichoke hearts.
AIP-friendly	Yes
SCD/GAPS	Yes
lower carb	Yes

make it a meal
This dish pairs perfectly with any of the Cauliflower Couscous recipes on page 332.

mediterranean burgers

prep time: 5 minutes | *cook time:* 4 to 6 minutes | *serves:* 4

We eat burgers every week in our house. We have a great time changing up the toppings, the spices, and even the meat, and the combination of Mediterranean spices in this recipe will liven up your burgers. It pairs well with Tahini Dipping Sauce (page 393), as pictured, or try it with Tzatziki Sauce (page 392) for an AIP-friendly sauce.

1 pound ground lamb or beef

1/2 medium white onion, minced

1 teaspoon ground cumin

1 teaspoon ground cinnamon

1/2 teaspoon ground nutmeg

1 teaspoon paprika

1/4 cup chopped fresh parsley

1 tablespoon chopped fresh cilantro

1 tablespoon chopped fresh mint

1/2 teaspoon fine sea salt

1/4 teaspoon ground black pepper

burger toppings of your choice

1. Place all of the ingredients, except the dipping sauce and toppings, in a large bowl and mix until well combined. Form the meat into 4 patties.

2. Heat a grill pan on the stovetop or an outdoor grill to medium-high heat.

3. Cook the burgers for 2 to 3 minutes on each side for medium doneness, or until they are cooked to your preferred temperature.

4. Serve with your toppings of choice.

nut-free	Yes
egg-free	Yes
low FODMAP	Use 1/2 cup chopped scallions in place of the onion.
AIP-friendly	Use 1 teaspoon ground turmeric in place of the cumin. Omit the nutmeg and paprika.
SCD/GAPS	Yes
lower carb	Yes

chef's tip

For the best flavor, choose meat that is at least 20 percent fat. Also, avoid overworking the burger with your hands because it emulsifies the fat, making the burger chewier.

nutritionist's note

The fat from 100 percent grass-fed beef is full of essential omega-3 fats, which help to lower inflammation in the body.

braised beef, artichokes, and peas (jelbana)

prep time: 10 minutes | *cook time:* 1 hour | *serves:* 4 to 6

Artichokes are native to the Mediterranean region and were featured in ancient Egyptian paintings as a symbol of health and fertility. They're also delicious. This flavorful stew combines them with peas, which give the dish its Arabic name: *jelbana*, "fresh peas."

1 tablespoon unsalted butter, ghee, or coconut oil

2 pounds beef or lamb stew meat (preferably on the bone)

1 medium white onion, diced

fine sea salt and ground black pepper

1 tablespoon ground cinnamon

6 cups Beef Broth (page 388)

2 tablespoons tomato paste

2 cups fresh or frozen peas

3 medium carrots, cut into 1/2-inch pieces

2 cups frozen artichoke hearts, defrosted and drained

1/3 cup chopped fresh cilantro, for garnish

1. Melt the fat in a stockpot over medium heat. Season the stew meat liberally with salt and pepper and brown for about 5 minutes.

2. Add the onion, a pinch of salt and pepper, and the cinnamon to the pot and sauté the mixture for 3 more minutes, until the onion is translucent.

3. Add the broth and tomato paste to the pot and stir to combine. Bring the mixture to a simmer with the lid on. Remove the lid and simmer for 30 minutes, or until the meat is very tender.

4. Add the peas, carrots, and artichoke hearts and continue to simmer the stew, still uncovered, for 20 minutes, or until the carrots are tender. Ladle the stew into bowls and top with the cilantro.

SLOW COOKER INSTRUCTIONS

Place the fat, stew meat, onion, spices, and beef broth in the slow cooker. Cook the mixture for 5 hours on low. Add the tomato paste, peas, carrots, and artichoke hearts and cook for 1 more hour. Garnish with the cilantro and serve.

nut-free	Yes
egg-free	Yes
low FODMAP	Omit the onion and add 1/2 cup chopped chives as a garnish. Use 2 cups cubed butternut squash in place of the artichokes. Use 1 cup chopped tomatoes in place of the tomato paste.
AIP-friendly	Use 1/2 cup canned pumpkin in place of the tomato paste. Use artichokes with no additives.
SCD/GAPS	Yes
lower carb	Use 1 carrot and 1 cup of peas.

chef's tip

If it is available in your area, try to get lamb or beef on the bone, which creates a richer sauce for this dish. If you cannot find it on the bone, boneless stew meat will still work.

nutritionist's note

Artichokes are a great source of soluble fiber, which is often lacking in the Western diet. Artichokes are well known for their digestive benefits, including reducing symptoms of IBS and aiding in fat digestion. They are also important for liver detoxification, which helps us maintain a healthy weight.

paleo moussaka

prep time: 15 minutes | *cook time:* 1 hour | *serves:* 4

Moussaka, a traditional dish of baked lamb and eggplant topped with a béchamel sauce made with cheese and wheat flour, is common throughout the Balkans and Middle East. We wanted to make a dairy-free Paleo version that could be enjoyed by low-carb dieters and SCD/GAPS followers and that would even fit the autoimmune protocol with just a few minor adjustments.

---

2 tablespoons unsalted butter, ghee, or coconut oil, divided, plus more for greasing the dish

1 medium white onion, diced

2 teaspoons minced garlic

1 pound ground lamb or beef

fine sea salt and ground black pepper

1 teaspoon ground cinnamon

1/2 cup tomato paste

1 large eggplant, cut into bite-sized piecest

3 tablespoons chopped fresh parsley

1 (13 1/2-ounce) can full-fat coconut milk, divided

1/4 cup arrowroot flour

1 large egg, beaten

1. Preheat the oven to 350°F. Grease a 9-inch square baking dish.

2. Melt 1 tablespoon of the fat in a large skillet over medium heat. Add the onion and garlic to the pan and sauté for 3 minutes. Add the ground meat, season liberally with pinches of salt and pepper, and add the cinnamon to the pan. Break up the meat with a spatula while continuing to cook until browned, about 8 minutes.

3. In a small bowl, combine the tomato paste with 1 cup of water and mix well. Add the diluted tomato paste to the meat mixture and stir until well combined. Transfer the meat mixture to a large bowl and set aside. (Do not clean the skillet; you will use it shortly.)

4. Sprinkle a few pinches of salt and pepper on the eggplant. Melt the remaining 1 tablespoon of fat in the same skillet you used to cook the meat and sauté the eggplant over medium heat for about 5 minutes, until it is barely softened. Transfer the eggplant to the prepared baking dish. (Reserve the skillet for later use.)

5. Pour the meat sauce mixture evenly over the eggplant and sprinkle on the parsley.

6. For the white sauce: In a small bowl, combine 1/4 cup of the coconut milk, the arrowroot flour, and a pinch of salt and pepper and stir well. Warm up the same skillet over medium heat and pour in the remaining coconut milk. When the coconut milk starts to bubble, stir in the arrowroot mixture. Stir the white sauce continuously until it begins to

chef's tip

When making a white sauce, be sure to dissolve the thickener in liquid away from heat before adding it to the pan. Otherwise, it will clump and not have the desired smooth texture.

nutritionist's note

The skin of an eggplant (or aubergine, as it is called in Algeria) contains important phytonutrients that act as antioxidants. Although eggplants are beneficial for most people, they do belong to the nightshades family, which can cause sore joints, skin irritation, and other problems in people who are sensitive to them.

nut-free	Yes
egg-free	Use the AIP-friendly modification for the white sauce.
low FODMAP	Use 2 cups chopped tomatoes, drained, in place of the paste and omit the water. Omit the onion and garlic. Use garlic-infused olive oil as the cooking fat.
AIP-friendly	Use 4 medium zucchini in place of the eggplant and 1 cup canned pumpkin in place of the tomato paste and omit the water. For the white sauce, mix 1 (13 1/2-ounce) can full-fat coconut milk, 1/4 cup arrowroot flour, 1 teaspoon baking soda, 1 teaspoon apple cider vinegar, and a pinch of salt and pepper in a bowl. Transfer to a saucepan over medium heat and stir continuously until the sauce begins to thicken. Follow the rest of directions as listed, resuming with Step 8.
SCD/GAPS	For the white sauce, omit the arrowroot flour. In the same skillet used in Step 7, mix 2 tablespoons coconut flour with 1 (13 1/2-ounce) can full-fat coconut milk over medium heat until it bubbles. Remove the sauce from the heat and whisk in 2 eggs. Follow the rest of directions as listed, resuming with Step 8.
lower carb	Use the SCD/GAPS version.

thicken, about 2 to 3 minutes. When it bubbles, remove the sauce from the heat and whisk in the egg until smooth and thick.

7.   Pour the white sauce evenly over the meat and eggplant in the baking dish. Bake the casserole for 40 minutes. Turn the oven to broil for 3 to 5 minutes to get a nice golden brown color on the top.

8.   Remove the moussaka from the oven and let it cool for 10 minutes before cutting into portions and serving.

seafood

salmon and crab roll-ups

prep time: 15 minutes, plus 5 minutes to make the aioli | *cook time:* n/a | *serves:* 4

Nabil: These roll-ups are similar to a dish that was on the menu at a restaurant where I used to work. Caitlin ordered it once and loved it so much that I created this version at home. The aioli in this recipe is made with higher-quality oils than most restaurants use, and at home you can make sure to use wild fish.

12 ounces cooked crabmeat

1/4 cup chopped fresh chives (about 1 bunch), divided

1/2 cup diced red bell pepper

1/2 cup diced celery

1 teaspoon paprika

fine sea salt and ground black pepper

2 tablespoons lemon juice

1/2 cup Aioli (page 384)

12 ounces smoked salmon, thinly sliced

1 lemon, cut into wedges, for serving

1. Drain the crabmeat and shred it with your fingers. In a medium bowl, mix the crab with half the chives, the bell pepper, celery, paprika, a pinch of salt and pepper, and the lemon juice. Add the aioli to the crab mixture and stir until well combined. Adjust the seasonings to taste.

2. Place a slice of salmon about the size of your palm on a plate. It may be necessary to place a few pieces end to end to make a slice large enough for rolling.

3. Put a scoop of dressed crabmeat in the middle of the salmon and carefully roll it up.

4. Repeat until all the crab salad and salmon are used up. Top the salmon rolls with the rest of the chives and serve with lemon wedges.

nut-free	Yes
egg-free	Use 1/3 cup full-fat, canned coconut milk in place of the aioli.
low FODMAP	Yes
AIP-friendly	Omit the paprika. Use 1/3 cup full-fat, canned coconut milk in place of the aioli. Use 1/2 cup diced red onion in place of the red bell pepper.
SCD/GAPS	Yes
lower carb	Yes

chef's tip

Fresh crab can be expensive, so make this dish when it's in season and more affordable. Chilled crabmeat (found at the seafood counter) or shelf-stable canned crabmeat can also be used to save time and money. Claw meat, which is usually costs a few dollars less per pound, will also work.

nutritionist's note

Use homemade aioli or mayonnaise to avoid canola and soybean oils, which are used in most store-bought versions.

fattoush shrimp salad

prep time: 10 minutes | *cook time:* 20 minutes to cook the shrimp | *serves:* 4

Fattoush salad is commonly served in Mediterranean restaurants with pita chips sprinkled over the top to add a nice crunch. We were thrilled when we discovered that our Cilantro Crackers (page 124) serve as an excellent stand-in for traditional wheat pita chips. Fattoush salad traditionally has chicken or is served without meat, but our version uses shrimp instead to give it a coastal feel.

FOR THE DRESSING

1/4 cup extra-virgin olive oil

2 tablespoons lemon juice

fine sea salt and ground black pepper to taste

FOR THE SALAD

1 cup pitted Kalamata olives

1 cup cherry tomatoes, halved

1 large cucumber, seeded and diced

8 cups chopped romaine lettuce

1/4 cup chopped fresh mint

1/4 cup chopped fresh cilantro

1 recipe Lemon Garlic Shrimp (page 264)

1/4 cup crumbled feta (optional)

6 Cilantro Crackers (page 124), crumbled (optional)

1. Whisk together the dressing ingredients in a small bowl.

2. Combine the olives, tomatoes, cucumber, lettuce, mint, and cilantro in a large bowl.

3. Toss the salad with the dressing until well coated.

4. Divide the salad among 4 plates.

5. Top the salads with the shrimp and feta, if using. Sprinkle on the crumbled crackers, if using, and serve.

nut-free	Use the nut-free modications for the crackers.
egg-free	Yes
low FODMAP	Omit the feta. Use the low FODMAP modifications for Lemon Garlic Shrimp (page 264) and Cilantro Crackers (page 124).
AIP-friendly	Use shredded carrots or beets in place of the tomatoes. Omit the feta.
SCD/GAPS	Omit the feta.
lower carb	Yes

chef's tip

Mint and cilantro add a bold freshness to salads that always wakes the palate.

lemon garlic shrimp

prep time: 10 minutes, plus up to 1 hour to marinate |
cook time: 10 minutes | *serves:* 4

These tasty shrimp work well as an appetizer or atop a salad for a main meal. We love to eat shrimp as often as we can; it's fast and easy to cook, and its protein is filling. Here, garlic and lemon naturally complement this healthy dish.

---

1 pound wild shrimp, peeled and deveined

2 teaspoons minced garlic

fine sea salt and ground black pepper

1/4 cup chopped fresh parsley

1 teaspoon paprika

1 teaspoon grated lemon zest

2 tablespoons unsalted butter, ghee, or coconut oil

3 tablespoons finely diced shallots

1 lemon, cut into wedges, for serving

1. Place the shrimp in a large bowl with the garlic, a few pinches of salt and pepper, the parsley, paprika, and lemon zest and stir well. Marinate the shrimp in the fridge for up to 1 hour.

2. Melt the fat in a sauté pan on medium-high heat. Add the shallots to the pan and cook for 2 minutes. Add the shrimp mixture to the pan.

3. Sauté the shrimp for about 5 minutes, until pink.

4. Transfer the shrimp to a plate and serve with the lemon wedges.

nut-free	Yes
egg-free	Yes
low FODMAP	Omit the garlic and shallots. Use garlic-infused olive oil as the cooking fat. Top with 1/4 cup chopped chives.
AIP-friendly	Omit the paprika.
SCD/GAPS	Yes
lower carb	Yes

chef's tip

To save time, look for shrimp that have already been peeled and deveined. If saving money is more important, peel and devein them yourself.

nutritionist's note

Shrimp are a great source of the antioxidant astaxanthin, which is hard to get in the diet. Shrimp are also rich in healthy omega-3 fats and selenium, which are important for overall health. Choose wild shrimp from North America to avoid contaminants and ensure sustainability.

mediterranean seafood salad

prep time: 10 minutes | *cook time:* 5 minutes, plus 20 minutes to cook the shrimp | *serves:* 4

Caitlin: During my first trip to Algeria, and my first visit with Nabil's family, we took a day trip from Algiers to the seaside village of Tipasa. There, at a small café, we ate a salad similar to this one, with fish cooked the same day it was caught. Whenever I eat this salad, I think of that timeless village, where the local fishermen bring in their fresh catches on the docks just as they have for hundreds of years. For even more protein, add a can of wild tuna with the anchovies and shrimp.

FOR THE DRESSING

1/4 cup extra-virgin olive oil

2 tablespoons lemon juice

fine sea salt and ground black pepper to taste

FOR THE SALAD

4 large eggs

4 Roma tomatoes, quartered

1 head romaine lettuce, cut into bite-sized pieces

1/2 cup pitted black olives

6 anchovy fillets

2 tablespoons capers, rinsed and drained

2 teaspoons minced garlic

1 recipe Lemon Garlic Shrimp (page 264)

1/2 cup thinly sliced roasted red peppers (see page 396 for roasting instructions)

2 tablespoons chopped fresh cilantro

1. Make the dressing: Whisk together the olive oil, lemon juice, and salt and pepper in a small bowl.

2. Hard-boil the eggs: Place the eggs in a saucepan, cover them with water, and bring to a boil, covered, over medium-high heat. As soon as the water comes to a boil, remove the pan from the heat. Let the eggs sit in the pan for 3 minutes with the lid on, then place the eggs under cold running water for 2 minutes. When cool, peel the eggs and slice in half lengthwise.

3. Arrange the eggs and tomatoes evenly around the edges of 4 plates. Season with salt and pepper.

4. Place the lettuce, olives, anchovies, capers, garlic, shrimp, red pepper, and cilantro in a large bowl. Pour the dressing over the top and toss to evenly coat.

5. Arrange the dressed salad on a platter to serve.

nut-free	Yes
egg-free	Omit the eggs.
low FODMAP	Use 1/2 cup chopped scallions in place of the garlic.
AIP-friendly	Omit the eggs, tomatoes, and roasted red pepper and use shredded carrots and beets instead.
SCD/GAPS	Yes
lower carb	Yes

chef's tip

Roasting peppers may seem like a lot of work, but it's actually really simple. Directions for making roasted peppers are on page 396. The sugars in the peppers become concentrated during roasting, creating an intense and unforgettable flavor. If you buy jarred roasted peppers, read the label to avoid vegetable oils and unhealthy preservatives.

nutritionist's note

Anchovies are a great source of vitamin A, which is very important for supporting reproduction. It's also important for supporting the protective linings of the gut, lungs, and sinuses, helping to ward off pathogens to keep us healthy all year long.

seared tuna salade niçoise

prep time: 5 minutes | *cook time:* 20 minutes | *serves:* 4

Caitlin: The culinary school Nabil attended had a restaurant where students cooked for the faculty and visitors. My parents and I once went there while Nabil was working and ordered the custom salade niçoise, which had tableside service, and Nabil impressed my parents by making this salad as they watched. I was so proud, and now every time we have this fresh, flavorful salad, I remember that happy day.

---

2 medium sweet potatoes, peeled and cut into bite-sized pieces

fine sea salt and ground black pepper

2 large eggs

4 ounces green beans, trimmed

1 head romaine lettuce, cut into bite-sized pieces

1/2 cup pitted Kalamata olives

1 cup cherry tomatoes, halved

1/2 medium red onion, thinly sliced

1/2 pound raw tuna fillet

1 tablespoon unsalted butter, ghee, or coconut oil

FOR THE DRESSING

2 tablespoons lemon juice

1/4 cup extra-virgin olive oil

fine sea salt and ground black pepper to taste

1. Steam the potatoes: Place the potatoes in the top of a steamer pot and season with salt and pepper. Add a few cups of water to the bottom of the steamer pot—just enough to come up to the bottom of the steamer basket or insert. Place the steamer pot over medium-high heat with the lid on and cook the potatoes until slightly soft but still firm, 5 to 7 minutes.

2. Hard-boil the eggs: Place the eggs in a saucepan, cover them with water, and bring to a boil, covered, over medium heat. As soon as the water comes to a boil, remove the pan from the heat. Let the eggs sit in the pan for 3 minutes with the lid on, then place the eggs under cold running water for 2 minutes. When cool, peel the eggs, slice lengthwise, and set aside.

3. Cook the green beans: In a saucepan, bring 3 cups of water to a boil. Add the green beans and a pinch of salt. Cook the green beans until slightly cooked but still firm, about 3 minutes. Transfer the beans to a bowl of ice water to stop the cooking process. Drain.

4. Place the lettuce on 2 plates. Arrange the olives, tomato halves, and onion slices in small piles on top of the lettuce. Add the eggs to the salad plates.

5. Whisk together the dressing ingredients in a small bowl.

6. Season the tuna liberally with salt and pepper.

7. Melt the fat in a skillet over high heat. Wait until the pan is very hot, about 2 minutes, and then place the tuna in the pan. Sear for 30 seconds on each side.

8. Slice the tuna crosswise into 1/2-inch-thick pieces and place on top of the salad in a fan shape.

9. Pour the dressing over the salad and enjoy.

nut-free	Yes
egg-free	Omit the eggs.
low FODMAP	Use 1/2 cup chopped scallions in place of the red onion.
AIP-friendly	Omit the tomatoes and eggs.
SCD/GAPS	Use butternut squash in place of the sweet potatoes.
lower carb	Omit the sweet potatoes.

chef's tip

When searing the tuna, make sure not to cook it too long. The goal is to just get some color on the outside, not to cook it through. Think of it as if you are framing the fillet with a 3/8-inch sear on all sides.

nutritionist's note

Choose wild seafood whenever possible, and check the Monterey Bay Aquarium Seafood Watch app to make sure whatever seafood you buy is sustainable.

sardine cakes

prep time: 10 minutes | *cook time:* 10 minutes | *yield:* 4 patties

If you've been wanting to eat more sardines but aren't sure how to make them appetizing or are intimidated by them, try these delicious cakes. They're a great way to work nutritious sardines into your weekly menu.

1/4 cup coconut flour

1/4 cup blanched almond flour

fine sea salt and ground black pepper

3 (4-ounce) cans wild sardines, packed in olive oil or spring water

2 tablespoons chopped fresh cilantro

2 teaspoons paprika

1 teaspoon grated lemon zest

1 tablespoon Dijon mustard (gluten-free)

3 large eggs, beaten

1/4 cup sustainable palm shortening or coconut oil

1/4 cup Aioli (page 384), for serving (optional)

1 lemon, cut into wedges, for serving

1. Mix the coconut and almond flours with a few pinches of salt and pepper in a shallow bowl.

2. Drain the oil or water from the sardine cans and place the sardines in a bowl. Mash them with a fork. Add the cilantro, paprika, lemon zest, mustard, and a pinch of salt and pepper. Stir the sardines and seasonings together until well combined.

3. Form the sardine mixture into 4 evenly sized patties. Dredge the patties in the eggs, then in the flour mixture, coating both sides. Carefully shake off the excess flour and set on a plate.

4. Melt the fat in a large skillet over medium heat. To check the temperature of the oil, insert the end of a wooden spoon handle into the oil; if bubbles form around the handle, it is ready to use. Add the patties to the pan and fry them for about 3 minutes, until golden brown. Flip with a slotted spoon or spatula and cook for another 3 minutes, or until golden brown.

5. Let the patties drain on a paper towel for a few minutes. Serve with the aioli and lemon wedges.

nut-free	Use finely ground sunflower seeds (see page 170) in place of the almond flour.
egg-free	Use 3/4 cup very ripe mashed plantains instead of the eggs. Serve with Tzatziki Sauce (page 392) in place of the aioli.
low FODMAP	Use cashew meal in place of the almond flour.
AIP-friendly	Use 3/4 cup very ripe mashed plantains instead of the eggs. Use 2 extra tablespoons coconut flour and omit the almond flour. Omit the paprika and mustard and use 1 tablespoon ground ginger. Serve with Tzatziki Sauce (page 392) in place of the aioli.
SCD/GAPS	Yes
lower carb	Yes

chef's tip

Sardines do tend to have a lot of tiny bones, but when they are made into cakes the bones become undetectable. This dish makes sardines more palatable for someone who is unfamiliar with this tasty fish.

nutritionist's note

Sardines are a rich source of anti-inflammatory omega-3 fatty acids, and since they are low on the food chain, they do not absorb a lot of mercury. Sardines are also a great source of selenium, which supports thyroid metabolism, and whole sardines are very rich in bone-building calcium.

zesty crab cakes with aioli

prep time: 10 minutes | *cook time:* 6 to 12 minutes | *serves:* 4

We have many fond memories of making crab cakes at our apartment in San Francisco. Dungeness crab are in season in the winter here, and we buy them fresh near our house and have fun picking out the meat from the cracked shells. When crab is out of season or we're short on time, we use canned crabmeat.

1 pound cooked crabmeat

2 tablespoons coconut flour

2 large eggs, beaten

1/4 cup chopped scallions

2 teaspoons garlic powder

1 teaspoon cayenne pepper

1 teaspoon paprika

fine sea salt and ground black pepper

1/4 cup coconut oil or sustainable palm shortening

1/2 cup Aioli (page 384), for garnish

1 cup arugula, for serving (optional)

2 lemons, cut into wedges, for serving

1. In a large bowl, combine the crabmeat, coconut flour, eggs, scallions, garlic powder, cayenne, paprika, and a pinch of salt and pepper. Use a fork to thoroughly mix the ingredients together.

2. Heat the oil in a large skillet over medium-high heat. While the oil is heating up, form the crab mixture into 3-inch patties and place them on a plate.

3. To check the temperature of the oil, insert the end of a wooden spoon handle into the oil; if bubbles form around the handle, it is ready to use. Carefully place the crab cakes into the pan with a slotted spatula. Do not overcrowd them. Cook the crab cakes for about 3 minutes on the first side, or until golden brown. Flip and cook on the other side until slightly browned, about 3 minutes.

4. Remove the cakes from the pan and put them on a serving plate. Cover the cakes with a towel to keep warm. Repeat until all the crab cakes are cooked.

5. Drizzle the crab cakes with the aioli and plate on small beds of arugula, if using. Serve with the lemon wedges.

nut-free	Yes
egg-free	Use 1 cup very ripe mashed plantains in place of the eggs and increase the coconut flour to 1/4 cup. Serve with Tzatziki Sauce (page 392) in place of the aioli.
low FODMAP	Omit the garlic powder. Use the low FODMAP modification for the aioli.
AIP-friendly	Use 1 tablespoon ground ginger in place of the cayenne and paprika. Use 1 cup very ripe mashed plantains in place of the eggs and increase the coconut flour to 1/4 cup. Serve with Tzatziki Sauce (page 392) in place of the aioli.
SCD/GAPS	Yes
lower carb	Yes

nutritionist's note

Most crab cakes at restaurants are filled with breadcrumbs. In this recipe, eggs and coconut flour are used as the binder instead of bread, which increases the dish's nutrient density. Unlike polyunsaturated vegetable oils—such as the highly processed soybean and corn oils restaurants often use—coconut and palm oils are stable at high heats, so they're an ideal choice for pan-frying.

sardine salad with capers and olives

prep time: 10 minutes | *cook time:* n/a | *serves:* 2

This dish is a more nutritious twist on tuna salad. It's easy to throw together and a great way to get more sardines in your diet. The lemon, capers, and olives we added bring bold flavors to the dish.

---

2 (4-ounce) cans sardines packed in olive oil or water, drained

fine sea salt and ground black pepper

2 tablespoons capers, rinsed and drained

1/4 cup diced red onion

1/4 cup sliced green olives

1/4 cup lemon juice (2 lemons)

2 tablespoons extra-virgin olive oil

4 cups sliced romaine lettuce

1 cup cherry tomatoes, halved

1. In a medium bowl, mash the sardines with a fork.

2. Add a few pinches of salt and pepper, the capers, onion, olives, lemon juice, and olive oil to the bowl and stir.

3. Arrange the lettuce and tomatoes on 2 plates and top with a scoop of the sardine salad.

nut-free	Yes
egg-free	Yes
low FODMAP	Use 1/2 cup chopped scallions in place of the red onion.
AIP-friendly	Omit the tomatoes.
SCD/GAPS	Yes
lower carb	Yes

chef's tip

When sardines are mashed, the bones and skin are not detectable, which makes them more appealing to people who are new to eating sardines. Once the sardines are mashed, this tasty salad looks similar to tuna salad.

nutritionist's note

It's a good idea to drain the sardines and add a higher-quality olive oil, or choose sardines packed in spring water. Avoid fish packed in cottonseed, canola, or soybean oils, which are poor-quality, inflammatory oils.

crispy fried sardines

prep time: 10 minutes | *cook time:* 10 minutes | *serves:* 4

Nabil: I have fond childhood memories of eating grilled sardines by the water after swimming and jumping off the cliffs into the Mediterranean Sea. Sardines are very available and affordable during the summer in the Mediterranean region. These small fish can be eaten with your hands by just pulling pieces off the bone. Or, if a sardine is very small, you can eat it whole, bones and all.

---

2 pounds sardines, cleaned (see Chef's Tip)

1 tablespoon garlic powder

1 tablespoon chili powder

1/2 teaspoon ground cumin

1/2 cup chopped fresh parsley, plus more for garnish

1 cup blanched almond flour

fine sea salt and ground black pepper

2 large eggs, beaten

1 teaspoon apple cider vinegar

up to 2 cups sustainable palm shortening or coconut oil

1 lemon, halved, for serving

1 recipe Aioli (page 384), for serving (optional)

1. Rinse the sardines and place them on a paper towel to drain.

2. In a medium bowl, mix the garlic powder, chili powder, cumin, parsley, almond flour, and a few pinches of salt and pepper.

3. In shallow bowl, mix the eggs with a pinch of salt and pepper and the apple cider vinegar.

4. Dip the sardines in the egg mixture until well coated. Dredge the sardines in the almond flour mixture, coating each fish on both sides.

5. Add the palm shortening to a deep skillet—it should be about 2 inches deep—and heat over medium-high heat until it is quite hot. To check the temperature of the oil, insert the end of a wooden spoon handle into the oil; if bubbles form around the handle, it is ready to use. Add the sardines to the pan and fry until golden brown, about 2 minutes on each side.

6. Drain the fried sardines on a paper towel, garnish with parsley, and serve with the lemon halves and aioli, if using.

chef's tip

Cleaning sardines is easy, but why waste your time when it can be done for free at the fish market? Ask the fishmonger to clean the sardines for you, which will make preparing this dish a breeze. If for some reason you need to clean the sardines yourself, lay each fish on its side on a cutting board. Insert a knife 1/4 inch into the bottom of the fish and cut from one end of the belly to the other, lengthwise. Remove the innards with your fingers, rinse the fish, and prepare as desired.

nutritionist's note

Sardines are one of the few fish that can supply a great deal of calcium because the bones are small enough to eat. Just 3 ounces of sardines supply 75 percent of the daily recommended intake of calcium.

nut-free	Use 1/2 cup coconut flour in place of the almond flour.
egg-free	No
low FODMAP	Omit the garlic powder and use cashew meal in place of the almond flour. Use the low FODMAP modification for the aioli.
AIP-friendly	No
SCD/GAPS	Yes
lower carb	Yes

seafood brochette

prep time: 10 minutes, plus up to 2 hours to marinate | *cook time:* 10 minutes | *serves:* 4

Brochette is a French word for meat cooked on a skewer. These brochettes are reminiscent of ones we had while visiting some Algerian friends in France last April. Our friends set up a tiny grill in a beautiful Paris park and we ate gourmet brochettes right on the lush spring grass. Here, we've added garlic, paprika, and parsley to accentuate the sweetness of the seafood.

---

1 tablespoon minced garlic

2 teaspoons paprika

1 pinch saffron

fine sea salt and ground black pepper

1/3 cup chopped fresh parsley

2 tablespoons extra-virgin olive oil

1/4 cup lemon juice

12 medium shrimp, peeled and deveined

12 large dry sea scallops (see Nutritionist's Note)

2 bell peppers, any color, cut into bite-sized pieces

1 medium red onion, cut into bite-sized pieces

1 tablespoon butter, ghee, or coconut oil

1. In a bowl, combine the garlic, paprika, saffron, a pinch of salt and pepper, the parsley, olive oil, and lemon juice and mix well. Add the seafood, bell pepper, and onion and mix until coated with the marinade. Place the mixture in the refrigerator to marinate for up to 2 hours.

2. If using wooden skewers, soak them for 10 minutes.

3. Take the seafood and veggies mixture out of the refrigerator and thread the pieces onto wooden or metal skewers, alternating the veggies and seafood.

4. To use a grill pan: Preheat the oven to 350°F. Melt the fat in a grill pan over medium-high heat. Sear the brochettes for 1 minute on each side. Put the grill pan into the oven and cook for 3 to 5 more minutes, until the seafood is cooked through.

5. To use an outdoor grill: Preheat the grill to medium-high heat. Grill the brochettes for 3 to 5 minutes on each side, until the seafood is cooked through.

chef's tip

If you prefer, you can use 1 1/2 pounds red snapper or other white fish fillets, cubed, in place of the shrimp and scallops.

nutritionist's note

Be sure to buy "dry" sea scallops rather than "wet" ones, which have been treated with sodium tripolyphosphate (STP) and are mushy and less flavorful. STP is a chemical that makes seafood appear fresher than it really is. It may also make fish, shrimp, or scallops absorb more water so they weigh more, increasing cost without adding value. In large quantities, STP is a suspected neurotoxin as well as a registered pesticide. In California, it's also considered an air contaminant. To tell if a fish has been soaked in STP, look for a milky white liquid oozing from the fish—unfortunately, it doesn't have to appear on the label.

nut-free	Yes
egg-free	Yes
low FODMAP	Omit the onion and garlic and use garlic-infused olive oil for the marinade.
AIP-friendly	Use zucchini in place of the peppers. Use 1 teaspoon ground ginger in place of the paprika.
SCD/GAPS	Yes
lower carb	Yes

almond-crusted cod

prep time: 10 minutes, plus 20 minutes to soak |
cook time: 12 minutes | *serves:* 4

Caitlin: Last year Nabil took me to Wine Country for a birthday getaway, and we ate at a cute café that served a version of this amazing fish dish. I was so impressed that I asked Nabil to re-create it when we got home, and this is the delicious result. The addition of olives gives the sauce a Mediterranean flavor.

---

4 (5-ounce) wild cod fillets, or other white fish

fine sea salt and ground black pepper

2 cups sliced almonds

2 large eggs, beaten

2 teaspoons garlic powder

1 teaspoon paprika

FOR THE SAUCE

1/2 cup extra-virgin olive oil

1 bunch fresh cilantro, stemmed

8 green olives, pitted

2 tablespoons lemon juice

1. Before cooking, soak the fish in salted ice water for 20 minutes; this will help it stay intact during cooking. Preheat the oven to 350°F. Line a rimmed baking sheet with parchment paper.

2. Season the cod fillets with a few pinches of salt and pepper. Place the almonds in a shallow bowl.

3. In a medium bowl, mix the eggs, garlic powder, paprika, and a pinch of salt and pepper. Dredge the cod fillets in the egg mixture, then coat with the almonds.

4. Place the coated fillets on the prepared baking sheet. Place in the oven and bake for 10 to 12 minutes, or until golden brown.

5. While the fish is baking, put the sauce ingredients in a food processor and pulse for a few seconds. When the fish is done, turn the oven to broil for 30 seconds to toast the almonds on the top side of the fish.

6. Plate the fish, top with a spoonful of the sauce, and serve.

nut-free	Use hulled pumpkin seeds in place of the sliced almonds.
egg-free	Omit the eggs and top the fish with a thin layer of almonds before baking.
low FODMAP	Omit the garlic powder. Use hulled pumpkin seeds in place of the almonds.
AIP-friendly	Omit the almonds, eggs, and paprika.
SCD/GAPS	Yes
lower carb	Yes

chef's tip

When purchasing cod, make sure it does not smell fishy. If fish has an odor, it is an indication that it is no longer fresh.

nutritionist's note

Eating wild fish, such as cod, as little as one to three times per month helps protect against strokes because it is high in anti-inflammatory omega-3s. Wild fish also helps to lower triglycerides, which reduces the risk of metabolic syndrome and type 2 diabetes.

cioppino

prep time: 20 minutes | *cook time:* 20 minutes | *serves:* 4

Cioppino, a classic San Francisco seafood soup created by Italian immigrants, has become one of our favorites. This recipe is our Paleo adaptation.

---

2 tablespoons unsalted butter, ghee, or coconut oil

1/2 cup diced shallots (2 shallots)

3 cloves garlic, minced

2 green or red bell peppers, seeded and diced

fine sea salt and ground black pepper

1 teaspoon dried thyme leaves

2 bay leaves

5 Roma tomatoes, diced

3 cups Fish Broth (page 389) or water

1 tablespoon tomato paste

8 ounces white fish (such as catfish, grouper, Pacific cod, or swordfish), cubed

1 pound medium shrimp, peeled and deveined

1 pound cooked crabmeat

4 cooked crab claws (optional)

1/4 cup chopped fresh parsley, for garnish

2 lemons, halved, for serving

1. Melt the fat in a stockpot over medium heat. Sauté the shallots, garlic, and peppers in the fat for about 1 minute, until the shallots are translucent. Add a few pinches of salt and pepper, the thyme, and the bay leaves to the pot and stir to combine.

2. Add the tomatoes to the pot and sauté for 5 minutes. Add the broth and the tomato paste and stir to incorporate the paste. Reduce the heat to medium-low and simmer for 10 minutes to combine the flavors.

3. Add the white fish to the pot and cook for 1 minute. Add the shrimp and cook for another 3 minutes. Add the crabmeat and claws, if using, and simmer for 1 minute, until warmed.

4. Adjust the seasonings to taste and remove the bay leaves. Divide among 4 serving bowls, top with the parsley, and serve with the lemon halves.

nut-free	Yes
egg-free	Yes
low FODMAP	Omit the garlic and shallots. Use garlic-infused olive oil as the cooking fat. Add 1 more tomato and omit the tomato paste.
AIP-friendly	Omit the peppers. Use 1 cup canned pumpkin in place of the diced tomatoes and tomato paste.
SCD/GAPS	Yes
lower carb	Yes

chef's tip

If you do not have fish broth, save your shrimp shells and boil them in a few cups of water for 10 minutes. Strain the liquid and discard the shells. Use the broth in seafood recipes such as this flavorful stew. It will add a ton of flavor and is very easy to make.

nutritionist's note

Shrimp are a great source of iodine, which is important for proper thyroid function. We need 150 micrograms per day to keep the thyroid on track, and 3 ounces of shrimp supplies about 25 micrograms.

pistachio-crusted sole

prep time: 10 minutes | *cook time:* 10 minutes | *serves:* 4

This dish showcases the subtle flavor of pistachios, a nut that has been a part of the human diet since the Paleolithic era. The modern pistachio nut, however, was first cultivated in the cooler parts of Iran, where it has long been a staple crop. From there the modern pistachio spread throughout the rest of the Mediterranean region, where they are grown widely.

4 (5-ounce) sole fillets, or other white fish

fine sea salt and ground black pepper

2 teaspoons paprika, divided

2 large eggs, beaten

2 teaspoons finely grated lemon zest

1 tablespoon garlic powder

2 cups shelled, raw pistachios

1/4 cup sustainable palm shortening or coconut oil

1/4 cup chopped fresh parsley, for garnish

2 lemons, cut into wedges, for serving

1. Sprinkle both sides of the fish with a few pinches of salt and pepper and 1 teaspoon of the paprika.

2. In a small shallow bowl, season the eggs with the remaining teaspoon of paprika, the lemon zest, the garlic powder, and a pinch of salt and pepper.

3. Put the pistachios in the food processor and pulse until roughly chopped. Spread the chopped pistachios on a plate. Dredge the fish through the egg mixture, then coat with the pistachios on both sides.

4. Melt the fat in a large skillet over medium-high heat for 2 minutes. When the oil is hot, place the fish in the skillet and pan-fry for 3 to 4 minutes, until golden brown. Flip carefully and fry on the other side for 3 minutes, or until done.

5. Garnish the fish with the parsley and serve with the lemon wedges.

nut-free	Use chopped pumpkin seeds in place of the pistachios.
egg-free	No
low FODMAP	Omit the garlic powder. Use chopped pumpkin seeds in place of the pistachios.
AIP-friendly	No
SCD/GAPS	Yes
lower carb	Yes

chef's tip

It's easy for nuts like pistachios to become stale, so it's important to keep them in an airtight container and store them in the refrigerator or freezer.

nutritionist's note

Pistachios are high in monounsaturated fats, which boast anti-inflammatory properties. They also contain vitamin E, a potent antioxidant that helps cellular function and has anti-aging benefits.

fennel and herb–stuffed fish (hout-fel-koucha)

prep time: 20 minutes | *cook time:* 50 minutes | *serves:* 4 to 6

Delicate white fish are easy to overcook, but with this recipe you'll get perfect results. The seasoned sweet potato stuffing and cooking method ensure the fish will be moist and flavorful.

---

1 whole, head-on white fish, such as haddock, cod, or snapper (about 4 to 5 pounds), scaled and gutted (see Chef's Tip)

2 medium sweet potatoes, peeled and cut into bite-sized pieces

1 medium fennel bulb, diced

1 cup tightly packed fresh parsley leaves

8 ounces mushrooms, sliced

2 cloves garlic, peeled

1 large egg, beaten

fine sea salt and ground black pepper

2 tablespoons butter, ghee, or coconut oil

1 lemon, sliced, divided

1/4 cup chopped fresh parsley, for garnish

1. Preheat the oven to 350°F.

2. Rinse off the fish, inside and out, and set aside.

3. Place the sweet potatoes in the top of a steamer pot with a few inches of water. Steam the sweet potatoes over medium heat until they are soft, 8 to 10 minutes.

4. In a food processor, combine the cooked sweet potatoes, fennel, parsley, mushrooms, garlic, egg, and a pinch of salt and pepper.

5. Stuff the fish with the potato mixture. Place the stuffed fish in the middle of a large sheet of parchment paper and season the outside with a pinch or two of salt and pepper.

6. Place the fat and half of the lemon slices on top of the fish. Grab the ends of the paper and fold them over towards the middle. Pinch the edges, fold them together, and roll them toward the center until they are secure enough to stay closed.

7. Place the wrapped fish packet on a rimmed baking dish and bake for 40 minutes. Unwrap the fish to serve and garnish with the rest of the lemon slices and the parsley.

nut-free	Yes
egg-free	Use 2 tablespoons arrowroot flour in place of the egg.
low FODMAP	Use 1/4 cup chopped chives in place of the garlic.
AIP-friendly	Use 2 tablespoons arrowroot flour in place of the egg.
SCD/GAPS	Use 2 cups cooked butternut squash in place of the sweet potato.
lower carb	Use 1 (15-ounce) can pumpkin in place of the sweet potato.

chef's tip

Most fish markets and higher-end supermarkets will clean the fish for you, making it easier to get started. But, though scaling and gutting fish can be intimidating at first, it's not hard to do. Holding the fish by its tail, use the edge of a knife to scrape the skin downwards, toward the head, to remove the scales. Rinse the fish off and insert the knife in the belly of the fish and cut all the way from the tail to the head. Pull out the gills and the guts with your fingers. Discard both and rinse out the inside of the fish. Cook the fish as desired.

creamy cilantro salmon

prep time: 10 minutes | *cook time:* 10 minutes | *serves:* 4

Caitlin: Salmon is an abundant and nutritious fish that's popular on the Paleo diet and that provides plenty of essential omega-3 fats. While it's not commonly used in the Mediterranean, the sauce in this recipe adds that Mediterranean flair. Nabil had fun teaching me how get the prized crispy skin on this dish. This recipe pairs well with Cauliflower Couscous (page 332), as pictured.

FOR THE SAUCE

4 cups loosely packed fresh cilantro leaves

4 cups loosely packed fresh parsley leaves

1 tablespoon minced garlic

3 tablespoons lemon juice (2 lemons)

1 cup full-fat, canned coconut milk

FOR THE SALMON

4 (5-ounce) wild salmon fillets, skin on

fine sea salt and ground black pepper

1 tablespoon butter, ghee, or coconut oil

1. Preheat the oven to 350°F.

2. Make the sauce: Put the cilantro, parsley, garlic, and lemon juice in a food processor. Pulse the herb mixture while slowly adding the coconut milk until the sauce is creamy. Set aside.

3. Prepare the salmon: Season the salmon liberally with salt and pepper on both sides. Heat a skillet over medium-high heat for 2 minutes. Add the fat to the pan and melt it. Sear the salmon in the skillet, skin side down, for 1 minute. Press down on the salmon to make sure the skin is touching the pan.

4. Transfer the skillet to the oven, leaving the skin side down, and cook for 3 to 4 minutes. Flip the salmon over and cook for 2 more minutes, leaving a little pink in the middle of the salmon. Be careful not to overcook the salmon or it will dry out.

5. Remove the salmon from the oven, top with the sauce, and serve.

nut-free	Yes
egg-free	Yes
low FODMAP	Use 1/2 cup chopped scallions in place of the garlic.
AIP-friendly	Yes
SCD/GAPS	Yes
lower carb	Yes

chef's tip

Top chefs always strive to get fish skin crispy because the contrast of moist flaky fish and crispy skin is so appealing. The key is to sear the fish, skin side down, on the stovetop before placing it the oven.

nutritionist's note

Wild salmon is a great source of immune-supporting vitamin D. It also provides selenium and omega-3 fatty acids, which both support memory and a healthy metabolism. Avoid Atlantic salmon, which sounds as if it is wild but is usually farm-raised.

spinach-stuffed calamari

prep time: 15 minutes, plus 10 minutes to cool and 40 minutes to make the sauce | *cook time:* 15 minutes | *serves:* 4

Sicily is an island in the Mediterranean Sea that is famous for stuffed calamari. Usually stuffed calamari has breadcrumbs, but this garlic-and-spinach filling provides plenty of freshness and flavor without them.

---

12 calamari, heads and tubes

1 pound fresh baby spinach

2 tablespoons butter, ghee, or coconut oil, divided

1 medium onion, diced

1 teaspoon minced garlic

2 tablespoons chopped fresh mint

2 teaspoons chopped fresh parsley

1 teaspoon chili powder

fine sea salt and ground black pepper

1 recipe Basic Tomato Sauce (page 182), for serving

1/4 cup chopped fresh parsley, for garnish

1. Rinse the calamari, making sure the tubes remain intact, and cut off the heads. Mince the heads and set aside.

2. Rinse and drain the spinach. Heat a steamer pot over medium heat and steam the spinach until soft, about 2 minutes.

3. In a skillet, melt 1 tablespoon of the fat over medium heat. Add the onion and sauté until translucent, about 3 minutes. Add the garlic, mint, parsley, chili powder, and a pinch of salt and pepper and sauté for 2 minutes.

4. Add the steamed spinach and the calamari heads and cook for 5 minutes. Remove the mixture from the pan and let cool for about 10 minutes. (Do not clean the pan, you will use it again.)

5. Stuff the calamari tubes with the spinach mixture until they are tightly packed.

6. Melt the remaining tablespoon of fat in the skillet over medium-high heat and sear the calamari tubes for a few seconds on each side. Add the tomato sauce and simmer the tubes for about 3 minutes to allow the flavors to combine. Plate the calamari, top with the tomato sauce, and garnish with the parsley to serve.

nut-free	Yes
egg-free	Yes
low FODMAP	Omit the garlic and onions. Use garlic-infused olive oil as the cooking fat.
AIP-friendly	Use the Autoimmune-Friendly No-Mato Sauce (page 187) in place of the tomato sauce. Use 1 teaspoon ground ginger in place of the chili powder.
SCD/GAPS	Yes
lower carb	Yes

chef's tip

The key to preventing calamari from becoming too chewy is to cook it at a higher temperature for less time.

nutritionist's note

Calamari is high in the B vitamin niacin, which promotes healthy cell metabolism. One serving of calamari contains 4 milligrams of niacin, which is 30 percent of the daily recommended niacin intake. Calamari also has vitamin B12, which supports proper nerve function and the growth of red blood cells.

paella

prep time: 30 minutes | *cook time:* 25 minutes | *serves:* 4

Caitlin: When Nabil made this paella during the photo shoot for this book, we all fought over the last spoonful. The garlic and the sweetness of the seafood is a heavenly flavor pairing. To stay Paleo-friendly, this dish replaces the traditional rice with shredded cauliflower.

---

2 tablespoons unsalted butter, ghee, or coconut oil

1 pound boneless, skinless chicken thighs, cubed

1 medium onion, diced

1 green bell pepper, diced

1 red bell pepper, diced

2 teaspoons minced garlic

2 bay leaves

1 pinch saffron

1 teaspoon dried thyme leaves

fine sea salt and ground black pepper

1 medium tomato, diced

1/4 cup tomato paste

1/2 cup Chicken Broth (page 386)

6 ounces medium shrimp, peeled and deveined

6 ounces calamari rings

3 cups shredded cauliflower (1 medium head)

1 cup frozen peas, defrosted and drained

8 ounces mussels, cleaned (see Chef's Tip)

1/2 cup chopped fresh cilantro, for garnish

1 lemon, sliced into wedges, for serving

1. In a large cast-iron or stainless steel skillet, melt the fat over medium-high heat. Add the chicken and sauté for 2 minutes. Add the onion and peppers to the pan and sauté for 2 minutes, or until the onion is translucent.

2. Add the garlic, bay leaves, saffron, thyme, and a pinch of salt and pepper to the pan and sauté for 2 more minutes. Add the tomato and sauté for 2 minutes. Add the tomato paste and chicken broth, stir to combine, and bring to a boil. Decrease the heat to medium-low and simmer for 5 minutes.

3. Add the shrimp and calamari to the pan and cook for 2 minutes, or until the shrimp is pink. Add the cauliflower and peas and cook for 3 more minutes. Place the mussels on top and cover with a lid. Cook for 3 minutes, or until cauliflower is cooked but not mushy. Discard any mussels that did not open.

4. Adjust the seasonings to taste, remove the bay leaves, and top with the cilantro. Serve straight from the pan with the lemon wedges for an impressive presentation.

nut-free	Yes
egg-free	Yes
low FODMAP	Add 1 tomato and omit the tomato paste. Omit the onion and garlic. Use garlic-infused olive oil as the cooking fat.
AIP-friendly	Omit the peppers and use 1/2 cup canned pumpkin in place of the tomato and tomato paste.
SCD/GAPS	Yes
lower carb	Omit the peas.

chef's tip

To clean the mussels: First, make sure they're all closed and discard any open ones. Soak them in cool water for about 20 minutes. Carefully remove the mussels from the water, leaving the sediment they released behind in the water. Remove the beard from each mussel by pulling it toward the hinge end. (The beard is the thick string that sticks out of the shell.) Clean off any dirt on the outside of the mussels with a brush and rinse them under cold water.

lemon-butter steamed mussels

prep time: 20 to 30 minutes | *cook time:* 10 minutes | *serves:* 4 as an appetizer

This is a simple dish that will wow your friends and family. We often make it at home as an appetizer because it's so quick and easy, and mussels are usually affordable and can be found easily at most grocery stores and wholesale clubs.

1/4 cup unsalted butter, ghee, or coconut oil

1 shallot, minced

fine sea salt and ground black pepper

2 teaspoons minced garlic

2 pounds mussels, cleaned (see Chef's Tip on page 292)

2 cups Fish Broth (page 389) or water

1/4 cup lemon juice

1/2 cup chopped fresh cilantro, divided

1 lemon, halved, for serving

1. In a deep sauté pan, melt the fat over medium heat. Add the shallot to the pan with a pinch of salt and pepper and sauté for 1 minute. Add the garlic to the pan and sauté for 1 more minute.

2. Add the mussels, broth, lemon juice, and half of the cilantro to the pan. Cover the sauté pan with a lid and steam the mussels for 3 to 5 minutes, until they open. Discard any that didn't open.

3. Transfer the mussels with the broth to a serving bowl. Sprinkle the mussels with the rest of the cilantro and serve with the lemon halves.

chef's tip

Fresh mussels should be closed tightly when purchased and stored in a breathable storage container until cooked. For tips on cleaning mussels, see the Chef's Tip on page 292.

nutritionist's note

Mussels and oysters can be farmed sustainably because they do not create a lot of pollution and actually can improve a habitat. Look for shellfish farmed in Canada or the United States, which have stricter safety and quality standards.

nut-free	Yes
egg-free	Yes
low FODMAP	Use garlic-infused olive oil as the cooking fat. Use 1/2 cup chopped scallions in place of the onions.
AIP-friendly	Yes
SCD/GAPS	Yes
lower carb	Yes

odd bits

Why Offal?

Traditional cultures prized organ meats because they are high in essential fats, including DHA and ALA, which are necessary for the brain and spinal cord. They are also rich sources of fat-soluble vitamins, which are important for a vital immune system, and minerals that are needed for strong bones and teeth. Offal has fallen out of favor in the low-fat and lean-meat paradigm of the last fifty years, which has demonized animal foods. But when seeking optimal health, it is very important to embrace offal because it is the most nutrient-dense group of foods on earth.

mediterranean chicken liver pâté

prep time: 10 minutes | *cook time:* 15 minutes | *serves:* 4 to 6

Nabil: In Algeria, most people—including children—eat liver weekly. I never knew that many people have an aversion to liver until moving to the United States. I find that marinating and grilling liver and adding spices or herbs can make it more palatable to most people. But of all the ways to disguise liver, pâté is one of the most popular. Here, we've used Mediterranean spices instead of parsley and thyme to change the flavor profile of this traditional French charcuterie.

---

6 tablespoons ghee, duck fat, or coconut oil, divided

1 medium white onion, diced

4 teaspoons minced garlic

2 teaspoons crushed bay leaves

fine sea salt and ground black pepper

1 pound chicken livers

1/4 cup chopped fresh cilantro

2 teaspoons ground cumin

1 teaspoon ground paprika

1/4 cup apple cider vinegar

assorted raw vegetables, for serving

1. Melt 1 tablespoon of the fat in a skillet over medium heat.

2. Add the onion, garlic, bay leaves, and a few pinches of salt and pepper to the skillet and sauté for 3 minutes.

3. Rinse and pat dry the chicken livers. Add the chicken livers to the skillet with another pinch of salt and pepper.

4. Sauté the livers for 5 minutes, then add the cilantro, cumin, paprika, and vinegar. When the vinegar has evaporated, after about 3 to 5 minutes, transfer the mixture to the food processor.

5. Add the remaining fat, 1 tablespoon at a time, to the warm liver while pulsing in the food processor. Run the food processor for several more seconds until a smooth consistency is reached.

6. Taste the mixture and adjust the seasonings to taste.

7. Serve warm or chill for an hour before serving. Serve the pâté with assorted crudités such as endive, carrots, celery, sliced green apple, or cucumber rounds.

nut-free	Yes
egg-free	Yes
low FODMAP	Omit the onions and garlic. Use garlic-infused olive oil as the cooking fat. Add 1/2 cup chopped scallions to the food processor.
AIP-friendly	Use 1 teaspoon ground turmeric in place of the cumin. Use 1 teaspoon ground ginger in place of the paprika.
SCD/GAPS	Yes
lower carb	Yes

nutritionist's note

The importance of organ meats in the diet cannot be overstated. Liver, for instance, is rich in vitamin A, which supports a healthy brain and nervous system.

braised liver and mushrooms

prep time: 15 minutes | *cook time:* 40 minutes | *serves:* 4

Caitlin: I was introduced to this braised liver and mushrooms dish on my first full day in Algeria, when Nabil's sisters took me to a lovely restaurant near their home. I'd never had liver cooked that way before, and I knew right away I wanted to include a version in this book.

---

1 tablespoon unsalted butter, ghee, or coconut oil

1/2 cup diced white onion

1 pound beef liver, cut into bite-sized pieces

fine sea salt and ground black pepper

3 teaspoons minced garlic

1 tablespoon ground cumin

1 teaspoon ground caraway seeds (optional)

8 ounces mushrooms, sliced

2 tablespoons tomato paste

1/4 cup chopped fresh cilantro, for garnish

1. In a sauté pan, melt the fat over medium heat. Add the onion and sauté for 2 minutes, until translucent. Add the liver and sauté for 1 minute. Add a few pinches of salt and pepper and the garlic, cumin, and caraway, if using, to the liver and sauté the mixture for 1 minute.

2. Add the mushrooms to the pan and cook for 3 more minutes. Stir in the tomato paste and 2 cups of water.

3. Simmer the liver, uncovered, for about 30 minutes, until tender. Adjust salt and pepper to taste.

4. Transfer the liver and mushrooms to a serving bowl and garnish with the cilantro.

SLOW COOKER INSTRUCTIONS

Place all of the ingredients except the cilantro in a slow cooker and cook on low for 4 to 5 hours. Garnish with the cilantro to serve.

nut-free	Yes
egg-free	Yes
low FODMAP	Omit the onion and garlic. Use garlic-infused olive oil as the cooking fat.
AIP-friendly	Use 1 teaspoon ground turmeric and 1 teaspoon ground ginger in place of the cumin, caraway seeds, paprika, and chili powder. Use 1/2 cup canned pumpkin in place of the tomato paste.
SCD/GAPS	Yes
lower carb	Yes

chef's tip

Braising liver in a sauce is a great way to improve its texture and flavor. The spices mask the liver flavor that some people do not like, and the slow cooking gives the liver a more pleasing texture.

nutritionist's note

A mere 3 1/2 ounces of liver has nearly 147 percent of the daily recommended value of folate, which is important for healthy reproductive function and proper fetal development. Folate is also crucial in preventing anemia and gingivitis, and it is helpful for digestive system disorders.

grilled liver kebabs (Kibda)

prep time: 5 minutes, plus up to 30 minutes to marinate |
cook time: 5 minutes | *serves:* 4

Caitlin: In the South, where I grew up, fried chicken restaurants often include fried liver on their menus, and that was my only exposure to liver until I started following the Paleo diet. Nabil, on the other hand, ate it every week growing up. He turned me on to different ways of eating liver, and now I even crave it. I particularly love these kebabs, which are especially good when dipped in Tahini Dipping Sauce (page 393).

---

1 tablespoon ground cumin

1 tablespoon paprika

1/4 teaspoon chili powder

fine sea salt and ground black pepper

1 tablespoon apple cider vinegar

1 tablespoon extra-virgin olive oil

1 pound calf's liver, cut into 1-inch cubes

1 tablespoon unsalted butter, ghee, or coconut oil, melted

1. In a bowl, combine the cumin, paprika, chili powder, a few pinches of salt and pepper, the vinegar, and the olive oil. Add the liver cubes and toss to evenly coat. Let the liver marinate for up to 30 minutes.

2. If using wooden skewers, soak them in water for about 10 minutes before you're ready to grill the liver.

3. Heat a grill pan on the stovetop or an outdoor grill to medium-high heat.

4. Put the liver onto wooden or metal skewers. Brush the grill with the melted fat. Sear the liver for 2 minutes on each side, or until browned.

chef's tip

Calf's liver is more tender, milder in flavor, and lighter in color than matured beef liver. Calf's liver is very tasty when pan-fried or grilled to medium temperature, while beef liver tastes best when slow-cooked to make it tender.

nutritionist's note

Just 3 1/2 ounces of liver provides 200 percent of the recommended daily allowance of B12 (cobalamin), an anemia-preventing vitamin that is synergistic with folate. B12 may also help prevent the brain plaque formation consistent with Alzheimer's disease. This important vitamin is only found in animal foods and is abundant in healthy, grass-fed liver.

nut-free	Yes
egg-free	Yes
low FODMAP	Yes
AIP-friendly	Use 1 teaspoon ground turmeric and 1 teaspoon ground ginger in place of the cumin, paprika, and chili powder.
SCD/GAPS	Yes
lower carb	Yes

algerian beef heart chili

prep time: 20 minutes | *cook time:* 40 minutes | *serves:* 4 to 6

Caitlin: Nabil loves to make hearty stews for me on cold and foggy San Francisco nights. This one uses ground beef heart, which is very lean and has a similar taste and texture to ground beef. Cinnamon and cumin give the stew a unique, spicy-sweet flavor.

---

1 tablespoon unsalted butter, ghee, or coconut oil

1/2 cup diced white onion

2 cups diced green bell pepper (2 large peppers)

2 teaspoons minced garlic

1 teaspoon ground chili powder

1 tablespoon ground cinnamon

1 tablespoon ground cumin

fine sea salt and ground black pepper

1 1/2 pounds ground beef heart (see Chef's Tip)

1/4 cup tomato paste

4 cups Beef Broth (page 388)

1 cup shredded carrots (2 medium)

1 cup shredded zucchini (2 medium)

1/4 cup chopped fresh cilantro, for garnish

1. Melt the fat in a stockpot over medium heat.

2. Add the onion and bell pepper to the pot and sauté for 3 minutes. Stir in the garlic, chili powder, cinnamon, cumin, and a few pinches of salt and pepper. Cook the seasoned vegetables for 2 more minutes.

3. Add the ground heart to the stockpot, season liberally with salt and pepper, and sauté for 5 minutes. Add the tomato paste and the beef broth to the pot and stir until dissolved. Add the carrots and zucchini and stir until well mixed.

4. Cover the meat mixture and simmer for 30 minutes, stirring every 10 minutes. Adjust the salt and pepper to taste.

5. Serve topped with the fresh cilantro.

SLOW COOKER INSTRUCTIONS

Place all the ingredients except the zucchini and cilantro in a slow cooker and cook for 6 hours on low. Add the zucchini and cook for 1 more hour. Top with the fresh cilantro and serve.

nut-free	Yes
egg-free	Yes
low FODMAP	Omit the onion and garlic. Use garlic-infused olive oil as the cooking fat. Use 2 cups chopped tomatoes in place of the tomato paste.
AIP-friendly	Omit the green pepper, cumin, and chili powder. Add 2 teaspoons ground ginger. Use 1 cup canned pumpkin in place of the tomato paste.
SCD/GAPS	Yes
lower carb	Yes

chef's tip

For convenience, ask your butcher to prepare the heart for you by cutting out the chewy parts and grinding the heart. If you are preparing the heart yourself, slice it into quarters and cut out any tough-looking veins or gristle. Then place the heart in a food processor, one quarter at a time, and pulse until it becomes very blended and mushy.

Beef heart can be found at specialty butchers or farmers markets. If you have trouble finding it, grass-fed ground beef or lamb can also be used in this recipe.

zesty liver and beef meatloaf

prep time: 20 minutes | *cook time:* 1 hour | *serves:* 4

The best way to get your family to eat more organ meats is to hide them in meatloaf, spaghetti sauce, and stews. This recipe has a high ratio of muscle meat to organ meat, which means that the taste of the liver will be undetectable.

---

1 tablespoon unsalted butter, ghee, or coconut oil, plus more for greasing the pan

1 green bell pepper

1 medium white onion

8 ounces mushrooms, sliced

2 teaspoons minced garlic

fine sea salt and ground black pepper

6 ounces calf's or beef liver

2 tablespoons coconut flour

2 large eggs

1 tablespoon ground cumin

1 teaspoon paprika

1 1/2 pounds ground beef

1 recipe Harissa Dipping Sauce (page 395; optional)

1. Preheat the oven to 350°F. Grease a 9-by-5-inch loaf pan.

2. Melt the fat in a sauté pan over medium heat.

3. Add the bell pepper, onion, and mushrooms and cook for 5 minutes, until the onions are translucent. Add the garlic and a few pinches of salt and pepper and sauté for 2 minutes. Remove the vegetables from heat and let the mixture cool for 5 to 10 minutes.

4. In a food processor, combine the liver, coconut flour, eggs, cumin, and paprika and pulse until smooth. Add the cooled vegetables and a few pinches of salt and pepper to the mixture and pulse a few more times.

5. In a large bowl, combine the mixture from the food processor with the ground beef.

6. Put the meatloaf mixture into the prepared loaf pan and bake for 40 minutes, or until the internal temperature reaches 160°F and a crust has formed on top.

7. Slice and serve with the dipping sauce, if desired.

nut-free	Yes
egg-free	Use the AIP-friendly modification.
low FODMAP	Omit the onion and garlic. Use garlic-infused olive oil as the cooking fat. Use Basic Tomato Sauce (page 182) in place of the dipping sauce.
AIP-friendly	Omit the eggs, green pepper, cumin, and paprika. Add 2 teaspoons ground ginger. Use 1/4 cup arrowroot flour and 1 1/2 cups canned pumpkin in place of the eggs and coconut flour. Top with Autoimmune-Friendly No-Mato Sauce (page 187).
SCD/GAPS	Yes
lower carb	Yes

nutritionist's note

Past generations ate liver on a regular basis, but it has fallen out of favor these days. Many people today think that organ meats are something to discard, but health experts believe that liver is our most potent superfood. Liver is high in fat-soluble vitamins that are critical to well being and should be obtained daily from animal sources. Vitamins A, D, and K2 work synergistically with minerals to support immune health and the growth and preservation of strong bones and teeth, and to protect blood vessels and arteries.

beef tongue with green olives

prep time: 20 minutes | *cook time:* 3 1/2 hours | *serves:* 4

Caitlin: I was afraid to prepare beef tongue when I first went Paleo because the outer covering was really intimidating. It turns out, though, that the skin is easily removed after a few hours of slow cooking. I was excited to try it, and I'm glad I did. The taste and texture of slow-cooked tongue are a lot like barbecue, and it has a lot of beneficial nutrients.

1 pound beef tongue (1 tongue)

fine sea salt and ground black pepper

3 bay leaves

2 cups pitted green olives

1 tablespoon unsalted butter, ghee, or coconut oil

1/2 cup diced shallots (4 large)

2 teaspoons minced garlic

1 teaspoon ground chili powder

1 tablespoon ground cumin

2 tablespoons tomato paste

1 pound green beans, cleaned and trimmed

1/4 cup fresh cilantro leaves, for garnish

SLOW COOKER INSTRUCTIONS

Cook the tongue for 8 hours on low with a few pinches of salt and pepper, the bay leaves, and 6 cups of water. After the beef tongue is cooked, proceed with Step 2.

1. Put the tongue, a pinch of salt and pepper, the bay leaves, and 6 cups of water in a large stockpot. Cook the tongue over medium heat, covered, for 3 hours, or until it is fork-tender.

2. Remove the tongue and place it on a cutting board, and save the broth for later use. Use 2 forks to remove the outer skin of the tongue—it should easily fall off—and discard. Cut the tongue meat into bite-sized pieces and set aside.

3. Put 3 cups of water in a saucepan and bring to a boil. Add the olives and continue to boil for 5 minutes. (This step is important because it removes the bitterness from the olives.) Drain the olives and set aside.

4. Melt the fat in a sauté pan over medium heat. Sauté the shallots for 1 minute. Add the garlic and sauté for 1 more minute.

5. Add the tongue pieces to the shallot mixture and sauté for 1 minute. Add the chili powder, cumin, and a few pinches of salt and pepper. Sauté the mixture for 2 more minutes.

6. Add the tomato paste and 3 to 4 cups of the tongue cooking liquid, until it just barely covers the tongue. Stir the mixture gently and bring it to a boil. Add the olives, reduce the heat, and simmer for 10 minutes.

7. Add the green beans to the pot and simmer for 10 more minutes. Adjust the salt and pepper to taste, remove the bay leaves, and transfer to a serving dish. Top with the fresh cilantro to serve.

nut-free	Yes
egg-free	Yes
low FODMAP	Omit the shallots and garlic. Use garlic-infused olive oil as the cooking fat. Use 1 cup chopped tomatoes in place of the tomato paste.
AIP friendly	Use 1 teaspoon ground turmeric and 1 teaspoon ground ginger in place of the cumin and chili powder. Use 1/2 cup canned pumpkin in place of the tomato paste.
SCD/GAPS	Yes
lower carb	Yes

chef's tip

This dish can be intimidating, but once you cook a tongue you will have it licked—pun intended! Beef tongue should be available at your natural grocery store or local farmers market, or by request from your butcher. It's very popular with gourmet cooks, so you may have to call ahead and ask a specialty meat market to save it for you.

nutritionist's note

Beef tongue is a good source of iron and zinc, both of which boost the immune system so that your body is able to fight off infection.

allspice oxtail soup

prep time: 10 minutes | *cook time:* 3 hours 45 minutes | *serves:* 4

Oxtail, the meat and bones from a cow's tail, is used in many Mediterranean dishes. It creates a flavorful broth because it is very high in gelatin, and after slow cooking, the meat is falling-off-the-bone tender. This dish also includes spices commonly used in southern Algeria, which is largely made up of the Sahara, for a flavorful, filling soup.

1 tablespoon unsalted butter, ghee, or coconut oil

3 pounds oxtail pieces

3 dried bay leaves

1 medium white onion, diced

2 teaspoons minced garlic

1 teaspoon chili powder

1 teaspoon dried thyme

1 teaspoon dried allspice

3 whole cloves

fine sea salt and ground black pepper

3 cups cooked fresh or canned pumpkin

1/4 cup chopped fresh cilantro, for garnish

1. Melt the fat in a large stockpot over medium heat. Place the pieces of oxtail in the pot, season liberally with salt and pepper, and sauté for 2 minutes. Add the bay leaves, onion, garlic, chili powder, thyme, allspice, and cloves. Sauté the meat until it is browned on all sides, about 10 minutes.

2. Cover the meat with 8 cups of water and bring to a boil. Reduce the heat to medium-low and simmer for 3 hours, covered. Check the pot periodically and add a cup of water if it looks like it's getting too low (the oxtail should be submerged at all times).

3. When the meat is tender, add the pumpkin and a pinch of salt and pepper and stir. Simmer the soup, uncovered, for 30 minutes. Adjust the seasonings to taste.

4. Remove the bay leaves and top with the cilantro.

SLOW COOKER INSTRUCTIONS
Place all of the ingredients except the cilantro in a slow cooker with 8 cups of water. Cook on low for 6 hours. Adjust the seasonings to taste and garnish with the cilantro to serve.

nut-free	Yes
egg-free	Yes
low FODMAP	Omit the onion and garlic. Use garlic-infused olive oil as the cooking fat.
AIP-friendly	Use 1 teaspoon ground turmeric in place of the chili powder.
SCD/GAPS	Yes
lower carb	Yes

chef's tip

Oxtail is economical, but it may be difficult to find. Try requesting it ahead of time at your butcher shop or from a local farmer.

nutritionist's note

Oxtail is a great source of gelatin, which is infused into the broth during cooking. Gelatin is very healing for the digestive tract and is full of minerals for strong bones, teeth, and nails.

liver meatballs with mushroom gravy

prep time: 15 minutes | *cook time:* 30 minutes | *serves:* 4

With the liver meatballs, this mushroom gravy becomes a filling, nutritious meal. It uses the texture of the vegetables instead of wheat flour to thicken the gravy, and since it combines liver with beef in the meatballs, even people who don't enjoy the taste of liver will like this dish.

FOR THE MEATBALLS

1 pound ground beef

4 ounces calf's liver

1 tablespoon ground cumin

fine sea salt and ground black pepper

FOR THE GRAVY

1 tablespoon unsalted butter, ghee, or coconut oil

1/2 cup diced shallot

1 teaspoon minced garlic

16 ounces mushrooms, sliced

2 bay leaves, crushed

fine sea salt and ground black pepper

2 cups Beef Broth (page 388)

1/4 cup chopped fresh cilantro, for garnish

1. Make the meatballs: Put the ground beef, liver, cumin, and a few pinches of salt and pepper in a food processor. Pulse until smooth and roll the mixture into 2-inch balls.

2. Make the gravy: In a large saucepan, melt the fat over medium heat. Add the shallot and garlic and sauté for 1 minute. Add the mushrooms, bay leaves, and a pinch of salt and pepper and sauté until the mushrooms are soft, about 5 minutes.

3. Add the broth to the pan and bring the mixture to a boil. Decrease the heat and simmer for 10 minutes, uncovered.

4. Add the meatballs to the mushroom sauce and simmer for 10 more minutes. Pour half the sauce into a blender, leaving the meatballs in the pan. Puree the sauce until smooth and add it back to the pan with the meatballs.

5. Stir the mixture while bringing the sauce to a simmer and remove it from heat. Add salt and pepper to taste, remove the bay leaves, and garnish with the cilantro to serve.

nut-free	Yes
egg-free	Yes
low FODMAP	Omit the shallot and garlic. Use garlic-infused olive oil as the cooking fat.
AIP-friendly	Use 1 teaspoon ground turmeric in place of the cumin.
SCD/GAPS	Yes
lower carb	Yes

grilled beef heart skewers

prep time: 5 minutes, plus up to 1 hour to marinate |
cook time: 5 minutes | *serves:* 4

Beef hearts are often discarded, so it is easy to get this great cut inexpensively from a specialty butcher or farmer. The texture is similar to lean chicken breast, but it's darker in color. This dish goes well with Minty Cucumber and Tomato Salad (page 134), Tzatziki Sauce (page 392), and Mini Pitas (page 142), as pictured.

---

1 tablespoon ground cumin

1 tablespoon paprika

1/2 teaspoon chili powder

fine sea salt and ground black pepper

1 tablespoon apple cider vinegar

1 pound beef or lamb heart, cut into 1-inch cubes

1 tablespoon unsalted butter, ghee, or coconut oil, melted

1. Combine the cumin, paprika, chili powder, and a few pinches of salt and pepper in a small bowl and mix together. Add the vinegar, mix, and add the cubed meat.

2. Let the meat marinate for up to 1 hour in the refrigerator. f using wooden skewers, soak them in water for 10 minutes

3. Heat a grill pan on the stovetop or an outdoor grill to medium-high heat. Put the cubes of meat onto wooden or metal skewers.

4. Brush the grill with the melted fat. Cook the skewers for 2 minutes on each side, or until browned.

nut-free	Yes
egg-free	Yes
low FODMAP	Yes
AIP-friendly	Use 1 teaspoon ground turmeric and 1 teaspoon ground ginger in place of the cumin, paprika, and chili powder.
SCD/GAPS	Yes
lower carb	Yes

chef's tip

Most of the time the butcher will prepare the heart for you, so all you have to do is slice and grill it. If you do need to prepare the heart, slice it in half and remove the connective tissue, valves, muscles, and tendons. You want to keep the dense muscle and the bits of fat for added flavor, but remove anything that looks tough. It will be pretty obvious by sight what is going to be tasty and what will be too chewy.

nutritionist's note

Stress and many common medications, such as statin drugs, deplete the body of coenzyme Q10, which is vital for heart health. Luckily, beef heart is one of the few cuts of meat that provide ample amounts of coenzyme Q10.

vegetable sides

sautéed green beans with lamb bacon

prep time: 5 minutes | *cook time:* 15 minutes | *serves:* 4

Green beans, called *lubia* in North Africa, are a summertime staple there. This recipe uses lamb bacon to flavor the beans. Traditional Mediterranean cooking uses a variety of animal fats, which infuse rich flavors into the vegetables.

1 pound green beans, trimmed

fine sea salt and ground black pepper

4 ounces lamb bacon or bacon of choice

2 teaspoons minced garlic

1 teaspoon paprika

1. Heat a steamer pot with 3 cups of water over medium heat. Place the green beans in the top with a pinch of salt and cover. Steam them for 5 minutes, or until slightly cooked.

2. Chop the lamb bacon into small pieces. Heat a skillet over medium heat. Add the bacon pieces and garlic to a skillet and cook for 5 minutes.

3. Add the green beans and paprika and stir. Sauté the mixture for 3 minutes to combine the flavors.

4. Add salt and pepper to taste and serve.

nut-free	Yes
egg-free	Yes
low FODMAP	Omit the garlic and cook in garlic-infused olive oil.
AIP-friendly	Use 1 teaspoon ground ginger in place of the paprika.
SCD/GAPS	Yes
lower carb	Yes

chef's tip

Lamb bacon can be found at specialty butcher shops or halal or kosher stores. Regular bacon can be used if desired.

perfect sweet potato fries

prep time: 5 minutes | *cook time:* 5 to 7 minutes | *serves:* 4

Caitlin: Nabil didn't grow up eating sweet potatoes, and he was not crazy about them before he went Paleo. Now he eats them about once a week and loves it when I make these fries. They're cut thin for even cooking and crispier fries.

---

4 large sweet potatoes

2 cups sustainable palm shortening, coconut oil, or beef tallow

fine sea salt to taste

paprika to taste

1. Peel the sweet potatoes and cut them lengthwise into thin strips.

2. In a deep skillet, heat the fat over medium-high heat until hot. To check the temperature, insert the end of a wooden spoon handle into the fat; if bubbles form all around it, the oil is ready to use. Add the sweet potatoes, making sure they don't clump together, and cover.

3. Cook for 5 to 7 minutes, until golden brown.

4. Transfer the fries to a paper towel to drain. Sprinkle with salt and paprika and serve immediately.

nut-free	Yes
egg-free	Yes
low FODMAP	Yes
AIP-friendly	Use ground ginger to taste in place of the paprika.
SCD/GAPS	Use butternut squash in place of the sweet potatoes.
lower carb	Use uncooked jicama strips instead.

nutritionist's note

Frying can be healthy when it is done with a natural oil or fat, such as coconut oil or beef tallow. Saturated fats are very stable at high heats, meaning they won't oxidize and cause free-radical damage inside our bodies. Avoid polyunsaturated oils, such as canola, corn, and soybean oils. They are heavily processed, making them oxidized before they reach your table.

savory sweet potato cakes

prep time: 10 minutes | *cook time:* 1 hour 10 minutes | *yield:* 6 cakes

Caitlin: These sweet potato cakes were a big hit with some non-Paleo friends at our Super Bowl party. Even though they're Paleo-friendly, they're also comfortingly starchy. The cilantro gives these savory cakes an unexpected but welcome twist. They pair well with Tzatziki Sauce (page 392), as pictured.

4 medium sweet potatoes

1/2 cup coconut flour

1 teaspoon paprika

2 teaspoons ground cumin

1 teaspoon cayenne pepper

fine sea salt and ground black pepper

2 large eggs, beaten

1/2 cup chopped fresh cilantro, plus more for garnish

1/4 cup sustainable palm shortening, coconut oil, or beef tallow

1. Preheat the oven to 350°F.

2. Bake the sweet potatoes for 1 hour, or until easily pierced with a knife. Allow to cool, then remove and discard the skin. Place the cooked sweet potatoes in a large bowl.

3. In a small bowl, use a fork to mix together the coconut flour, paprika, cumin, cayenne pepper, a pinch of salt and pepper, the eggs, and the cilantro.

4. Pour the egg mixture into the bowl with the sweet potatoes and mix well. Form the sweet potatoes into 6 evenly sized patties.

5. Melt the fat in a skillet over medium heat. Add the patties and cook for 3 to 4 minutes on each side, until golden brown. The cakes will be crispy on the outside and soft in the middle when done.

6. Garnish with the cilantro to serve.

nut-free	Yes
egg-free	Use 1/4 cup arrowroot flour in place of the eggs.
low FODMAP	Yes
AIP-friendly	Use 1 tablespoon ground ginger in place of the paprika, cumin, and cayenne. Use 1/4 cup arrowroot flour in place of the eggs.
SCD/GAPS	Use 4 cups cooked butternut squash in place of the sweet potato.
lower carb	Use 4 cups canned pumpkin in place of the sweet potato.

nutritionist's note

Sweet potatoes are high in beta-carotene, an antioxidant, and should be eaten with fats such as olive oil or grass-fed butter to increase its absorption.

warm eggplant and tomato salad with mint (zaalouk)

prep time: 10 minutes | *cook time:* 20 to 25 minutes | *serves:* 4

This warm Moroccan salad has flavors of both North Africa and the Middle East. The cumin makes it earthy, and the mint refreshes the palate.

---

1 tablespoon unsalted butter, coconut oil, or ghee

1 medium white onion, diced

1 tablespoon minced garlic

3 Roma tomatoes, chopped

fine sea salt and ground black pepper

1 large eggplant

2 medium zucchini

1 teaspoon ground cumin

1 teaspoon chili powder

1/2 cup chopped fresh parsley

1 tablespoon apple cider vinegar

1/4 cup extra-virgin olive oil, for garnish

1/4 cup chopped fresh mint leaves, for garnish

1. Melt the fat in a skillet over medium heat.

2. Add the onion, garlic, and tomatoes with a few pinches of salt and pepper. Sauté the onion mixture for 10 minutes.

3. While the onion and tomatoes are cooking, dice the eggplant and zucchini into bite-sized pieces. Add the eggplant, zucchini, cumin, chili powder, and parsley to the skillet. Sauté the mixture for 10 to 15 more minutes, or until the vegetables are well cooked.

4. Add the vinegar to the pan and stir.

5. Garnish the dish with the olive oil and mint leaves.

nut-free	Yes
egg-free	Yes
low FODMAP	Use 1/2 cup chopped scallions in place of the onion. Omit the garlic and use garlic-infused olive oil in place of the regular olive oil.
AIP-friendly	Omit the eggplant and add 4 zucchini, for a total of 6. Use 1/2 cup canned pumpkin in place of the tomatoes. Use 1 teaspoon ground ginger in place of the chili powder. Use 1/2 teaspoon ground cardamom in place of the cumin.
SCD/GAPS	Yes
lower carb	Yes

chef's tip

Eggplant is a versatile vegetable that easily absorbs other flavors and can be used in main dishes and sides. It works well as a stuffing or thickener in many dishes, such as moussaka (page 256).

mock potato salad

prep time: 10 minutes | *cook time:* 20 minutes | *serves:* 4

Nabil: Affordable and plentiful, turnips are a popular vegetable in North Africa in the fall and winter. The best thing about this wonderful vegetable is that it takes on the flavor of the spices and herbs it is cooked with. Since I grew up eating turnips in soup every week, this salad makes me feel right at home.

---

6 to 8 medium turnips (about 2 pounds), peeled and cut into bite-sized pieces

fine sea salt and ground black pepper

1/4 cup Aioli (page 384)

1 teaspoon dry mustard

2 tablespoons apple cider vinegar

1/2 cup fresh cilantro leaves, chopped

1 medium red onion, minced (optional)

1. Place the turnips in a stockpot, cover with water, and bring to a boil. Boil the turnips until fork-tender, about 20 minutes.

2. Transfer the turnips to a bowl and let cool for 5 minutes.

3. Make the dressing: In a small bowl, mix together a pinch of salt and pepper and the aioli, dry mustard, vinegar, and cilantro.

4. Add the red onion, if using, to the bowl of turnips. Add the dressing and toss well to coat.

5. Serve warm or chilled.

nut-free	Yes
egg-free	Follow the AIP-friendly modification.
low FODMAP	Use 1/2 cup chopped scallions in place of the red onion.
AIP-friendly	Use 1/4 cup olive oil and 3 tablespoons lemon juice or 1/4 cup Tzatziki Sauce (page 392) in place of the aioli.
SCD/GAPS	Yes
lower carb	Yes

chef's tip

To make sure your turnips are very fresh, check that the greens on the top look vibrant. A good trick to reduce the bitterness of turnips is to boil a potato in the water with the turnips.

nutritionist's note

Turnips have a quarter of the carbohydrates in white potatoes, so they are popular with low-carb dieters. This recipe is a great way to enjoy the taste of potato salad if you're sensitive to carbohydrates.

roasted eggplant casserole

prep time: 5 minutes | *cook time:* 50 minutes | *serves:* 4

Caitlin: Eggplant has a special texture that gives this dish the feel of lasagna without the unhealthy wheat noodles.

---

1 tablespoon unsalted butter, ghee, or coconut oil, for greasing the dish

2 large eggplants

4 cloves garlic, peeled

1/4 cup extra-virgin olive oil

1 teaspoon dried thyme leaves

1 tablespoon tomato paste

2 large eggs, beaten

2 tablespoons grated Parmesan cheese (optional)

1. Preheat the oven to 350°F. Grease a 2-quart casserole dish or 8-inch-square glass baking dish.

2. Poke 2 holes in each eggplant with a knife and stuff in the garlic cloves. Place the eggplants in the prepared baking dish.

3. Roast the eggplants for 30 minutes, or until soft. Let them cool and remove the skin. (Do not wash the baking dish; you will use it again.)

4. In a large bowl, mash the eggplant flesh with a fork. Add the olive oil, thyme, tomato paste, and eggs and stir until well combined.

5. Pour the mixture into the baking dish. Bake for 20 minutes, or until cooked through.

6. If using the cheese, turn the oven to broil. Remove the dish and sprinkle the cheese over the top. Return it to the oven and broil for 2 minutes, or until browned.

nut-free	Yes
egg-free	No
low FODMAP	Omit the garlic. Use garlic-infused olive oil in place of the olive oil. Omit the cheese. Use 1/2 cup chopped tomatoes in place of the tomato paste.
AIP-friendly	No
SCD/GAPS	Yes
lower carb	Yes

golden raisin slaw

prep time: 15 minutes, plus 1 hour to refrigerate | *cook time:* n/a | *serves:* 4

Caitlin: I grew up loving coleslaw made with lots of store-bought mayonnaise. Nabil has reimagined it in this healthier version with Mediterranean flavors and no processed oils.

---

1 medium head cabbage, shredded

2 medium carrots, shredded

1 cup golden raisins

1/4 cup extra-virgin olive oil

1/4 cup lemon juice

2 tablespoons finely chopped fresh mint

2 tablespoons finely chopped fresh cilantro

1 teaspoon Herbes de Provence (page 401; see Chef's Tip, page 78)

fine sea salt and ground black pepper to taste

Place all the ingredients in a large bowl and toss until well combined. Adjust the seasonings to taste. Let the salad chill for 1 hour in the refrigerator before serving.

nut-free	Yes
egg-free	Yes
low FODMAP	No
AIP-friendly	Yes
SCD/GAPS	Yes
lower carb	Omit the raisins.

cauliflower couscous

prep time: 10 minutes | *cook time:* 8 minutes | *serves:* 4

In North Africa, couscous made from wheat is a staple food that is served with slow-cooked tajines. Our version of this side dish has a similar texture and makes a tasty, healthy substitute.

---

1 large head cauliflower, cored

fine sea salt and ground black pepper

1/4 cup chopped fresh cilantro

1. Rinse the cauliflower and let it drain. Cut the cauliflower into florets.

2. Use a food processor with a shredder blade to shred the florets.

3. Put the shredded cauliflower in a steamer pot with 3 cups of water over medium heat. Season with a few pinches of salt and pepper and steam for 5 to 8 minutes, until cooked but still firm to the bite, not mushy.

4. Place the cauliflower in a large bowl. Add the cilantro and stir to combine.

RAISIN AND PINE NUT COUSCOUS
To the cooked and still-warm cauliflower, add 1/2 cup raisins and 1/2 cup pine nuts and toss for a sweet and crunchy change of pace. Top with the fresh cilantro.

SAFFRON COUSCOUS
Steep 1/2 teaspoon saffron threads and 1 teaspoon turmeric in 2 tablespoons of boiling water. Pour the spiced water over the cooked and still-warm cauliflower and toss until well combined. Top with the fresh cilantro.

nut-free	Yes. (If making Raisin and Pine Nut Couscous, omit the pine nuts or use pumpkin seeds in their place.)
egg-free	Yes
low FODMAP	Yes. (If making Raisin and Pine Nut Couscous, omit the raisins.)
AIP-friendly	Yes. (If making Raisin and Pine Nut Couscous, omit the pine nuts.)
SCD/GAPS	Yes
lower carb	Yes

charmoula roasted vegetables

prep time: 10 minutes, plus 15 minutes to marinate |
cook time: 25 to 30 minutes | *serves:* 4

Roasted root vegetables have always been a favorite of ours because oven-roasting brings out the sweetness in the vegetables. This dish adds charmoula, a marinade used in Algerian, Moroccan, and Tunisian cooking, for a new spin on an old favorite. There are many different regional variations, and other seasonings can include lemon, cumin, chili pepper, saffron, and onion. These spiced vegetables pair well with Lamb-Stuffed Chicken Thighs (page 212), as pictured.

1 tablespoon coconut oil, for greasing the pan

3 medium turnips, peeled and cut into bite-sized pieces

3 large carrots, peeled and cut into bite-sized pieces

2 stalks celery, diced

1 medium fennel bulb, diced

2 teaspoons minced garlic

1 tablespoon ground cumin

1 teaspoon paprika

1 teaspoon cayenne pepper

3 cups tightly packed fresh cilantro leaves

fine sea salt and ground black pepper

2 tablespoons lemon juice

1/2 cup extra-virgin olive oil

1.   Preheat the oven to 350°F. Grease a rimmed sheet pan or glass baking dish.

2.   In a large bowl, combine the turnips, carrots, celery, and fennel.

3.   Put the garlic, cumin, paprika, cayenne pepper, cilantro, a pinch of salt and pepper, the lemon juice, and the olive oil in a food processor and pulse until smooth.

4.   Pour the sauce over the vegetables and toss until they are fully coated. Let the vegetables marinate at room temperature for about 15 minutes.

5.   Pour the vegetables into the prepared pan and spread them out evenly. Bake the vegetable mixture for 25 to 30 minutes, until tender.

nut-free	Yes
egg-free	Yes
low FODMAP	Omit the garlic. Use garlic-infused olive oil in place of the regular olive oil.
AIP-friendly	Use 2 teaspoons ground ginger in place of the paprika and cayenne. Use 1 teaspoon ground turmeric in place of the cumin.
SCD/GAPS	Yes
lower carb	Use 1 carrot and 4 stalks celery.

nutritionist's note

Carrots are often touted as having vitamin A, but that vitamin A is usually poorly converted within the body, unless you're in optimal health. Usable vitamin A is better provided by animal foods such as eggs, chicken, fish, and ruminant animals, and it's especially abundant in liver.

marinated olives

prep time: 5 minutes, plus up to 8 hours to marinate | *cook time:* n/a | *serves:* 6 to 8

Olives are very bitter when they are picked and must be cured with salt for several weeks before they're eaten. This curing process dates back to ancient times, and in Algeria, Morocco, and Tunisia, people still cure their own olives when they are in season. Store-bought olives have already been cured, but they tend to be plain and bland. This recipe spices them up for a tasty appetizer or side dish.

2 pounds unpitted green olives

1/2 cup diced red onion

3 tablespoons minced garlic

1 cup extra-virgin olive oil

2 bay leaves, crushed

2 teaspoons finely grated lemon zest

1 lemon, thinly sliced

1 cup diced sundried tomatoes

1 teaspoon paprika

1/2 cup fresh cilantro, chopped

1. Rinse the olives in cool water and drain. Place them in a large bowl.

2. Add the rest of the ingredients to the bowl. Stir until well mixed and refrigerate for up to 8 hours.

nut-free	Yes
egg-free	Yes
low FODMAP	Omit the onion and garlic. Use garlic-infused olive oil in place of the regular olive oil.
AIP-friendly	Make sure the only additives to the olives are salt and water. Omit the tomatoes and use 1 teaspoon ground ginger in place of the paprika.
SCD/GAPS	Yes
lower carb	Yes

nutritionist's note

Avoid olives with preservatives or artificial colors. Look for canned or jarred olives that have only salt and water added.

fermented probiotic pickles

prep time: 5 minutes, plus 2 weeks to ferment | *cook time:* n/a | *serves:* 4

Ancient cultures in the Mediterranean used fermentation to preserve foods. This easy recipe yields tasty pickles with a Mediterranean flavor in a very short time. Plus, you'll save money by getting your probiotics and pickles in one simple recipe. Probiotics are formed during the fermentation process and promote healthy digestion.

5 to 7 Persian cucumbers

2 tablespoons fine sea salt

1 tablespoon cumin seeds

1 tablespoon minced garlic

2 sprigs fresh dill

1 cup tightly packed fresh cilantro leaves

1 grape or cabbage leaf

1. Rinse the cucumbers and put them in a 2-quart jar.

2. In a medium bowl, mix the salt with 4 cups of water until the salt dissolves. Pour the salt water into the jar with the cucumbers. Add the cumin seeds, garlic, dill, and cilantro to the jar and stir slightly. Add the grape leaf and push the cucumbers down until they are covered with brine.

3. Seal the jar and leave at room temperature. Pickles will ferment in 1 to 2 weeks. Periodically check to make sure the cucumbers are still submerged under the brine. If they're sticking out of the brine, just push them back down or add a little water until water and the grape leaf cover them.

4. Monitor the cucumbers for desired taste and texture. After sitting for about 2 weeks, they will be ready to eat. Store in the fridge to slow the fermentation. Enjoy as a side dish or a snack.

nut-free	Yes
egg-free	Yes
low FODMAP	Omit the garlic.
AIP-friendly	Omit the cumin seeds.
SCD/GAPS	Yes
lower carb	Yes

nutritionist's note

Naturally fermented foods are one of the few sources of vitamin K2, which is important for bone health. Naturally fermented foods also provide beneficial bacteria for the colon, which can become out of balance from antibiotics and a typical American diet. Pickling does not provide the same probiotic benefits as fermenting.

desserts

pistachio and chocolate biscotti

prep time: 15 minutes | *cook time:* 20 minutes, plus 45 minutes to cool |
yield: 12 biscotti

Biscotti are classic crisp cookies that are served with coffee and tea all over the Mediterranean. In this version we used pistachios, which are abundant in Turkey.

1 1/2 cups blanched almond flour

1/2 cup coconut flour

3 tablespoons cocoa powder

1/2 teaspoon baking soda

1/4 teaspoon sea salt

1 teaspoon vanilla extract (gluten-free)

3/4 cup honey

1/2 cup roughly chopped raw pistachios

1. Preheat the oven to 350°F. Line a baking sheet with parchment paper.

2. Put the almond flour, coconut flour, cocoa powder, baking soda, and salt in a food processor and pulse until combined. With the machine running, add the vanilla extract and honey in a thin stream. Continue running the processor until a thick, pasty dough is formed.

3. Scrape the dough from the food processor into a large bowl. Work the pistachios into the dough with a spatula or by hand.

4. Place the dough on the prepared baking sheet. Form it into a flat rectangle no more than 1 inch thick.

5. Bake the dough for 15 minutes and turn off the oven. Allow the biscotti to cool for 30 minutes in the oven, then remove from the oven and let cool for another 10 minutes. Cut the biscotti into 1-inch-thick slices and turn the slices on their sides, spaced 1 inch apart.

6. Heat the oven back up to 350°F. Put the sliced biscotti back in the oven for 5 minutes to crisp. Remove from the oven and let cool for 5 minutes. Serve with coffee or tea.

nut-free	Use finely ground sunflower seeds (see page 170) in place of the almond flour.
egg-free	Yes
low FODMAP	Use lower carb modification and use cashew meal in place of the almond flour. Use pumpkin seeds in place of the pistachios.
AIP-friendly	No
SCD/GAPS	Omit the cocoa powder and increase the almond flour by 3 tablespoons. Use the scraped seeds of 1 vanilla bean in place of the vanilla extract.
lower carb	Omit the honey, and add 2 beaten eggs and 1 teaspoon stevia extract powder to the egg/nut flour mixture.

nutritionist's note

Vanilla extract is often made with alcohol that has been distilled from wheat, oats, barley, or rye, which have gluten. It is important to find an extract that is labeled "gluten-free" or that is alcohol-free to avoid contamination. You can also use the contents of a scraped vanilla bean that has not had any contact with gluten.

lemon pound cake (mouskoutchou)

prep time: 15 minutes | *cook time:* 35 minutes | *yield:* 1 (10-inch) cake

This beloved North African dessert is typically served with mint tea or Turkish coffee. It is usually made with wheat flour, but we've adapted it to be gluten- and grain-free.

1/2 cup melted unsalted butter, coconut oil, or sustainable palm shortening, plus more for greasing the pan

1 tablespoon arrowroot flour, for dusting the pan

6 large eggs

1 teaspoon rose water (optional; see Chef's Tip, page 95)

1/2 cup honey

2 tablespoons finely grated lemon zest

1 teaspoon lemon juice

2 cups blanched almond flour

3 tablespoons coconut flour

2 teaspoons baking soda

1 recipe Cashew Cream Icing (page 376; optional)

1. Preheat the oven to 350°F. Grease a Bundt cake pan and dust it with arrowroot flour to keep the cake from sticking.

2. Crack the eggs into a mixing bowl and add the rose water, if using, honey, melted fat, lemon zest, and lemon juice. Beat the mixture with an electric mixer until foamy.

3. In a separate bowl, mix the almond flour, coconut flour, and baking soda. Add the dry ingredients to the egg mixture and mix until well combined.

4. Pour the batter into the prepared cake pan and bake for 30 to 35 minutes, until the cake is golden brown and a toothpick inserted in the middle comes out clean.

5. Remove the cake from the oven and let it cool in the pan for 15 minutes. Place a plate over the cake pan and carefully flip it over so the cake comes out onto the plate. Let it cool completely. Top with the icing, if desired.

nut-free	No
egg-free	No
low FODMAP	Use cashew meal in place of the almond flour and follow the lower carb modification.
AIP-friendly	No
SCD/GAPS	Omit the arrowroot flour. Follow the guidance in the Chef's Tip when removing the cake from the pan.
lower carb	Use 2 teaspoons stevia extract powder in place of honey. Reduce the coconut flour by 1 tablespoon.

chef's tip

If the Bundt cake is hard to remove from the pan, place the cake pan upside down on a serving plate. Drape a cloth soaked in boiling water on the bottom and sides of the pan, not touching the cake, for 5 minutes. This allows steam to create space between the pan and the cake, which helps free the cake so it will come out in one piece.

almond tea cookies (el mechewak)

prep time: 15 minutes | *cook time:* 15 minutes | *yield:* 18 cookies

These classic Algerian tea cookies can be seen in every bakery window in Algiers. Made with almonds and honey, they also usually have some wheat flour in them, but we've adapted them to be Paleo-friendly.

---

3 1/2 cups blanched almond flour

1 cup honey

1 teaspoon vanilla extract (gluten-free)

1 teaspoon rose water (see Chef's Tip, page 95) or finely grated lemon zest

2 large eggs, beaten

1 cup slivered almonds

1/4 cup dried apricots

1. Preheat the oven to 300°F. Line a baking sheet with parchment paper.

2. In large bowl, mix the almond flour, honey, vanilla, and rose water until well combined. Gradually add the eggs to the mixture.

3. Stir the mixture with a spatula or knead by hand until a paste forms. Using your hands, roll the dough into 1-inch balls and set aside.

4. Roughly chop the slivered almonds. Roll each dough ball in the chopped almonds until lightly coated.

5. Place the dough balls on the prepared baking sheet and press a small indention in the top with your finger. Cut the apricots into slivers and push a piece of the dried apricot into the top of each dough ball.

6. Bake the cookies for 12 to 15 minutes, until golden brown. Cool on a cooling rack for 10 minutes before serving.

nut-free	Use finely ground sunflower seeds (see page 170) in place of the almond flour.
egg-free	No
low FODMAP	No
AIP-friendly	No
SCD/GAPS	Use the scraped seeds of 1 vanilla bean in place of the vanilla extract.
lower carb	Use 2 teaspoons stevia extract powder in place of the honey. Add 1 egg. Increase the almond flour by 1/2 cup.

fig brownies

prep time: 10 minutes | *cook time:* 30 minutes, plus 30 minutes to cool | *yield:* 18 small or 9 large brownies

This spin on a classic American dessert uses figs, which have hundreds of tiny edible seeds that give these brownies a unique pop and crunch. Fresh figs are available in the Mediterranean region during the summer but are less common in North America, so we've used dried figs here.

3/4 cup unsalted butter, ghee, or coconut oil, melted, plus more for greasing the dish

1 teaspoon vanilla extract (gluten-free)

3 large eggs, beaten

1 cup honey

1 teaspoon lemon juice

2 1/2 cups blanched almond flour

1 1/2 cups cocoa powder

1 teaspoon baking soda

1 cup chopped dried figs

1. Preheat the oven to 350°F. Grease a 9-inch-square glass or ceramic baking dish.

2. In a medium bowl, whisk together the melted fat, vanilla, eggs, honey, and lemon juice until well combined.

3. In a small bowl, mix the almond flour, cocoa, and baking soda. Add the dry mixture to the wet and stir until well combined. Stir in the figs and pour the mixture into the prepared baking dish.

4. Bake for 30 minutes, or until a knife inserted in the center comes out clean. Remove from the oven and cool in the baking dish for 30 minutes. Cut into squares before serving.

nut-free	Use finely ground sunflower seeds (see page 170) in place of the almond flour.
egg-free	No
low FODMAP	Use cashew meal in place of the almond flour. Use 2 teaspoons stevia extract powder in place of the honey. Use 1 cup canned pumpkin in place of the figs.
AIP-friendly	No
SCD/GAPS	No
lower carb	Use 2 teaspoons stevia extract powder in place of the honey. Use 1 cup canned pumpkin in place of the figs. Reduce the almond flour by 1/2 cup.

chocolate pot de crème

prep time: 5 minutes, plus 2 hours to refrigerate | *cook time:* 15 minutes | *serves:* 4

Pot de crème is a classic French dessert that we adapted to include Mediterranean flavors, such as cinnamon, nutmeg, and rose water. It is usually made with cream, but our version is dairy-free. Even though it tastes sinful, it is actually quite nutritious.

---

3 1/2 ounces unsweetened baking chocolate (100% cacao)

2 cups full-fat, canned coconut milk

3 large eggs, beaten

1 teaspoon ground cinnamon

1 teaspoon ground nutmeg

1 teaspoon vanilla extract (gluten-free)

3 tablespoons honey

1 teaspoon rose water or orange zest (optional)

whipped cream, for topping (optional)

1. Heat 2 cups of water in the bottom of a double boiler over medium heat. If you do not have a double boiler, use a heatproof glass mixing bowl over a saucepan filled with a few cups of water, making sure the water does not touch the bottom of the bowl. Melt the chocolate in the top of the double boiler.

2. Gradually add the coconut milk and eggs to the melted chocolate, stirring continuously with a whisk, still over medium heat.

3. Add the cinnamon, nutmeg, vanilla, honey, and rose water, if using, to the chocolate and stir continuously until it is thick, about 15 minutes. Pour the chocolate mixture into 4 (6-ounce) custard cups and refrigerate until set, about 2 hours. Top with whipped cream, if using, and serve.

chef's tip

Many pot de crème recipes are made in the oven, but this recipe is a little easier because it uses a double boiler. Make sure the water does not touch the top part of the double boiler or the pudding will cook too quickly and is likely to burn.

nutritionist's note

Many people are sensitive to dairy, which can cause sinus problems, headaches, muscle tension, joint inflammation, and weight gain. It is a good idea to eliminate it for thirty days to see how you feel, then slowly add it back into your diet. Coconut milk is a perfect substitute in many recipes and even tastes great in coffee.

nut-free	Yes
egg-free	No
low FODMAP	Use lower carb modification.
AIP-friendly	No
SCD/GAPS	No
lower carb	Use 1 teaspoon stevia extract powder in place of the honey.

chocolate tahini truffles

prep time: 10 minutes, plus 1 hour to chill | *cook time:* 10 minutes | *yield:* 12 truffles

Caitlin: When we were deciding which recipes to include in this book, I made these truffles for my little brothers, and they went crazy for them. They're twenty-two and twenty-four years old, and both are into Paleo and always ready to eat. They ate the entire batch of these tasty treats in no time, and we knew right away the truffles had made the cut.

2 ounces unsweetened baking chocolate (100% cacao), roughly chopped

1/4 cup coconut butter or manna

2 tablespoons tahini (sesame seed paste)

2 tablespoons full-fat, canned coconut milk

3 tablespoons honey

1/2 cup shredded coconut or 1 tablespoon slivered almonds (optional)

1. Prepare a double boiler with 2 cups of water over medium heat. If you do not have a double boiler, use a heatproof glass mixing bowl over a saucepan filled with a few cups of water, making sure the water does not touch the bottom of the bowl. Melt the chocolate in the double boiler.

2. Add the coconut butter, tahini, coconut milk, and honey to the chocolate, stirring constantly. Once all the ingredients are melted and well combined, remove the bowl from the heat and place in the refrigerator for 1 hour.

3. Using your hands, form the chilled chocolate mixture into 1-inch balls and either roll them in the shredded coconut or top with the slivered almonds, if using. Place on a platter and serve immediately, or chill until it is time to eat. These truffles will keep in a refrigerator for 1 week.

chef's tip

Coconut butter is the meat of the coconut pureed into a consistency similar to almond butter. It works much like peanut butter in many recipes where a thick paste is needed. While it's not commonly used in the Mediterranean, it's a favorite for Paleo recipes because it can replace nut butters and add a mild sweetness that isn't overpowering. It can be found at natural and organic food markets like Whole Foods or ordered from Amazon, usually at a discount.

nutritionist's note

Tahini is a nutrient-dense paste made of ground sesame seeds. Sesame seeds are a good source of calcium and magnesium, and they have protective properties that prevent oxidation when heated. Sesame seeds are easier to digest when soaked and ground, which makes their nutrients more available.

nut-free	Omit the almonds.
egg-free	Yes
low FODMAP	Use 1 teaspoon stevia extract powder in place of the honey. Omit the almonds.
AIP-friendly	No
SCD/GAPS	Omit the chocolate and increase the coconut butter to 1/2 cup.
lower carb	Use 1 teaspoon stevia extract powder in place of the honey.

crème caramel

prep time: 15 minutes | *cook time:* 40 minutes, plus 1 hour to chill | *serves:* 6

Caitlin: Many countries have a similar version of this dessert—flan in Spain, crème brûlée in France. Nabil and I both love puddings and crème desserts, so we had a great time testing this recipe. With its combination of vanilla-flavored cream and caramelized sauce, we know you will love it, too.

1 tablespoon coconut oil, for greasing the ramekins

3 cups full-fat, canned coconut milk

3 tablespoons honey

1 teaspoon vanilla extract (gluten-free)

5 large eggs

1 cup coconut sugar

1. Preheat the oven to 325°F. Grease 6 (6-ounce) ramekins and set aside.

2. Whisk the coconut milk, honey, vanilla, and eggs in a mixing bowl until well combined and set aside.

3. In a saucepan, melt the coconut sugar over medium heat with 1 teaspoon of water until dissolved.

4. Fill each ramekin 1/4 inch with the melted sugar. Divide the coconut milk mixture evenly between the ramekins.

5. Fill a baking dish with about an inch of water to make a water bath. Lower the ramekins into the water. (The water should come halfway up the sides of the cups; if it doesn't, add a little more.) Bake for 35 to 40 minutes, until the custard is set.

6. Remove from the oven and let the custard chill in the refrigerator for 1 hour. Run a knife around the side of the ramekins between the custard and the dish, then turn out onto a plate to serve.

nut-free	Yes
egg-free	No
low FODMAP	Use the lower carb modification.
AIP-friendly	No
SCD/GAPS	Omit the coconut sugar sauce. Use the seeds of 1 scraped vanilla bean in place of the vanilla extract.
lower carb	Use 1 teaspoon stevia extract powder in place of the honey. Omit the coconut sugar sauce.

pâte d'amande

prep time: 5 minutes | *cook time:* 5 minutes, plus 1 hour to rest | *yield:* 1 cup

Nabil: *Pâte d'amande*, also known as marzipan, is a French dessert that is very common in North Africa. It's often used as a filling for desserts, but it's also wonderful on its own. There are many different versions of *pâte d'amande*, and every Mediterranean mom and grandma has her own way of making it. This is the version my mother makes, and it's delicious in the stuffed dates, pictured at right.

2 tablespoons unsalted butter, ghee, or coconut oil

1/4 cup coconut sugar

1 tablespoon rose water (see Chef's Tip, page 95)

3/4 cups blanched almond flour

1/4 teaspoon vanilla extract (gluten-free)

natural food coloring (optional)

1. In a saucepan, melt the fat over medium heat. Add the sugar and rose water and stir until smooth, about 2 minutes.

2. Add the almond flour and vanilla and keep stirring over low heat until the mixture begins to thicken, about 3 minutes.

3. Remove the mixture from the heat and pour into an 8-by-8-inch glass baking dish. Let the mixture rest for 1 hour. It is now ready to be used as a filling in other confections or formed into decorative shapes and enjoyed.

4. Optional: If you're forming the paste into decorative shapes, such as fruit, use a mold and a few drops of natural food coloring, such as India Tree brand.

nut-free	No
egg-free	Yes
low FODMAP	No
AIP-friendly	No
SCD/GAPS	Use 1/2 cup honey in place of the coconut sugar. Use the scraped seeds of 1 vanilla bean in place of the vanilla extract.
lower carb	No

stuffed dates

prep time: 10 minutes, plus 1 hour 10 minutes to make the pâte d'amande | *cook time:* n/a | *yield:* 12 to 15 dates

Although easy to make, this dish will impress your guests. The Mediterranean flavors of dates and almonds combine to make this a dessert that will perk up your taste buds.

1/2 pound large Medjool dates

1 recipe Pâte d'Amande (page 354)

1 cup unsweetened shredded coconut

1. Slice the dates vertically and pull out the pit.

2. Stuff each date with 1 tablespoon of the pâte d'amande.

3. Roll the dates in the coconut and serve.

nut-free	Use coconut butter in place of the pâte d'amande.
egg-free	Yes
low FODMAP	No
AIP-friendly	Use coconut butter in place of the pâte d'amande.
SCD/GAPS	Use the SCD/GAPS modification for the pâte d'amande.
lower carb	No

flourless chocolate cake

prep time: 30 minutes | *cook time:* 50 minutes | *yield:* 1 (9-inch) cake

Caitlin: My mom and sister make a similar version of this cake for special occasions, but Nabil has added his own Mediterranean twist with orange blossom water and orange zest.

---

1 tablespoon unsalted butter, ghee, or coconut oil, for greasing the cake pan

1 tablespoon cocoa powder, for dusting the cake pan

11 ounces dark chocolate (80% cacao), roughly chopped

1 cup coconut oil

1/2 teaspoon vanilla extract (gluten-free)

3/4 cup maple syrup or honey

1/2 teaspoon orange blossom water (see Chef's Tip, page 98)

1 teaspoon orange zest

1/4 teaspoon fine sea salt

6 large eggs

1 recipe Chocolate Dip (page 377), for topping (optional)

1. Preheat the oven to 275°F. Grease a 9-inch round cake pan with the fat and dust it with cocoa powder.

2. Melt the chocolate and coconut oil in a double boiler, stirring constantly. If you do not have a double boiler, use a heatproof glass mixing bowl over a saucepan filled with a few cups of water, making sure the water doesn't touch the bottom of the bowl. Remove the bowl from the heat when the chocolate is fully melted.

3. Stir in the vanilla, maple syrup, orange blossom water, orange zest, 2 tablespoons of water, and the salt. One by one, whisk the eggs into the chocolate mixture until completely incorporated.

4. Pour the cake batter into the prepared pan.

5. Fill a large baking dish with 1/2 inch of water and place the cake pan into the baking dish. The water should come halfway up the side of the cake pan. Place the cake pan and baking dish in the oven and bake for 45 to 50 minutes, until the cake is set.

6. Remove the cake pan from the water bath and let the cake cool in the pan at room temperature for about an hour. Tip the cake out onto a platter. Drizzle with the chocolate dip, if using, slice, and serve. Store leftovers in the refrigerator.

nut-free	Yes
egg-free	No
low FODMAP	Follow lower carb modification.
AIP-friendly	No
SCD/GAPS	No
lower carb	Use 1 teaspoon stevia extract powder in place of the honey. Add 1 egg for a total of 7 eggs.

chef's tip

A bain-marie, often called a water bath, is a kind of double boiler created by putting one baking dish inside another baking dish containing a few inches of water and then placing it over heat or, as here, in the oven. It helps a custard or cake cook slowly and evenly without burning.

chocolate pistachio bites

prep time: 15 minutes, plus 1 hour 15 minutes to chill |
cook time: 10 minutes | *yield:* 36 bites

Caitlin: These cookies are based on a recipe I saw in an Algerian cookbook, re-created to be Paleo-friendly. They combine the richness of dark chocolate with the buttery taste of pistachios.

1/3 cup full-fat, canned coconut milk

16 ounces dark chocolate (80% cacao), chopped

1/4 cup unsalted butter, ghee, or coconut oil

2 large eggs, beaten

2 teaspoons grated lemon zest

2 cups coconut sugar

1 1/2 cups blanched almond flour

1 3/4 cups cocoa powder

1 teaspoon vanilla extract (gluten-free)

2 cups raw pistachios

1. In a saucepan over medium heat, warm the coconut milk for 3 minutes. Add the chocolate and fat to the pan while stirring. Continue stirring and heating the mixture for 2 minutes. Remove the saucepan from the heat. Stir in the eggs and lemon zest and stir for 1 minute.

2. Put the saucepan back on the burner, still over medium heat, and add the coconut sugar, almond flour, cocoa powder, and vanilla. Stir the mixture well for 2 minutes and then remove from the heat. Let the mixture cool for 15 minutes.

3. Place the pistachios in a food processor and pulse until they are finely ground, about the consistency of a coarse powder.

4. Form the chocolate mixture into 1-by-2-inch rectangles with your hands and then roll them in the chopped pistachios. Place the squares on a platter and let them chill in the refrigerator for 1 hour before serving.

nut-free	No
egg-free	No
low FODMAP	Follow lower carb modification. Use cashew meal in place of the almond flour. Use chopped walnuts in place of the pistachios.
AIP-friendly	No
SCD/GAPS	No
lower carb	Use unsweetened baking chocolate with 100% cacao instead of 80%. Use 2 teaspoons stevia extract powder in place of the coconut sugar. Add 2 eggs and 1/3 cup coconut milk.

samia's crescent cookies

prep time: 40 minutes, plus 15 minutes to rest and 1 hour 10 minutes to make the pâte d'amande | *cook time:* 20 minutes | *yield:* 24 cookies

Nabil: These cookies are similar to a North African cookie that is usually made with wheat flour. They are filled with a sweet almond paste and have a crunchy outside layer. Samia is one of my four sisters, and she loves making cookies like these for special occasions.

FOR THE DOUGH

5 cups tapioca flour, plus extra for rolling out the dough

2 cups packed blanched almond flour

1/2 cup honey

2 large eggs

1 tablespoon vanilla extract (gluten-free)

1 tablespoon rose water (see Chef's Tip, page 95) or finely grated lemon zest

3/4 cup melted unsalted butter, ghee, or coconut oil

FOR THE FILLING

2 cups Pâte d'Amande (page 354)

FOR THE TOPPING

1 large egg yolk, beaten

1/2 cup sliced raw almonds

1. Make the dough: In a large bowl, mix the tapioca flour and almond flour. In another large bowl, mix the honey, eggs, vanilla, and rose water. Add the dry mixture to the wet mixture and mix well.

2. Make a well in the middle of the batter and pour in the melted fat.

3. Continue mixing the batter by hand until well combined. If the dough is dry, add a few tablespoons of water to make it easier to work with. Form the dough into 4 balls and let them rest for 15 minutes.

4. Assemble and bake the cookies: Preheat the oven to 350°F. Line a baking sheet with parchment paper. Dust a clean, dry surface with tapioca flour to keep the dough from sticking.

5. Roll out a ball of dough until it is about 1/4 inch thick. Cut a piece of the dough into a triangle that's about 3 inches wide and 5 inches tall.

6. Form 1 to 2 tablespoons of the filling into a 2-inch cylinder. Place the filling on the wide end of the triangle, then roll up the dough around the filling. Turn the edges in to form a crescent shape. Repeat the process until all the dough and filling have been used.

7. Using a brush, cover the cookies with the beaten egg yolk.

8. Place the almonds on a plate. Dip the cookie into the chopped almonds to coat.

9. Arrange the cookies on the prepared baking sheet. Bake the cookies until golden brown, about 20 minutes. Let cool and serve with tea or coffee.

nut-free	No
egg-free	No
low FODMAP	No
AIP-friendly	No
SCD/GAPS	No
lower carb	No

pistachio tapioca pudding

prep time: 10 minutes, plus 2 hours to set | *cook time:* n/a | *serves:* 4

Caitlin: Nabil and I love puddings—especially those with Mediterranean flavors such as rose water and pistachios, like this one. It reminds me of a rice pudding that we used to eat at a Turkish restaurant in downtown San Francisco and makes a great Paleo-friendly replacement.

1 cup shelled raw pistachios

3/4 cup tapioca flour

2 cups full-fat, canned coconut milk

1 teaspoon ground cinnamon

1 teaspoon rose water (see Chef's Tip, page 95)

1/4 cup honey

1. Pulse the pistachios in a food processor until finely chopped. Divide the chopped pistachios into 2 equal portions and set them aside.

2. Mix the tapioca flour, coconut milk, cinnamon, rose water, and honey in a large bowl until well combined. Add half the pistachios to the bowl and mix well.

3. Pour the pudding into 4 (6-ounce) custard cups. Refrigerate for 2 hours, or until set. Garnish with the remaining pistachios before serving.

nut-free	Use pumpkin seeds in place of the pistachios.
egg-free	Yes
low FODMAP	Use 1 teaspoon stevia extract powder in place of the honey. Use chopped macadamia nuts or pumpkin seeds in place of the pistachios.
AIP-friendly	Omit the pistachios.
SCD/GAPS	No
lower carb	No

almond squares (el makhabaz)

prep time: 15 minutes | *cook time:* 10 minutes | *yield:* 18 cookies

Nabil: In Algeria, cookie-making is an art that is taken very seriously and passed down from mothers to daughters. Before going Paleo, I would return from a visit home with a huge box of ornate cookies. These gluten-free almond squares are a blend of the Middle Eastern–style cookies I grew up with and the Paleo ingredients Caitlin introduced me to.

---

3 cups blanched almond flour

2 teaspoon finely grated lemon zest

1 cup coconut sugar

3 large eggs, beaten

1 tablespoon orange blossom water (see Chef's Tip, page 98) or orange zest

1 recipe Chocolate Dip (page 377), for topping (optional)

1. Preheat the oven to 275°F. Line a baking sheet with parchment paper.

2. Mix the almond flour, lemon zest, and coconut sugar in a large bowl. Gradually mix the eggs and orange blossom water into the almond flour mixture until well combined.

3. Use your hands to shape the dough into 2-inch squares that are about 1/4 inch thick and place them on the prepared baking sheet. Bake the cookies for 10 minutes, or until golden brown. Let them cool for 15 minutes on a cooling rack.

4. Drizzle the squares with the chocolate dip and serve.

nut-free	No
egg-free	No
low FODMAP	No
AIP-friendly	No
SCD/GAPS	Use 1/2 cup honey in place of the coconut sugar. Use the scraped seeds of 1 vanilla bean in place of the vanilla extract. Omit the chocolate dip.
lower carb	Use 2 teaspoons stevia extract powder in place of the coconut sugar. Increase the almond flour by 3/4 cups.

chef's tip

While coconut sugar is not a traditional ingredient in North African cooking, it gives these cookies a unique, almost liqueur-like flavor.

chocolate-kissed coconut macaroons

prep time: 15 minutes, plus 10 minutes to make the chocolate dip |
cook time: 15 minutes | *yield:* 18 cookies

Caitlin: Nabil made these cookies for my sister's Paleo-friendly, gluten-free bridal shower, and they were a big hit. The ladies loved the hints of cinnamon and vanilla combined with chocolate and coconut.

---

4 large egg whites, room temperature

1/4 teaspoon fine sea salt

scraped seeds of 1 vanilla bean

1 teaspoon ground cinnamon

1/4 cup organic cane sugar

3 cups unsweetened shredded coconut

1 recipe Chocolate Dip (page 377)

1. Preheat the oven to 325°F. Line a baking sheet with parchment paper.

2. Whip the egg whites with a hand mixer until they form medium-firm peaks. Whisk the salt, vanilla seeds, and cinnamon into the egg whites. Whisk the sugar slowly into the egg white mixture, 1 tablespoon at a time.

3. Carefully fold in the shredded coconut, little by little, with a spatula.

4. Spoon the batter onto the baking sheet in 2-tablespoon mounds.

5. Bake the cookies for 15 minutes, until golden brown. Remove the cookies from the oven and place them on a cooling rack.

6. Let the cookies cool for 10 minutes, then dip them in the chocolate dip. Place each dipped cookie on parchment for 5 minutes to allow the chocolate to set before serving.

nut-free	Yes
egg-free	Mix 2 tablespoons beef or other gelatin with 1/2 cup boiling water in a large bowl to replace the eggs. See "A Note on Gelatin" on page 95.
low FODMAP	Use lower carb modification.
AIP-friendly	Mix 2 tablespoons beef or other gelatin with 1/2 cup boiling water in a large bowl. Add the vanilla seeds, cinnamon, and 1/4 cup warm honey and stir. Add the coconut and mix until well combined. Spoon the coconut mixture into 2-inch mounds on a baking sheet. Refrigerate the cookies for 2 hours and serve.
SCD/GAPS	Omit the chocolate dip and use 1/3 cup warmed honey in place of the sugar.
lower carb	Use 1 teaspoon stevia extract powder in place of the sugar and add 2 egg whites.

chef's tip

Egg whites form peaks more easily when they are not cold. About 1 hour before making the recipe, place the eggs on the counter to come to room temperature.

nutritionist's note

Coconut is known for its ability to boost the immune system against parasites and pathogens. It is always a good idea to eat coconut products daily for immune support and whenever you feel a cold coming on.

sesame candies

prep time: 5 minutes, plus 1 hour to cool | *cook time:* 10 minutes | *yield:* 18 candies

Nabil: Sesame candies are common throughout the Middle East and North Africa. As a kid, I used to buy them, individually wrapped in red and yellow cellophane, as an after-school treat at the corner shop in my neighborhood.

---

2 1/2 cups raw sesame seeds

1 cup honey

2 teaspoons ground cinnamon

2 teaspoons ground ginger

1/2 teaspoon fine sea salt

1. Line a large rimmed baking sheet with parchment paper.

2. Heat a large stainless-steel skillet over medium heat. Toast the sesame seeds in the pan, stirring them constantly. The seeds will change color and become golden. When a majority of them look toasted, after about 3 to 5 minutes, pour the seeds into a bowl.

3. Pour the honey into the same skillet, still over medium heat, and stir it until it boils, about 2 to 3 minutes. Add the toasted sesame seeds, cinnamon, ginger, and salt to the skillet and stir until combined.

4. Pour the sesame seeds onto the parchment paper and press into a smooth square shape with your hands.

5. Let the sesame candy sit on the counter for 1 hour to cool and harden. It will still be soft and pliable, not crunchy, but firm enough to handle. Cut the candy into diamond shapes with a sharp knife before serving. Store in the refrigerator.

nut-free	Yes
egg-free	Yes
low FODMAP	No
AIP-friendly	No
SCD/GAPS	Yes
lower carb	No

strawberry tart

prep time: 15 minutes, plus 1 hour to chill | *cook time:* 30 minutes | *yield:* 1 (10-inch) tart

Nabil: This is a favorite of mine and my sister's. During her visit to San Francisco, every afternoon we'd sit down and chat over a piece of strawberry tart. The creaminess of the custard is accented perfectly by the sweet tartness of the strawberries.

FOR THE CRUST

2 cups blanched almond flour

1 tablespoon honey

1 tablespoon unsalted butter, ghee or coconut oil, room temperature, plus more for greasing the pan

1/4 teaspoon sea salt

1 teaspoon vanilla extract (gluten-free)

1 large egg, beaten

FOR THE PASTRY CREAM

2 cups full-fat, canned coconut milk

1/4 cup honey

4 large egg yolks

1/4 teaspoon sea salt

1/4 cup tapioca flour

2 tablespoons unsalted butter, ghee, or coconut oil

1 teaspoon vanilla extract (gluten-free)

2 cups halved strawberries

nut-free	Use finely ground sunflower seeds (see page 170) in place of the almond flour.
egg-free	No
low FODMAP	Follow lower carb modification and use cashew meal in place of the almond flour.
AIP-friendly	No
SCD/GAPS	Omit the tapioca flour and add 2 egg yolks to the cream. Use seeds scraped from 1 vanilla bean in place of the vanilla extract.
lower carb	Use 1/4 teaspoon stevia extract powder in the crust instead of honey. Use 2 teaspoons stevia extract powder in the pastry cream instead of honey. Omit the tapioca flour and add 2 egg yolks to the cream.

1. Preheat the oven to 350°F. Grease a 10 1/4-inch tart pan with a removable bottom. (If you don't have a tart pan, see the Chef's Tip.)

2. Make the crust: Mix all of the ingredients in a large bowl with a whisk. Form the dough into a ball.

3. Place a large piece of parchment paper on a flat surface. Place the dough on the parchment and roll it out to 1/4 inch thick.

4. Turn the parchment paper over onto the prepared tart pan and press the dough into the pan to remove any bubbles. Fill in any small spaces with extra pieces of dough with your fingers. Discard any leftover dough.

5. Bake the crust for 15 minutes, or until golden brown. Remove the crust from the oven and set aside.

6. Make the pastry cream: Place a few cups of water in the bottom of a double boiler over medium heat. Make sure the water does not touch the bottom of the bowl. Place the coconut milk, honey, egg yolks, and salt in the top of the double boiler. Whisk the mixture continuously until the custard begins to thicken, about 15 minutes. Whisk in the tapioca flour until smooth. The tapioca will continue to thicken the mixture, and it will set completely in the refrigerator.

7. Remove the custard from the heat and mix in the fat and vanilla until well combined.

8. Lay a piece of plastic wrap or parchment on top of the custard to prevent a skin from forming. Make sure the plastic wrap is completely touching the top of the custard. Place in the fridge for 1 hour to cool.

9. Spread the cooled custard evenly into the crust and top with the halved strawberries. Keep the tart in the refrigerator until serving. The tart will keep in the refrigerator for 3 to 4 days.

chef's tip

Regular almond flour will work in this recipe, but blanched almond flour makes the crust lighter in color, so it resembles a conventional crust, and gives it a lighter texture. If you don't have a tart pan, use a greased 9-inch pie pan and serve the tart directly from the pan. Most berries or thinly sliced, peeled fruit, such as kiwis or bananas, will also work well in place of the strawberries.

nutritionist's note

Strawberries are a great source of vitamin C and have almost equal amounts of fructose and glucose, which helps maintain normal blood sugar. Choose organic berries whenever possible because they are thin-skinned and absorb pesticide residue easily.

turkish apricot ice cream

prep time: 5 minutes, plus 30 minutes to freeze | *cook time:* n/a |
yield: 3 cups | *serves:* 4

Apricots and cardamom combine to create an ice cream with quintessential Middle Eastern flavors. Apricots are found in many Mediterranean dishes because they're grown widely in Turkey. Cardamom, which hails from northern Persia, has a long history of use in the Middle East.

6 fresh apricots, pitted, plus more for topping

1/2 cup honey

1 teaspoon lemon juice

2 cups full-fat, canned coconut milk

1/2 teaspoon sea salt

1 teaspoon vanilla extract (gluten-free)

1 teaspoon ground cardamom

3 tablespoons gelatin (see "A Note on Gelatin" on page 95)

1/4 cup boiling water

4 sprigs fresh mint, for garnish

1. Put the canister from your ice cream maker in the freezer at least 2 days before you plan to make the ice cream. (If you don't have an ice cream maker, see the Chef's Tip.)

2. Place the apricots, honey, lemon juice, coconut milk, sea salt, vanilla, and cardamom in a blender and blend until smooth.

3. Mix the gelatin with the boiling water and stir until dissolved. Add the gelatin mixture to the blender and blend for 10 seconds.

4. Pour into the ice cream machine and churn, per the manufacturer's instructions. Eat right away or freeze to enjoy later.

nut-free	Yes
egg-free	Yes
low FODMAP	Use 1 teaspoon stevia extract powder in place of the honey. Use 2 cups berries in place of the apricots.
AIP-friendly	Yes
SCD/GAPS	Use the scraped seeds of 1 vanilla bean in place of the vanilla extract.
lower carb	Use 1 teaspoon stevia extract powder in place of the honey.

chef's tip

If you do not have an ice cream maker, pour the mixture into a bowl after Step 3 and place the bowl in the freezer. Stir every 30 minutes for 2 hours.

nutritionist's note

The high fiber content of the apricots in this recipe brings down the usable carb count, making a small portion acceptable for a lower-carb diet (1/2 cup has 7 grams of net carbs). Apricots also are a rich source of potassium, which is important in blood pressure regulation.

madeleines

prep time: 25 minutes | **cook time:** 12 minutes | **yield:** 12 cookies

Madeleines are a classic French cookie that is often made in Algeria, Tunisia, and Morocco, reflecting centuries of French influence. This version is made with almond flour and orange zest, traditional Mediterranean ingredients that are also Paleo-friendly.

2 tablespoons unsalted butter, ghee, or coconut oil, melted, plus more for greasing the pan

2 large eggs

1/4 cup honey

1 teaspoon vanilla extract (gluten-free)

1/2 teaspoon finely grated orange zest

1 1/4 cups blanched almond flour

1 recipe Chocolate Dip (page 377; optional)

1. Preheat the oven to 375°F. Grease a 12-cup madeleine pan.

2. Crack the eggs into a bowl and whip them with an electric beater for 2 minutes. Add the honey, melted fat, vanilla, and orange zest to the eggs and mix until eggs are foamy. Then very slowly add the almond flour while stirring with a spatula.

3. Pour the batter into the prepared madeleine pan, filling each cup two-thirds full. Place in the oven and bake for 12 minutes, or until golden brown. Remove the cookies from the pan and let them cool on a baking rack for 10 minutes.

4. Dip each cookie halfway into the chocolate dip, if desired. Allow the chocolate-dipped cookies to set on a plate for 10 minutes to harden the chocolate before serving.

nut-free	Use finely ground sunflower seeds (see page 170) in place of the almond flour.
egg-free	No
low FODMAP	Use cashew meal in place of the almond flour. Use 1 teaspoon stevia extract powder in place of the honey.
AIP-friendly	No
SCD/GAPS	Omit the chocolate dip.
lower carb	Use 1 teaspoon stevia extract powder in place of the honey.

special equipment

• 1 (12-cup) madeleine pan

cashew cream icing

prep time: 5 minutes | *cook time:* n/a | *yield:* 2 cups

We created this creamy icing for Lemon Pound Cake (page 342), but it can also be used for Paleo pancakes, such as Cinnamon Spice Pancakes (page 96), Orange Blossom Pancakes (page 98), or Autoimmune-Friendly Banana Pancakes (page 100), or as a fruit dip.

1/4 cup honey

1 cup raw cashews

2/3 cup full-fat, canned coconut milk

1 teaspoon orange blossom water (see Chef's Tip, page 98)

1 teaspoon finely grated lemon zest

1 teaspoon lemon juice

Place all the ingredients in a food processor and pulse until smooth. Pour the icing over the cake or pancakes, or use as a fruit dip.

nut-free	Use 1 cup sesame tahini in place of the raw cashews.
egg-free	Yes
low FODMAP	Use lower carb modification.
AIP-friendly	No
SCD/GAPS	Yes
lower carb	Use 1 teaspoon stevia extract powder in place of the honey and add 1/4 cup coconut milk.

chocolate dip

prep time: 5 minutes | *cook time:* 5 minutes | *yield:* 1/2 cup

This sauce makes a perfect dip for cookies or fruit; it's also delicious drizzled over cake. It uses dark chocolate for a lot of cocoa flavor without overpowering sweetness.

6 ounces dark chocolate (70% to 100% cacao), chopped

honey to taste

1. Melt the chocolate in a double boiler over medium heat. If you do not have a double boiler, use a heatproof glass mixing bowl over a saucepan filled with a few cups of water, making sure the water doesn't touch the bottom of the bowl. Add the honey and stir until well combined.

2. Remove from the heat and dip cookies or fruit in the chocolate while it is still warm. Store leftovers in the refrigerator. To reheat, melt the chocolate over a double boiler.

nut-free	Yes
egg-free	Yes
low FODMAP	Follow lower carb modification.
AIP-friendly	No
SCD/GAPS	No
lower carb	Use very dark chocolate with over 85% cacao content. Use stevia extract powder to taste in place of the honey.

nutritionist's note

Make sure to choose organic chocolate to avoid pesticides. Fair-trade chocolate usually results in a more nutritious and delicious product. Dark chocolate of 70% to 100% cacao is rich in magnesium and antioxidants, which make it a healthy choice as an occasional treat.

the basics

easy pomegranate sauce

prep time: 10 minutes | *cook time:* 10 minutes | *yield:* 1/2 cup

Pomegranates, a wonderfully tart fruit, are used abundantly in the Mediterranean region, and they're easy to find year-round in California, so we like to come up with new ways to incorporate them into meals. This sauce is delicious on the crêpes on page 102, on pancakes, or with grilled meats.

---

2 pomegranates

1 tablespoon honey

1. Halve the pomegranates crosswise and, working over a large bowl, bang on the back of the shell to dislodge the seeds. Break open the white shell with your fingers to free the rest of the seeds, discarding the white pith.

2. Place the pomegranate seeds and 1 cup of water in a blender and blend until almost smooth. Pour the mixture through a wire-mesh strainer set over a bowl, pressing against the seeds to extract as much liquid as possible. Discard the seeds.

3. Place the mixture in a small saucepan and bring to a simmer over medium heat. Add the honey and continue to simmer, uncovered, until the mixture thickens into a sauce and coats the back of the spoon, 7 to 10 minutes.

4. Leftovers can be stored in the refrigerator for 3 days.

nut-free	Yes
egg-free	Yes
low FODMAP	Use stevia extract powder to taste in place of the honey.
AIP-friendly	Yes
SCD/GAPS	Yes
lower carb	Use stevia extract powder to taste instead of the honey.

blueberry sauce

prep time: 5 minutes | *cook time:* 7 minutes | *yield:* 1 cup

This naturally sweet blueberry sauce goes great with Orange Blossom Pancakes (page 98) or the crêpes on page 102.

2 cups fresh blueberries

1 teaspoon grated orange zest

1/2 teaspoon orange blossom water (optional; see Chef's Tip, page 98)

1. In a medium saucepan, combine 1 cup of water, the blueberries, orange zest, and orange blossom water, if using.

2. Stir the mixture and bring it to a simmer over medium heat. Cover and continue to simmer for 5 to 7 minutes, or until the blueberries are soft and the sauce thickens slightly. Leftovers can be stored in the refrigerator for 3 to 4 days.

nut-free	Yes
egg-free	Yes
low FODMAP	Yes
AIP-friendly	Yes
SCD/GAPS	Yes
lower carb	Yes

béarnaise sauce

prep time: 5 minutes | *cook time:* 10 minutes | *yield:* scant 1 cup

Béarnaise sauce is a descendant of hollandaise sauce; both are made with butter and egg yolks, but the addition of pepper and tarragon sets béarnaise apart. Because Algeria was a French colony for 130 years, it is common to find classic French sauces like these served in restaurants in the capital, Algiers. Béarnaise sauce goes well with steak (such as Marinated Filet Mignon, page 228, pictured below), poached eggs, and baked fish, and it's also good cold as a dressing or dip.

5 large egg yolks

1/2 cup melted unsalted butter or ghee

fine sea salt and ground white pepper

1 teaspoon lemon juice

2 tablespoons minced fresh tarragon

1. Bring 2 cups of water to a simmer in a saucepan over medium heat. Put the egg yolks and a tablespoon of water in a heatproof glass mixing bowl.

2. Put the bowl of eggs over the simmering water to create a double boiler. Do not let the water touch the bottom of the bowl.

3. Whisk the egg yolks until they become stiff and begin to coat the whisk, about 3 minutes. Remove the egg mixture from heat. Whisk the melted butter into the egg yolks, pouring it in very slowly in a continuous stream.

4. When the mixture becomes thick, add a generous pinch of salt and white pepper, the lemon juice, and the tarragon and whisk until combined.

5. If the sauce is too thick, add a tablespoon of water to thin it out. Keep the sauce warm in a bowl of hot water to prevent it from separating before serving.

6. Leftovers can be kept in the refrigerator for 3 or 4 days. Gently reheat the sauce over a double boiler.

nut-free	Yes
egg-free	No
low FODMAP	Yes
AIP-friendly	No
SCD/GAPS	Yes
lower carb	Yes

chef's tip

The sauce can sit out for 20 to 30 minutes once it is made, which is helpful when you're cooking multiple dishes. If there is any sauce left over, it can be kept in the refrigerator for 3 to 4 days and reheated in a double boiler.

hollandaise sauce

prep time: 5 minutes | *cook time:* 10 minutes | *yield:* scant 1 cup

Hollandaise sauce is a breakfast classic and a must-have on any morning menu. We love poached eggs with hollandaise for brunch Sunday mornings, Crab Hash with Poached Eggs and Hollandaise (page 80), pictured below, or Eggs Florentine (page 84).

5 large egg yolks

1/2 cup melted unsalted butter or ghee

fine sea salt and ground white pepper

1 teaspoon lemon juice

1 teaspoon paprika

1. Bring a few inches of water to a simmer in a saucepan over medium heat. Put the egg yolks and 2 teaspoons of water in a heatproof glass mixing bowl.

2. Put the bowl of eggs over the simmering water to create a double boiler. Do not let the water touch the bottom of the bowl.

3. Whisk the egg yolks until they become stiff and begin to coat the whisk, about 3 minutes. Remove the egg mixture from heat. Whisk the melted butter into the egg yolks, pouring it in very slowly in a continuous stream.

4. When the mixture becomes thick, add a pinch of salt and white pepper, the lemon juice, and the paprika and whisk until combined.

5. If the sauce is too thick, add a tablespoon of water to thin it out. Keep the sauce warm in a bowl of hot water to prevent it from separating before serving.

6. Leftovers can be kept in the refrigerator for 3 or 4 days. Gently reheat the sauce over a double boiler.

nut-free	Yes
egg-free	No
low FODMAP	Yes
AIP-friendly	No
SCD/GAPS	Yes
lower carb	Yes

aioli

prep time: 5 minutes | *cook time:* n/a | *yield:* 2 cups

Aioli is a classic sauce made from garlic, olive oil, lemon juice, and egg yolks. (Sometimes mustard is added, but we've omitted it here.) It is usually served at room temperature and has its roots in Spanish and French cooking.

1 tablespoon lemon juice

1 tablespoon minced garlic

5 large egg yolks, room temperature

1/2 teaspoon fine sea salt

1/4 teaspoon ground white pepper

up to 2 cups extra-virgin olive oil

1. Put the lemon juice, garlic, egg yolks, salt, and white pepper in a food processor. Pulse the ingredients for about 10 seconds.

2. With the food processor running, very slowly add the olive oil in a thin, continuous stream.

3. When the aioli thickens, stop adding the oil. You may have some oil left over. If the mixture becomes too thick, add a few teaspoons of water and pulse until it reaches the desired consistency.

4. Keep the aioli in the refrigerator for up to 1 week.

chef's tip

If you do not like the flavor of olive oil, you can also use macadamia oil or avocado oil, both of which have a more neutral flavor, to make aioli or mayonnaise.

nutritionist's note

It is a good idea to use pastured eggs in recipes where the eggs are not cooked, like this one, because they are from healthier and more robust chickens.

nut-free	Yes
egg-free	No
low FODMAP	Use 2 tablespoons chopped scallions in place of the garlic.
AIP-friendly	No
SCD/GAPS	Yes
lower carb	Yes

easy homemade olive oil mayo

prep time: 5 minutes | *cook time:* n/a | *yield:* 2 cups

It can be intimidating to make mayonnaise the first time, but after that you will be a mayo master. This olive oil mayonnaise has a unique Mediterranean flavor and is great in lunches and salads.

---

1 tablespoon lemon juice

5 large egg yolks, room temperature

1/2 teaspoon sea salt

1/2 teaspoon ground white pepper

up to 2 cups extra-virgin olive oil

1. Put the lemon juice, egg yolks, salt, and white pepper in a food processor. Pulse the ingredients until well mixed.

2. With the food processor running, very slowly add the olive oil in a thin, continuous stream.

3. When the mixture thickens, stop adding oil. You may have some oil left over. If the mixture becomes too thick, add a few teaspoons of water until it reaches the desired consistency.

4. Keep the mayonnaise in the refrigerator for up to 1 week.

chef's tip

Using room temperature egg yolks helps the mayo to emulsify. Make sure to pour in the oil in a slow continuous stream for best results.

nutritionist's note

Almost all store-bought mayonnaise is made from soybean, corn, or canola oil. These oils are made genetically modified plants, which have not been thoroughly tested for safety. For optimal health, and to avoid adulterated ingredients, it is best to make your own mayonnaise at home.

nut-free	Yes
egg-free	No
low FODMAP	Yes
AIP-friendly	No
SCD/GAPS	Yes
lower carb	Yes

chicken broth

prep time: 15 minutes | *cook time:* at least 3 hours | *yield:* 10 to 12 cups

Bone broth was traditionally used as a starter for soups and stews because it concentrates the flavors from the bones. In the Middle East and North Africa, it's also common to use bone-in meat for cooking. All too often, in North America, bones are discarded, but that means missing out on the intensified flavor and nutritional benefits that come from bones. With this chicken broth, you get all the benefits of bone broth and the comforting taste of classic chicken soup.

filtered water

3 pounds chicken bones

1 tablespoon fine sea salt

2 tablespoons apple cider vinegar

OPTIONAL

1 teaspoon whole cloves

5 sprigs fresh thyme

3 bay leaves

1 teaspoon black peppercorns

1 cup tightly packed fresh parsley leaves

1 medium white onion, halved

3 stalks celery, roughly chopped

2 medium carrots, roughly chopped

SLOW COOKER INSTRUCTIONS

Put all the ingredients in a slow cooker and simmer on low for 8 to 12 hours. If using the optional ingredients, remove them after 3 hours to keep the broth from becoming bitter. Continue with Step 4.

1. Fill a large stockpot three-quarters full with filtered water. Place the chicken bones, salt, and apple cider vinegar in the pot.

2. If using the optional ingredients, place the cloves, thyme, bay leaves, peppercorns, and parsley in cheesecloth and tie with cotton string to make a sachet. Put the sachet and the vegetables in the pot.

3. Cover the pot with a lid and simmer for 3 hours over medium-low heat. If cooking longer, remove the sachet and vegetables at the 3-hour mark; otherwise, the broth may become bitter.

4. After 30 minutes, use a large spoon to skim off any scum that has risen to the top. Repeat this process after 1 hour and again right before removing the pot from the stove.

5. Strain the broth through a wire-mesh strainer. Discard the sachet and cooked vegetables.

6. If not using immediately, refrigerate the broth for 8 hours or overnight, then remove any of the fat that has hardened on the top.

7. Drink the broth plain or seasoned with salt to taste, or use it unseasoned as a base for soups or stews.

chef's tip

For broth that is sure to gel, use plenty of chicken heads and feet. Good-quality, inexpensive ones can often be found at farmers markets. Although you don't have to use the herbs and vegetables for this broth to work well in recipes, they add a rich flavor that's especially welcome if you're drinking the broth plain.

nutritionist's note

The importance of broth cannot be overstated, and the absence of this traditional food from the modern diet is a big contributor to the decline in modern health. Bone broth is a rich source of calcium, magnesium, and potassium, which support healthy blood pressure and normal blood sugar and help prevent cavities and osteoporosis. The gelatin in broth can help heal the digestive tract in people with IBS, and its cartilage and collagen can help people with joint aches and pains, including arthritis. Collagen can also help reduce the appearance of wrinkles and cellulite.

nut-free	Yes
egg-free	Yes
low FODMAP	Omit the onion.
AIP-friendly	Yes
SCD/GAPS	Yes
lower carb	Yes

beef broth

prep time: 30 minutes | *cook time:* 8 to 12 hours | *yield:* 10 to 12 cups

Beef bones are large and full of flavor that becomes intensified when roasted. While roasting the bones isn't critical, broth made from roasted bones does enhance the flavor of soups and stews. Other large bones can also be used to make this broth, such as lamb or goat.

3 pounds beef bones

filtered water

1 tablespoon sea salt

3 tablespoons apple cider vinegar

OPTIONAL

1 teaspoon whole cloves

5 sprigs fresh thyme

3 bay leaves

1 teaspoon black peppercorns

1 cup tightly packed fresh parsley leaves

1 medium white onion, halved

3 stalks celery, roughly chopped

2 medium carrots, roughly chopped

SLOW COOKER INSTRUCTIONS

Skip the step of roasting the bones to save time. Put all the ingredients in a slow cooker and simmer on low for 8 to 12 hours. If using the optional ingredients, remove them after 3 hours to keep the broth from becoming bitter. Continue with Step 5.

1. Preheat the oven to 350°F. Roast the beef bones on a rimmed sheet pan until brown, about 30 minutes.

2. Fill a large stockpot three-quarters full with filtered water. Place the roasted bones, salt, and apple cider vinegar in the pot.

3. If using the optional ingredients, place the cloves, thyme, bay leaves, peppercorns, and parsley in cheesecloth and tie with cotton string to make a sachet. Put the sachet and the vegetables in the pot.

4. Cover the pot with a lid and simmer for 8 to 12 hours over medium-low heat.

5. After 30 minutes, use a large spoon to skim off any scum that has risen to the top. Repeat this process after 1 hour.

6. If using the optional ingredients, remove the sachet and vegetables at the 3-hour mark; otherwise, the broth may become bitter.

7. After 8 to 12 hours, skim off any scum once more and strain the broth through a wire-mesh strainer.

8. If not using immediately, refrigerate the broth overnight, then remove any of the fat that has hardened on the top.

9. Drink the broth plain or seasoned with salt to taste, or use it as an unseasoned base for soups or stews.

chef's tip

Making broth yourself is a great way to save money because you can use bones and cartilage that are usually discarded. I grew up eating lots of broth, because it fills you up without the need for a large portion of meat, and for my family of eleven, meat was very expensive.

nutritionist's note

Bones are full of minerals that are infused into the broth, and they can be used over and over until they disintegrate. Save the bones from each batch of broth in a freezer bag and add new ones from other meals. Broth can be cooked for 6 to 48 hours, depending on your preference, and the longer it cooks, the more minerals become infused in the broth.

nut-free	Yes
egg-free	Yes
low FODMAP	Omit the onion.
AIP-friendly	Yes
SCD/GAPS	Yes
lower carb	Yes

fish broth

prep time: 15 minutes | *cook time:* 1 hour | *yield:* 10 to 12 cups

Fish broth is a wonderful way to add flavor to dishes such as Cioppino (page 282) or Paella (292). It may seem unpleasant to work with fish bones or heads at first, but it will be worth it the effort when the final dish is on the table.

---

filtered water

3 pounds fish bones or heads

1 teaspoon sea salt

1 tablespoon apple cider vinegar

OPTIONAL

1 teaspoon whole cloves

5 sprigs fresh thyme

3 bay leaves

1 teaspoon black peppercorns

1 handful fresh parsley stems

3 stalks celery, roughly chopped

1 medium white onion, roughly chopped

1. Fill a large stockpot three-quarters full with filtered water. Place the fish bones, salt, and apple cider vinegar in the pot.

2. If using the optional ingredients, place the cloves, thyme, bay leaves, peppercorns, and parsley stems in cheesecloth and tie with cotton string to make a sachet. Put the sachet and vegetables in the pot.

3. Cover the pot with a lid and bring the liquid to a simmer over medium heat. After 30 minutes, use a large spoon to skim off any scum or foam that has formed on the top. Continue to simmer, covered, for another 30 minutes.

4. Skim the surface of the broth once more with a spoon. Strain the broth through a fine wire-mesh strainer. Discard the bones and sachet.

5. If not using immediately, refrigerate the broth for 8 hours or overnight, then discard any fat that has formed on the top. Use the broth in seafood recipes or drink it, seasoned to taste with salt.

SLOW COOKER INSTRUCTIONS

Place all the ingredients in a slow cooker and fill it three-quarters of the way full with filtered water. Cook for 4 to 6 hours on low and strain through a fine-mesh strainer. Continue with Step 5.

chef's tip

The fat that forms on the broth during refrigeration can be saved and used for cooking later, but some people feel it has an off flavor. I tend to discard it or feed it to pets.

nutritionist's note

Broth is well known for its healing properties, which include building strong nails, teeth, and bones. It also has benefits for healing the digestive tract, which can become irritated from years of eating hard-to-digest foods such as grains, vegetable oils, and sugar.

nut-free	Yes
egg-free	Yes
low FODMAP	Omit the onion.
AIP-friendly	Yes
SCD/GAPS	Yes
lower carb	Yes

ghee

prep time: n/a | *cook time:* 20 to 30 minutes | *yield:* 4 cups

Clarified butter is butter that has been heated, which causes the dairy proteins to separate and sink to the bottom of the pan and creates a richer flavor. It's used in many traditional cooking preparations. Ghee is clarified butter that has been cooked a little longer to remove all the moisture and caramelize the milk solids, which are then strained out. The extended cooking time also creates a unique nutty flavor. Ghee has a long shelf life and can be stored, in or out of the refrigerator, for several months.

---

2 pounds unsalted butter

1. Melt the butter in a heavy saucepan over low heat. Continue to cook at a gentle simmer for about 20 to 30 minutes.

2. Use a large spoon to skim the white foam from the surface every few minutes. Once all the white foam is removed and any remaining solids are browned and have sunk to the bottom of the pan, strain the ghee through a cheesecloth-lined strainer over a bowl. Discard any solids remaining at the bottom of the pan.

3. Transfer the ghee to a glass container for storing. Refrigeration is optional because ghee is very shelf-stable.

SLOW COOKER INSTRUCTIONS

Due to the large size of most slow cookers and the long cooking time involved, you'll need 4 pounds unsalted butter, not 2, and the yield is 8 cups ghee.

Place 4 pounds unsalted butter in a slow cooker. Cook for 3 hours on low. Carefully pour the golden liquid into a bowl, leaving the dairy proteins behind in the bottom of the slow cooker. Strain the ghee through cheesecloth to remove any remaining solids. Continue with Step 3.

nutritionist's note

Ghee is a traditional fat that is tolerated by many people with dairy sensitivity because the dairy protein, casein, has mostly been removed. It is also ideal for high-heat cooking because it has a very high smoke point, meaning it will not oxidize and create free radicals. Always choose butter from grass-fed cows, which is higher in fat-soluble vitamins and conjugated linoleic acid, which are both important for a healthy immune system and weight regulation.

special equipment

- *1 (12-inch square) piece cheesecloth*

nut-free	Yes
egg-free	Yes
low FODMAP	Yes
AIP-friendly	No
SCD/GAPS	Yes
lower carb	Yes

tzatziki sauce

prep time: 10 minutes, plus 8 hours to chill the coconut milk (if using) |
cook time: n/a | *yield:* 2 1/2 cups

Tzatziki is a traditional Greek condiment used with meats (such as Grilled Beef Heart Skewers, page 314, pictured below), as a dip, or for salad dressing. It's refreshing and light, and it's perfect for summer barbecues.

---

1 1/2 cups plain full-fat yogurt or cream from 2 (13 1/2-ounce) cans full-fat coconut milk, chilled overnight

1 cucumber, peeled, seeded, and quartered

juice from 1/2 lemon

fine sea salt and ground black pepper to taste

1 handful fresh dill

1/4 cup tightly packed fresh mint leaves

2 to 3 cloves garlic, peeled

1. If using coconut milk, make sure it is very cold. Scoop off the cream that has risen to the top of the can and save the coconut water for another use.

2. Place all the ingredients in a food processor and pulse until smooth. Store leftovers in the refrigerator for 3 to 4 days.

nut-free	Yes
egg-free	Yes
low FODMAP	Omit the garlic. Add 1/2 cup chopped scallions to the food processor.
AIP-friendly	Use the coconut milk option in place of the yogurt.
SCD/GAPS	Yes
lower carb	Yes

tahini dipping sauce

prep time: 2 minutes | *cook time:* n/a | *yield:* 1 cup

Perfectly creamy and with a hint of garlic, this sauce gets most of its great flavor from the sesame seeds. It makes a delicious salad dressing as well as a dip.

1 cup tahini (sesame seed paste)

fine sea salt and ground black pepper to taste

1/4 cup lemon juice

1 tablespoon garlic powder or 1 clove garlic, minced

1/4 cup chopped fresh cilantro, for garnish

Whisk all the ingredients together in a small bowl with 1/2 cup water. If it's too thick, add more water as needed. It will keep for 4 to 5 days in the refrigerator. Garnish with the cilantro to serve.

nut-free	Yes
egg-free	Yes
low FODMAP	Use 1/4 cup chopped fresh cilantro in place of the garlic.
AIP-friendly	No. Use Tzatziki Sauce (page 392) instead.
SCD/GAPS	Yes
lower carb	Yes

harissa

prep time: 5 minutes, plus 1 hour to soak the peppers |
cook time: n/a | *yield:* 2 1/2 cups

Harissa is a very strong, hot condiment that is used in North Africa and the Middle East. A little goes a long way to spice up tajines and soups.

---

6 ounces dried red chili peppers

1 tablespoon ground caraway

1 tablespoon ground coriander

1 tablespoon ground cumin

1 tablespoon dried mint leaves

1 teaspoon fine sea salt

1 teaspoon ground black pepper

1/4 cup extra-virgin olive oil, plus more for the top

1 tablespoon tomato paste

5 cloves garlic, peeled

2 tablespoons lemon juice

1. Remove the stems from the chili peppers and shake out as many seeds as possible. Discard the seeds. Soak the chili peppers in 2 cups of water for 1 hour.

2. Place the chili peppers with the soaking water, caraway, coriander, cumin, mint, salt, pepper, olive oil, tomato paste, garlic, and lemon juice in the food processor and pulse until smooth. The texture should be similar to a thick tomato sauce. Add a few tablespoons of water if it is too thick.

3. Transfer the paste to a glass storage container and top with a thin layer of olive oil to preserve it. It will keep for several weeks in the refrigerator.

nut-free	Yes
egg-free	Yes
low FODMAP	Use 1 tablespoon garlic-infused olive oil in place of the garlic and 1/2 cup chopped tomatoes in place of the tomato paste.
AIP-friendly	No
SCD/GAPS	Yes
lower carb	Yes

harissa dipping sauce

prep time: 5 minutes | *cook time:* n/a | *yield:* 1 1/2 cups

Harissa is very hot by itself, so this recipe tones it down with more neutral ingredients. This dipping sauce pairs well with meats, including Crispy Fried Chicken Tenders (page 218) and the meatloaf on page 306.

6 ounces tomato paste

2 tablespoons honey

1/2 cup Harissa (page 394)

1 tablespoon ground cumin

1 teaspoon ground paprika

1/2 teaspoon fine sea salt

1/2 teaspoon ground black pepper

1. In a small bowl, mix together all of the ingredients. Add a few tablespoons of water until it reaches desired consistency, if needed

2. Transfer the sauce to a glass storage container and top with a thin layer of olive oil to preserve it. It will keep for several weeks in the refrigerator.

nut-free	Yes
egg-free	Yes
low FODMAP	No. Use Tahini Dipping Sauce (page 393) instead.
AIP-friendly	No
SCD/GAPS	Yes
lower carb	Use 1/2 teaspoon stevia extract powder in place of the honey.

roasted pepper tutorial

prep time: 5 minutes | *cook time:* 20 minutes | *yield:* 2 to 3 cups

Caitlin: I never used to want to go to the effort of roasting peppers, but ever since Nabil taught me how easy it is, I don't think twice about it. And it's definitely worth taking the extra step: roasting intensifies the flavor of the peppers and makes every recipe better. These colorful, delicious peppers are used in Mediterranean Seafood Salad (page 266) and Roasted Pepper Dip (page 122).

2 tablespoons coconut oil or ghee, melted, for greasing the pan

4 to 6 bell peppers, assorted colors, washed and dried

1. Preheat the oven to 400°F. Grease a rimmed baking sheet with the melted fat. Place the peppers on the baking sheet.

2. Place the peppers in the oven and bake for 10 minutes, or until slightly browned on top. Flip the peppers over with tongs and cook for 5 more minutes. Then flip them again to an area that does not look browned and cook for 5 more minutes. When the peppers have deflated and the skin is starting to peel off, remove them from the oven.

3. Place the peppers in a container with a lid, such as a Dutch oven or covered casserole dish, for 10 minutes. This will trap the steam inside and make the skins easier to remove.

4. Place the peppers on a plate and peel off the skins. Discard the skins, stems, and seeds. Slice the peppers into thin strips and use them for salads or in dips.

5. Store for up to 5 days in the refrigerator.

nut-free	Yes
egg-free	Yes
low FODMAP	Yes
AIP-friendly	No
SCD/GAPS	Yes
lower carb	Yes

Place the peppers on the prepared baking sheet.

When the peppers are slightly browned on top, flip them over with tongs.

When the peppers have deflated and the skin is starting to peel off, remove them from the oven.

Place the peppers in a container with a lid, cover, and let sit for 10 minutes.

Peel the peppers and discard the skins, stems, and seeds.

Slice the peppers into thin strips and use them for salads or in dips.

harissa spice blend

prep time: 5 minutes | *cook time:* n/a | *yield:* about 3/4 cup

This is the blend of spices used in the North African hot sauce called harissa (see page 394). When you want to add some spice to grilled or slow-cooked meats, this is the blend to turn to.

3 tablespoons crushed red pepper

3 tablespoons dried mint

1 tablespoon ground caraway seeds

1 tablespoon ground cumin

1 tablespoon ground coriander

1 tablespoon garlic powder

1 tablespoon dried grated lemon peel

1 tablespoon fine sea salt

1 tablespoon ground black pepper

1. Mix the spices and herbs in a small bowl until well combined.

2. To use, rub the mixture on meat or mix it with ground meat before cooking.

nut-free	Yes
egg-free	Yes
low FODMAP	Use 3 tablespoons dried chives in place of the garlic.
AIP-friendly	Use 3 tablespoons ground ginger in place of the red pepper, caraway, and cumin. Use 3 tablespoons dried cilantro leaves in place of the coriander.
SCD/GAPS	Yes
lower carb	Yes

chef's tip

If you want to use this spice blend wet—for instance, as a marinade or drizzled over vegetables or meat—just add a few tablespoons of extra-virgin olive oil.

Although you can dry and grate your own lemon peel, you can also buy it at many grocery stores and online (try thespicehouse.com).

ras el hanout

prep time: 5 minutes | *cook time:* n/a | *yield:* about 3/4 cup

Traditionally, this spice blend is made by the owner of a spice shop or a restaurant as a representation of the best the owner has to offer. It is used in North Africa in savory dishes and can have many variations. In southeastern Algeria, it is used in as a spice for tajines.

---

1 tablespoon ground cardamom

1 tablespoon ground nutmeg

1 tablespoon ground allspice

1 tablespoon cayenne pepper

1 tablespoon ground coriander

1 tablespoon ground cinnamon

1 tablespoon ground turmeric

1 tablespoon ground ginger

1 tablespoon fine sea salt

1 tablespoon ground black pepper

1 1/2 teaspoons ground star anise

1 1/2 teaspoons ground cloves

In a small bowl, blend together the spices. Store in an airtight container in a cupboard, away from light. This quantity is enough to season 6 pounds of meat.

nut-free	Yes
egg-free	Yes
low FODMAP	Yes
AIP-friendly	Omit the nutmeg, cayenne pepper, and coriander. Add 1 teaspoon sumac.
SCD/GAPS	Yes
lower carb	Yes

tajine spice blend

prep time: 5 minutes | *cook time:* n/a | *yield:* about 3/4 cup

This spice blend can be used as the base of slow-cooked meat dish or as a rub for grilled meat.

1/4 cup ground cumin

2 tablespoons paprika

2 tablespoons fine sea salt

1 tablespoon ground coriander

1 tablespoon ground black pepper

1 tablespoon dried grated lemon peel (see Chef's Tip, page 398)

4 pinches saffron

In a small bowl, blend together the spices. Store in an airtight container in a cupboard, away from light. This quantity is enough to season 6 pounds of meat.

nut-free	Yes
egg-free	Yes
low FODMAP	Yes
AIP-friendly	Omit the cumin, coriander, and paprika. Add 1/4 cup ground ginger and 1/4 cup turmeric.
SCD/GAPS	Yes
lower carb	Yes

za'atar spice blend

prep time: 5 minutes | *cook time:* n/a | *yield:* 1 cup

This Arabic spice blend is used all over the Middle East and Africa. The ingredients vary by region, but the focus is always on the oregano and sesame seeds. This savory spice blend is wonderful on roasted chicken or duck.

3 tablespoons dried ground oregano

3 tablespoons dried mint leaves

3 tablespoons sesame seeds

1 tablespoon sumac

1 tablespoon ground cumin

1 tablespoon fine sea salt

1 tablespoon ground black pepper

1 tablespoon dried ground thyme

1 tablespoon ground coriander

1 tablespoon ground star anise

In a small bowl, blend together the spices. Store in an airtight container in a cupboard, away from light. This quantity is enough to season 6 pounds of meat.

nut-free	Yes
egg-free	Yes
low FODMAP	Yes
AIP-friendly	Use 3 tablespoons dried cilantro leaves in place of the cumin and coriander. Omit the sesame seeds.
SCD/GAPS	Yes
lower carb	Yes

herbes de provence

prep time: 5 minutes | *cook time:* n/a | *yield:* about 3/4 cup

This is a wonderful savory blend used in Provence, a coastal region of France that is known for its food and agriculture. Provence is on the Mediterranean Sea, near Corsica, and it shares a border with Italy. Herbes de Provence goes well with fish and shellfish.

2 tablespoons crushed bay leaves

2 tablespoons dried thyme leaves

2 tablespoons dried savory

2 tablespoons ground marjoram

2 tablespoons dried oregano leaves

2 tablespoons dried ground sage

2 tablespoons dried rosemary leaves

In a small bowl, blend together the spices. Store in an airtight container in a cupboard, away from light. This quantity is enough to season 6 pounds of meat.

nut-free	Yes
egg-free	Yes
low FODMAP	Yes
AIP-friendly	Yes
SCD/GAPS	Yes
lower carb	Yes

breakfast index

76 Meatball Chakchouka

78 Herbes de Provence Biscuits

80 Crab Hash with Poached Eggs and Hollandaise

82 Fried Sweet Potato Omelet

84 Eggs Florentine

86 Swiss Chard and Garlic Frittata

88 Savory Breakfast Sausage

90 Spinach and Olive Scramble

92 Cumin and Cauliflower Frittata

94 Pomegranate-Blueberry Smoothie

94 Apricot-Orange Smoothie

96 Cinnamon Spice Pancakes

98 Orange Blossom Pancakes

100 Autoimmune-Friendly Banana Pancakes

102 Crêpes with Pomegranate Sauce

104 Cinnamon-Apricot Breakfast Cookies

106 Gingery Sweet Potato Muffins

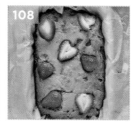
108 Strawberry Coffee Cake

110 Apricot Breakfast Bread

112 Easy Cinnamon and Ginger Granola

114 Vanilla Coconut Yogurt

115 Coconut Icing

appetizers index

118
Roasted Garlic
Cauliflower Hummus

120
Eggplant Dip
(Baba Ghanoush)

122
Roasted Pepper Dip
(Hmis)

124
Cilantro Crackers

126
Tabouli Salad

128
Beet and Carrot Salad

130
Easy Paleo Falafel

132
Easy Sweet Potato
Salad

134
Minty Cucumber and
Tomato Salad

136
Arugula and
Artichoke Salad with
Citrus Dressing

138
Shaved Jicama
Salad with Citrus
Vinaigrette

140
Caprese Salad with
Basil Dressing

142
Mini Pitas

soups index

146

Tangy Lamb Stew with Saffron and Ginger (Harira)

148

Cumin Cauliflower Soup

150

Cabbage and Meatball Soup

152

Cilantro Pumpkin Soup

154

Basil Minestrone Soup

156

Nora's Green Bean Soup

158

Caramelized Onion Soup

160

Almond Meatball Soup (M'touam)

pizza & pasta index

166
Mediterranean Paleo Pizza

170
Cashew Pizza Crust

170
Sunflower Pizza Crust

171
Lower Carb Pizza Crust

171
AIP Pizza Crust

172
Paleo Pasta

176
Ravioli

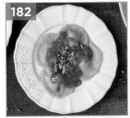
178
Zucchini Noodles

182
Basic Tomato Sauce

183
Puttanesca Sauce

184
Alfredo Clam Sauce

185
Mushroom Sauce

186
Mint Pesto

187
Autoimmune-Friendly No-Mato Sauce

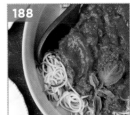
188
Bolognese Meat Sauce

190
Shrimp Alfredo

192
Spaghetti and Cumin-Spiced Meatballs

poultry index

196

Chicken and Olive
Tajine

198

Harissa-Spiced
Chicken Wings

200

Savory Chicken
Kebabs

202

Spicy Chicken Tajine

204

Fig and Ginger
Chicken Tajine

206

Saffron Braised
Chicken

208

Za'atar and Garlic
Roasted Duck

210

Kabylie Cinnamon
Chicken Tajine

212

Lamb-Stuffed Chicken
Thighs

214

Nacera's Lemon
Ginger Chicken Tajine

216

Za'atar Brick Chicken

218

Crispy Fried Chicken
Tenders

red meat index

222 Peppers and Zucchini Stuffed with Lamb (Lamb Dolmas)

224 Cinnamon Braised Beef Tajine

226 Top Sirloin with Mushroom Reduction Sauce

228 Marinated Filet Mignon with Béarnaise Sauce

230 Harissa Braised Short Ribs

232 Lamb and Vegetable Tajine

234 Siva's Cauliflower and Meatballs

236 Lamb Kebabs

238 Sweet Lamb Stew (L'ham Hlou)

240 Rosemary Leg of Lamb

242 Spiced Rack of Lamb

244 Kefta Lamb Kebabs (Persian Version)

246 Stuffed Cabbage (Cabbage Dolmas)

248 Shish Kebabs

250 Beef and Artichokes

252 Mediterranean Burgers

254 Braised Beef, Artichokes, and Peas (Jelbana)

256 Paleo Moussaka

seafood index

Salmon and Crab
Roll-Ups

Fattoush Shrimp
Salad

Lemon Garlic Shrimp

Mediterranean
Seafood Salad

Seared Tuna Salade
Niçoise

Sardine Cakes

Zesty Crab Cakes
with Aioli

Sardine Salad with
Capers and Olives

Crispy Fried Sardines

Seafood Brochette

Almond-Crusted Cod

Cioppino

Pistachio-Crusted
Sole

Fennel and Herb–
Stuffed Fish (Hout-
Fel-Koucha)

Creamy Cilantro
Salmon

Spinach-Stuffed
Calamari

Paella

Lemon-Butter
Steamed Mussels

odd bits index

298
Mediterranean
Chicken Liver Pâté

300
Braised Liver and
Mushrooms

302
Grilled Liver Kebabs
(Kibda)

304
Algerian Beef Heart
Chili

306
Zesty Liver and Beef
Meatloaf

308
Beef Tongue with
Green Olives

310
Allspice Oxtail Soup

312
Liver Meatballs with
Mushroom Gravy

314
Grilled Beef Heart
Skewers

vegetable sides index

318
Sautéed Green Beans with Lamb Bacon

320
Perfect Sweet Potato Fries

322
Savory Sweet Potato Cakes

324
Warm Eggplant and Tomato Salad with Mint (Zaalouk)

326
Mock Potato Salad

328
Roasted Eggplant Casserole

330
Golden Raisin Slaw

332
Cauliflower Couscous

334
Charmoula Roasted Vegetables

335
Marinated Olives

336
Fermented Probiotic Pickles

desserts index

340
Pistachio and Chocolate Biscotti

342
Lemon Pound Cake (Mouskoutchou)

344
Almond Tea Cookies (El Mechewak)

346
Fig Brownies

348
Chocolate Pot de Crème

350
Chocolate Tahini Truffles

352
Crème Caramel

354
Pâte d'Amande

355
Stuffed Dates

356
Flourless Chocolate Cake

358
Chocolate Pistachio Bites

360
Samia's Crescent Cookies

362
Pistachio Tapioca Pudding

364
Almond Squares (El Makhabaz)

366
Chocolate-Kissed Coconut Macaroons

368
Sesame Candies

370
Strawberry Tart

372
Turkish Apricot Ice Cream

374
Madeleines

376
Cashew Cream Icing

377
Chocolate Dip

the basics index

380

Easy Pomegranate
Sauce

381

Blueberry Sauce

382

Béarnaise Sauce

383

Hollandaise Sauce

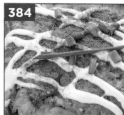
384

Aioli

385

Easy Homemade
Olive Oil Mayo

386

Chicken Broth / Beef
Broth / Fish Broth

390

Ghee

392

Tzatziki Sauce

393

Tahini Dipping Sauce

394

Harissa

395

Harissa Dipping
Sauce

396

Roasted Pepper
Tutorial

398

Harissa Spice Blend

400

Ras El Hanout and
Tajine Spice Blend

401

Za'atar Spice Blend
and Herbes de
Provence

some of our favorite, not-to-be missed recipes

mediterranean paleo menus

 cook DAY OF This dish can be cooked the day of the event.

make AHEAD This dish should be cooked prior to the day of the event.

aip

This assortment of dishes is a fantastic way to entertain while sticking to your autoimmune Paleo plan. The wonderful flavors of the Mediterranean, such as sweet cinnamon, tangy cilantro, and spicy garlic, fit beautifully on the AIP plan.

154 — make AHEAD
Basil Minestrone Soup

264 — cook DAY OF
Lemon Garlic Shrimp

171 — make AHEAD
AIP Pizza Crust

256 — make AHEAD
Paleo Moussaka

372 — make AHEAD
Turkish Apricot Ice Cream

brunch

This menu is perfect for a special Sunday brunch, whether it's for Mother's Day, a bridal or baby shower, or just a get-together with family and friends. It's a great mixture of breakfast favorites and a few light lunch dishes, such as peppery arugula salad and paprika-spiced fries.

90 — cook DAY OF
Spinach and Olive Scramble

78 — make AHEAD
Herbes de Provence Biscuits

82 — cook DAY OF
Fried Sweet Potato Omelet

320 — cook DAY OF
Perfect Sweet Potato Fries

102 — cook DAY OF
Crêpes with Pomegranate Sauce (can be served at room temp)

106 — make AHEAD
Gingery Sweet Potato Muffins

136 — cook DAY OF
Arugula and Artichoke Salad with Citrus Dressing

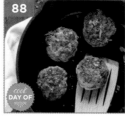
88 — cook DAY OF
Savory Breakfast Sausage

sunday family supper

These casual and comforting dishes, such as stuffed peppers and sweet potato cakes, will have everyone in your family asking for seconds.

266
Mediterranean Seafood Salad

146
Tangy Lamb Stew with Saffron and Ginger (Harira)

128
Beet and Carrot Salad

208
Za'atar and Garlic Roasted Duck

222
Peppers and Zucchini Stuffed with Lamb (Lamb Dolmas)

332
Cauliflower Couscous

322
Savory Sweet Potato Cakes

360
Samia's Crescent Cookies

tapas party

If you're hosting a cocktail party, this small-dishes menu is ideal—guests can easily eat while standing up, and the food can be passed around on trays or arranged on platters. Your guests will be delighted with the heat of the harissa wings followed by the garlic cauliflower hummus on top of crunchy cilantro crackers.

198
Harissa-Spiced Chicken Wings

335
Marinated Olives

140
Caprese Salad with Basil Dressing

118
Roasted Garlic Cauliflower Hummus

120
Eggplant Dip (Baba Ghanoush)

126
Tabouli Salad

142
Mini Pitas

124
Cilantro Crackers

130
Easy Paleo Falafel (make sauce ahead of time)

casual dinner party

With this menu, you don't need to be a professional chef to impress your friends at a dinner party. The flavor of the roasted peppers combines perfectly with the mint in the kebabs and the cucumber salad.

158
Caramelized Onion Soup (make ahead, finish day of)

138
Shaved Jicama Salad with Citrus Vinaigrette

122
Roasted Pepper Dip (Hmis)

124
Cilantro Crackers

244
Kefta Lamb Kebabs

134
Minty Cucumber and Tomato Salad

292
Paella

356
Flourless Chocolate Cake

food nerd party

This is the perfect combination of dishes to serve to the foodies and gourmet cooks in your life. They'll be impressed with all the exotic flavors and eclectic cuts of meat in these hearty offerings.

298
Mediterranean Chicken Liver Pâté

124
Cilantro Crackers

138
Shaved Jicama Salad with Citrus Vinaigrette

314
Grilled Beef Heart Skewers

312
Liver Meatballs with Mushroom Gravy

270
Sardine Cakes

308
Beef Tongue with Green Olives

204
Fig and Ginger Chicken Tajine

358
Chocolate Pistachio Bites

sources

Calton, Jason, and Mira Calton. *Rich Food Poor Food: The Ultimate Grocery Purchasing System (GPS)*. Malibu, CA: Primal Blueprint Publishing, 2013.

Gedgaudas, Nora. *Primal Body, Primal Mind: Beyond the Paleo Diet for Total Health and a Longer Life*. Rochester, VT: Healing Arts Press, 2011.

Kresser, Chris. *Your Personal Paleo Code: The 3-Step Plan to Lose Weight, Reverse Disease, and Stay Fit and Healthy for Life*. New York: Little, Brown and Company, 2013.

Moore, Jimmy, and Eric Westman. *Keto Clarity: Your Definitive Guide to the Benefits of a Low-Carb, High-Fat Diet*. Las Vegas: Victory Belt Publishing, 2014.

Sisson, Mark. *The Primal Blueprint: Reprogram Your Genes for Effortless Weight Loss, Vibrant Health, and Boundless Energy*. Malibu, CA: Primal Nutrition, 2009.

Wolfe, Liz. *Eat the Yolks: Discover Paleo, Fight Food Lies, and Reclaim Your Health*. Las Vegas: Victory Belt Publishing, 2014.

The World's Healthiest Foods (www.whfoods.com). George Mateljan Foundation for the World's Healthiest Foods.

resources

Where to Find High-Quality Foods

Meat, Poultry, and Eggs

Tropical Traditions (www.tropicaltraditions.com)

U.S. Wellness Meats (www.grasslandbeef.com)

Seafood

Tropical Traditions (www.tropicaltraditions.com)

Vital Choice (www.vitalchoice.com)

Fats and Oils

Coconut butter, coconut oil, palm oil, palm shortening: Tropical Traditions (www.tropicaltraditions.com)

Coconut milk: Amazon.com

Ghee: Pure Indian Foods (www.pureindianfoods.com), Tin Star Foods (www.tinstarfoods.com)

Olive oil: Kasandrinos (kasandrinos.com)

Flours

Blanched almond flour: Honeyville (shop.honeyville.com)

Tapioca starch: Nuts.com

Sweeteners

Coconut sugar: Madhava (www.madhavasweeteners.com)

Honey, maple syrup: Tropical Traditions (www.tropicaltraditions.com)

Stevia powder extract: SweetLeaf (sweetleaf.com)

Other

Almond butter: Artisana (www.artisanafoods.com)

Coconut aminos: Coconut Secret (www.coconutsecret.com)

Grass-fed gelatin: Great Lakes Gelatin (www.greatlakesgelatin.com)

Sea salt: Real Salt (realsalt.com)

Helpful Websites and Blogs

Balanced Bites (balancedbites.com)

Chris Kresser (chriskresser.com)

Ditch the Wheat (ditchthewheat.com)

Grass Fed Girl (grassfedgirl.com)

Healthy Living How To (healthylivinghowto.com)

Holistically Engineered (holisticallyengineered.com)

Just in Health Wellness Clinic (justinhealth.com)

Meatified (meatified.com)

Nourishing Our Children (nourishingourchildren.org)

The Paleo Mom (paleomom.com)

Paleo Parents (paleoparents.com)

Popular Paleo (popularpaleo.com)

Primal Palate (primalpalate.com)

Real Food Liz (realfoodliz.com)

Rubies & Radishes (rubiesandradishes.com)

The Spunky Coconut (thespunkycoconut.com)

Zenbelly (zenbelly.com)

Recommended Reading

Ballantyne, Sarah. *The Paleo Approach: Reverse Autoimmune Disease and Heal Your Body.* Las Vegas: Victory Belt Publishing, 2013.

Ballantyne, Sarah. *The Paleo Approach Cookbook: A Detailed Guide to Heal Your Body and Nourish Your Soul.* Las Vegas: Victory Belt Publishing, 2013.

Broznya, Kelly V. *The Paleo Chocolate Lovers' Cookbook.* Las Vegas: Victory Belt Publishing, 2013.

Joulwan, Melissa. *Well Fed: Paleo Recipes for People Who Love to Eat.* Austin, TX: Smudge Publishing, 2011.

Kresser, Chris. *Your Personal Paleo Code: The 3-Step Plan to Lose Weight, Reverse Disease, and Stay Fit and Healthy for Life.* New York: Little, Brown and Company, 2013.

Mayfield, Julie and Charles. *Paleo Comfort Foods: Homestyle Cooking for a Gluten-Free Kitchen.* Las Vegas: Victory Belt Publishing, 2011.

Sanfilippo, Diane. *Practical Paleo: A Customized Approach to Health and a Whole-Foods Lifestyle.* Las Vegas: Victory Belt Publishing, 2012.

Sanfilippo, Diane. *The 21-Day Sugar Deotx: Bust Sugar & Carb Cravings Naturally.* Las Vegas: Victory Belt Publishing, 2013.

Sanfilippo, Diane. *The 21-Day Sugar Deotx Cookbook: Over 100 Recipes for Any Program Level.* Las Vegas: Victory Belt Publishing, 2013.

Staley, Bill, and Hayley Mason. *Gather: The Art of Paleo Entertaining.* Las Vegas: Victory Belt Publishing, 2013.

Staley, Bill, and Hayley Mason. *Make It Paleo: Over 200 Grain-Free Recipes for Any Occasion.* Las Vegas: Victory Belt Publishing, 2011.

Tam, Michelle, and Henry Fong. *Nom Nom Paleo: Food for Humans.* Kansas City, MO: Andrews McMeel Publishing, 2013.

Vartanian, Arsy. *The Paleo Slow Cooker: Healthy, Gluten-Free Meals the Easy Way.* Minneapolis, MN: Race Point Publishing, 2013.

Walker, Danielle. *Against All Grain: Delectable Paleo Recipes to Eat Well and Feel Great.* Las Vegas: Victory Belt Publishing, 2013.

Wolf, Robb. *The Paleo Solution: The Original Human Diet.* Las Vegas: Victory Belt Publishing, 2010.

Wolfe, Liz. *Eat the Yolks: Discover Paleo, Fight Food Lies, and Reclaim Your Health.* Las Vegas: Victory Belt Publishing, 2014.

recipe allergen index

breakfast

	page number	nut-free	egg-free	low FODMAP	AIP-friendly	SCD/GAPS	lower carb
Meatball Chakchouka	76		M	M			
Herbes de Provence Biscuits	78			M		M	M
Crab Hash with Poached Eggs and Hollandaise	80			M		M	M
Fried Sweet Potato Omelet	82					M	
Eggs Florentine	84						
Swiss Chard and Garlic Frittata	86			M			
Savory Breakfast Sausage	88				M		
Spinach and Olive Scramble	90				M	M	
Cumin and Cauliflower Frittata	92			M			
Pomegranate-Blueberry Smoothie	94			M			M
Apricot-Orange Smoothie	94			M			M
Cinnamon Spice Pancakes	96			M			
Orange Blossom Pancakes	98	M		M			
Autoimmune-Friendly Banana Pancakes	100			M		M	
Crêpes with Pomegranate Sauce	102					M	M
Cinnamon-Apricot Breakfast Cookies	104	M		M			
Gingery Sweet Potato Muffins	106			M		M	M
Strawberry Coffee Cake	108			M			
Apricot Breakfast Bread	110	M		M			
Easy Cinnamon and Ginger Granola	112	M		M		M	M
Vanilla Coconut Yogurt	114						
Coconut Icing	115			M		M	M

appetizers

	page number	nut-free	egg-free	low FODMAP	AIP-friendly	SCD/GAPS	lower carb
Roasted Garlic Cauliflower Hummus	118			M	M		
Eggplant Dip (Baba Ghanoush)	120			M			
Roasted Pepper Dip (Hmis)	122			M			
Cilantro Crackers	124	M		M		M	
Tabouli Salad	126			M	M		
Beet and Carrot Salad	128						
Easy Paleo Falafel	130	M	M	M			
Easy Sweet Potato Salad	132			M		M	
Minty Cucumber and Tomato Salad	134			M	M		
Arugula and Artichoke Salad with Citrus Dressing	136			M	M		
Shaved Jicama Salad with Citrus Vinaigrette	138			M			M
Caprese Salad with Basil Dressing	140			M	M		
Mini Pitas	142	M		M			

soups

	page number	nut-free	egg-free	low FODMAP	AIP-friendly	SCD/GAPS	lower carb
Tangy Lamb Stew with Saffron and Ginger (Harira)	146			M	M		
Cumin Cauliflower Soup	148			M	M		
Cabbage and Meatball Soup	150			M	M		
Cilantro Pumpkin Soup	152	M		M	M		
Basil Minestrone Soup	154			M			
Nora's Green Bean Soup	156			M	M		
Caramelized Onion Soup	158				M		
Almond Meatball Soup (M'touam)	160	M		M	M		

pizza and pasta

	page number	nut-free	egg-free	low FODMAP	AIP-friendly	SCD/GAPS	lower carb
Mediterranean Paleo Pizza	166	M	M	M	M	M	M
Cashew Pizza Crust	170						
Sunflower Pizza Crust	170						
Lower Carb Pizza Crust	171						
AIP Pizza Crust	171						
Paleo Pasta	172			M			
Ravioli	176			M			
Zucchini Noodles	178						
Basic Tomato Sauce	182			M			
Puttanesca Sauce	183			M	M		
Alfredo Clam Sauce	184			M			
Mushroom Sauce	185			M			
Mint Pesto	186	M		M	M		
Autoimmune-Friendly No-Mato Sauce	187			M			
Bolognese Meat Sauce	188			M	M		
Shrimp Alfredo	190			M		M	M
Spaghetti and Cumin-Spiced Meatballs	192			M	M		

poultry

	page number	nut-free	egg-free	low FODMAP	AIP-friendly	SCD/GAPS	lower carb
Chicken and Olive Tajine	196			M	M		
Harissa-Spiced Chicken Wings	198			M	M		
Savory Chicken Kebab	200			M	M		
Spicy Chicken Tajine	202			M	M		
Fig and Ginger Chicken Tajine	204			M	M		
Saffron Braised Chicken	206			M	M		
Za'atar and Garlic Roasted Duck	208			M	M		
Kabylie Cinnamon Chicken Tajine	210			M	M		M
Lamb-Stuffed Chicken Thighs	212			M	M		
Nacera's Lemon Ginger Chicken Tajine	214			M			
Za'atar Brick Chicken	216				M		
Crispy Fried Chicken Tenders	218	M		M			

red meat

	page number	nut-free	egg-free	low FODMAP	AIP-friendly	SCD/GAPS	lower carb
Peppers and Zucchini Stuffed with Lamb (Lamb Dolmas)	222			M	M		
Cinnamon Braised Beef Tajine	224			M			
Top Sirloin with Mushroom Reduction Sauce	226			M	M		
Marinated Filet Mignon with Béarnaise Sauce	228						
Harissa Braised Short Ribs	230			M	M		
Lamb and Vegetable Tajine	232			M	M		
Siva's Cauliflower and Meatballs	234			M	M		
Lamb Kebab	236			M	M		
Sweet Lamb Stew (L'ham Hlou)	238						
Rosemary Leg of Lamb	240				M	M	
Spiced Rack of Lamb	242	M			M		
Kefta Lamb Kebab (Persian Version)	244			M			
Stuffed Cabbage (Cabbage Dolmas)	246				M		
Shish Kebab	248			M	M		
Beef and Artichokes	250			M			
Mediterranean Burgers	252			M	M		
Braised Beef, Artichokes, and Peas (Jelbana)	254			M	M		M
Paleo Moussaka	256		M	M	M	M	M

seafood

	page number	nut-free	egg-free	low FODMAP	AIP-friendly	SCD/GAPS	lower carb
Salmon and Crab Roll-Ups	260		M		M		
Fattoush Shrimp Salad	262	M		M	M	M	
Lemon Garlic Shrimp	264			M	M		
Mediterranean Seafood Salad	266		M	M	M		
Seared Tuna Salade Niçoise	268		M	M	M	M	M
Sardine Cakes	270	M	M	M	M		
Zesty Crab Cakes with Aioli	272		M	M	M		
Sardine Salad with Capers and Olives	274			M	M		
Crispy Fried Sardines	276	M		M			
Seafood Brochette	278			M	M		
Almond-Crusted Cod	280	M	M	M	M		
Cioppino	282			M	M		
Pistachio-Crusted Sole	284	M		M			
Fennel and Herb–Stuffed Fish (Hout-Fel-Koucha)	286		M	M	M	M	M
Creamy Cilantro Salmon	288			M			
Spinach-Stuffed Calamari	290			M	M		
Paella	292			M	M		M
Lemon-Butter Steamed Mussels	294			M			

odd bits

	page number	nut-free	egg-free	low FODMAP	AIP-friendly	SCD/GAPS	lower carb
Mediterranean Chicken Liver Pâté	298			M	M		
Braised Liver and Mushrooms	300			M	M		
Grilled Liver Kebabs (Kibda)	302				M		
Algerian Beef Heart Chili	304			M	M		
Zesty Liver and Beef Meatloaf	306		M	M	M		
Beef Tongue with Green Olives	308			M	M		
Allspice Oxtail Soup	310			M	M		
Liver Meatballs with Mushroom Gravy	312			M	M		
Grilled Beef Heart Skewers	314				M		

vegetable sides

	page number	nut-free	egg-free	low FODMAP	AIP-friendly	SCD/GAPS	lower carb
Sautéed Green Beans with Lamb Bacon	318			M			
Perfect Sweet Potato Fries	320				M	M	
Savory Sweet Potato Cakes	322		M		M	M	M
Warm Eggplant and Tomato Salad with Mint (Zaalouk)	324			M	M		
Mock Potato Salad	326	M	M		M		
Roasted Eggplant Casserole	328			M			
Golden Raisin Slaw	330						M
Cauliflower Couscous	332						
Charmoula Roasted Vegetables	334			M	M		M
Marinated Olives	335			M	M		
Fermented Probiotic Pickles	336			M	M		

index